T0408118

Promoting Religious Freedom in an Age of Intolerance

ELGAR STUDIES IN HUMAN RIGHTS

Discourse on human rights has grown ever more visible and essential, with human rights principles being discussed and scrutinized on both the international and national stage. This series brings together high-quality works of scholarship in the field of human rights, primarily in law, but particularly those with a critical or analytical edge, or those taking innovative and interdisciplinary approaches. Books in the series also address concerns at the intersection of human rights and other fields such as trade, the environment, international investment and religion, thus contributing to the depth and breadth of scholarship so vital to understanding the complicated matters at stake.

Titles in the series include:

Human Rights and Islam
An Introduction to Key Debates between Islamic Law and International Human Rights Law
Abdullah Saeed

The Social Rights Jurisprudence in the Inter-American Court of Human Rights
Shadow and Light in International Human Rights
Isaac de Paz González

Contesting Human Rights
Norms, Institutions and Practice
Edited by Alison Brysk and Michael Stohl

Behind the Veil
A Critical Analysis of European Veiling Laws
Neville Cox

Gender and Human Rights
Expanding Concepts
Ekaterina Yahyaoui Krivenko

Reconciling Religion and Human Rights
Faith in Multilateralism
Ibrahim Salama and Michael Wiener

Promoting Religious Freedom in an Age of Intolerance
Barbara Ann Rieffer-Flanagan

Promoting Religious Freedom in an Age of Intolerance

Barbara Ann Rieffer-Flanagan

Professor of Political Science, Department of Political Science, Central Washington University, USA

ELGAR STUDIES IN HUMAN RIGHTS

Cheltenham, UK • Northampton, MA, USA

Published by
Edward Elgar Publishing Limited
The Lypiatts
15 Lansdown Road
Cheltenham
Glos GL50 2JA
UK

Edward Elgar Publishing, Inc.
William Pratt House
9 Dewey Court
Northampton
Massachusetts 01060
USA

A catalogue record for this book
is available from the British Library

Library of Congress Control Number: 2022941186

This book is available electronically in the **Elgar**online
Political Science and Public Policy subject collection
http://dx.doi.org/10.4337/9781803925875

Printed on elemental chlorine free (ECF)
recycled paper containing 30% Post-Consumer Waste

ISBN 978 1 80392 586 8 (cased)
ISBN 978 1 80392 587 5 (eBook)

Printed and bound in the USA

For BM

You were my safe harbor from the storms that raged around me

Contents

Preface

I started on the road to what would become this book roughly a decade ago. I have been interested in religion and human rights for some time and wondered why more was not being done to protect religious freedom. No one seemed to be against religious freedom, unlike some political issues, such as abortion or vaccine mandates. Despite the lack of a devoted opposition, somehow protecting individuals' ability to believe, to gather, and to express their faith was not a priority. The more I explored this issue, the more horrific violations of this fundamental right I encountered.

So, I pursued a path to understand the causes and consequences of religious intolerance and religious persecution. Along the way, a number of people took time to talk to me and share their views and experiences. They deserve more gratitude than can be measured in a few sentences. I am grateful to Jean Cahan, Elizabeth Cassidy, James Chen, Elizabeth Clark, Tom Farr, Felice Gaer, Dennis Hoover, Karin Kittelmann Flensner, Katrina Lantos Swett, Jessica Lieberman, Karen Marsh, Greg Mitchell, Mahmood Monshipouri, Chris Seiple, Knox Thames, and Kurt Werthmuller for helping me to understand aspects of religious freedom. Others will remain anonymous, given the restrictions and threats in the countries in which they live.

A special debt of gratitude is owed to David Forsythe and Rhoda Howard-Hassmann. Both read numerous chapters in this manuscript and offered extensive comments that ultimately improved the writing and organization of this work. Their feedback was vital. This book is better because of their efforts. In addition, both were incredibly kind as I dealt with the loss of my mother in 2020. Perhaps it is not surprising that two prominent scholars of human rights are also generous and compassionate human beings. Thank you.

I was fortunate to deal with supportive people at Elgar, including Alex Pettifer, Finn Halligan, Paulina Cossette, and Emily Wright.

Abbreviations

CPC	Country of Particular Concern
EU	European Union
FBOs	Faith-Based Organizations
FoRB	Freedom of Religion or Belief
GRI	Government Restrictions Index (Pew Research Center)
ICCPR	International Covenant on Civil and Political Rights
IGO	Intergovernmental Organizations
IIFFMM	Independent International Fact-Finding Mission on Myanmar
IPPFoRB	International Panel of Parliamentarians for Freedom of Religion or Belief
ISIS/IS/ISIL	Islamic State
Ma Ba Tha	The Committee for the Protection of Race and Religion in Myanmar
NGO	Non-Governmental Organization
OHCHR	Office of the High Commissioner for Human Rights
SHI	Social Hostility Index (Pew Research Center)
UN	United Nations
USCIRF	US Commission on International Religious Freedom

1. Building religious freedom

INTRODUCTION

After having an argument with Zainuddin, a caretaker of a shrine in Kabul, Farkhunda Malikzada, a teacher's assistant, was accused of burning a Qur'an. Incensed by the (false) charge that she has desecrated the holy book, an angry mob set upon her: "She was beaten with sticks and boards, kicked, run over by a car and dragged, thrown into a dry riverbed, stoned, and finally set on fire as bystanders recorded the crime and police watched every act of barbarity."[1]

Unfortunately, this needless death is not a thing of the past or simply a moral lesson offered on how things are in a far-off land. The names and places may change, but the religious hostility that produces the denial of the fundamental right to freedom of religion or belief is widespread.[2] We continuously see reports of religious intolerance, whether it be attacks on Christians in Sri Lanka or Indonesia, Jews in France, Muslim Uyghurs in China, or Yazidi in Iraq. Various politicians lament the fact that individuals around the world are not able to practice the tenets of their faith due to government persecution or hostility from non-state actors.

This chapter begins by documenting the extent of religious persecution throughout the world. Next, it offers a means to addressing religious intolerance and developing religious freedom. My approach explains what factors are needed to see progress on the protection of this fundamental human right. This chapter then distinguishes between religious tolerance and freedom of religion or belief. Understanding this distinction has important policy implications. Lastly, this chapter offers an overview of the chapters that follow.

---

[1] State Department, "Executive Summary," *International Religious Freedom Report for 2015*. See also Joseph Goldstein and Ahmad Shakib, "A Day After a Killing Afghans React in Horror, but Some Show Approval," *New York Times*, March 20, 2015.

[2] The language used in international treaties, including the International Covenant on Civil and Political Rights (ICCPR), is freedom of religion or belief. I use religious freedom interchangeably with freedom of religion or belief, or FoRB.

PERSISTENT RELIGIOUS PERSECUTION

David Saperstein, the former American Ambassador at Large for International Religious Freedom, lamented the intolerance he witnessed around the world: "we are talking about people [in other parts of the world] being brutalized, we're talking about people who are being imprisoned, we're talking about people being tortured. We're talking about people being ethnically cleansed and victims of genocide."[3]

COVID-19 added to these difficulties. The pandemic and the restrictions many governments enacted to control it disrupt normal religious activities. Limiting social gatherings, including religious services, is not by itself a denial of religious freedom if applied uniformly throughout society. If government policies focus on health priorities and are applied in a neutral and non-discriminatory manner, there is no violation of an individual's rights. Unfortunately, many governments did not apply these policies in a neutral manner. Some countries denied religious minorities access to health care. Other states targeted, scapegoated, and blamed religious minorities for the spread of the virus.[4]

Intolerance toward individuals and groups with different beliefs, practices, and identities is widespread. The Pew Research Center noted that over 80 percent of the world's population lived in a country that substantially limited or prohibited religious activity.[5] As the United States Commission on International Religious Freedom (USCIRF), an independent, federal commission noted,

> The state of affairs for international religious freedom is worsening in both the depth and breadth of violations. The blatant assaults have become so frightening—attempted genocide, the slaughter of innocents, and the wholesale destruction of places of worship—that less egregious abuses go unnoticed or at least unappreciated. Many observers have become numb to violations of the right to freedom of thought, conscience, and religion.[6]

---

[3] David Saperstein, Panel Discussion, "Tolerance: A Key to Religious Freedom," February 9, 2017, Washington, D.C.

[4] Samuel Brownback, Ambassador at Large for International Religious Freedom, Briefing, May 14, 2020 (via teleconference).

[5] "Since some of these countries are among the world's most populous (such as China and India), this means that a large share of the world's population in 2016—83 percent—lived in countries with high or very high religious restrictions." Pew Research Center, "Global Uptick in Government Restrictions," June 21, 2018, https://www.pewforum.org/2018/06/21/global-uptick-in-government-restrictions-on-religion-in-2016/.

[6] USCIRF, 2017 Annual Report, http://www.uscirf.gov/sites/default/files/2017.USCIRFAnnualReport.pdf.

Various states and non-state actors from China to Cuba to Saudi Arabia to the Islamic State to Boko Haram engage in activities that deny individuals and communities the ability to live and act in accordance with a set of freely chosen beliefs. Whether these ideas revolve around a deity or the absence of a supernatural power, the fundamental right to freedom of religion or belief was articulated in the Universal Declaration of Human Rights, and then instituted in international laws (specifically Article 18 of the ICCPR).

The articles in the Universal Declaration articulate how individuals' dignity is established in a range of social, political, and economic activities and circumstances.[7] The preamble of the Declaration begins: "Whereas recognition of the inherent dignity and of the equal and inalienable rights of all members of the human family is the foundation of freedom, justice and peace in the world."[8] Article 18 of the Universal Declaration specifies how individuals ought to be treated with respect to their beliefs: "Everyone has the right to freedom of thought, conscience and religion; this right includes freedom to change his religion or belief, and freedom, either alone or in community with others and in public or private, to manifest his religion or belief in teaching, practice, worship and observance."[9] The normative aspirations of the Universal Declaration were codified in international law. Article 18 of the Covenant on Civil and Political Rights articulates freedom of religion or belief as follows:

1. Everyone shall have the right to freedom of thought, conscience and religion. This right shall include freedom to have or to adopt a religion or belief of his choice, and freedom, either individually or in community with others and in public or private, to manifest his religion or belief in worship, observance, practice and teaching.
2. No one shall be subject to coercion which would impair his freedom to have or to adopt a religion or belief of his choice.
3. Freedom to manifest one's religion or beliefs may be subject only to such limitations as are prescribed by law and are necessary to protect public safety, order, health, or morals or the fundamental rights and freedoms of others.
4. The State Parties to the present Covenant undertake to have respect for the liberty of parents and, when applicable, legal guardians to ensure the religious and moral education of their children in conformity with their own convictions.[10]

---

[7] Heiner Bielefeldt and Michael Wiener, *Religious Freedom Under Scrutiny* (Philadelphia: University of Pennsylvania Press, 2020), p. 22.

[8] See https://www.un.org/en/universal-declaration-human-rights/. For an in-depth account of the development of Article 18 of the Universal Declaration of Human Rights, see Linde Lindkvist, *Religious Freedom and the Universal Declaration of Human Rights* (New York: Cambridge University Press, 2017).

[9] See https://www.un.org/en/universal-declaration-human-rights/index.html.

[10] See http://www.ohchr.org/en/professionalinterest/pages/ccpr.aspx. In total, 169 states are party to this treaty.

This fundamental human right is often violated. The disregard for religious freedom is true whether the Islamic State[11] is enslaving Yazidis or killing Christians and Shiites and claiming they are heretics or infidels, or when China's secular Communist Party prevents Christians from independent communal worship and destroys churches or places over a million Muslim Uyghurs in "reeducation camps." The denial of freedom of religion or belief was also evident when French policies prevented Muslim women from wearing a burkini on a beach,[12] or when individuals from a religious minority endured physical violence or had their sacred sites desecrated. Physical attacks on Jewish individuals and on synagogues occurred in various states in Europe.[13] Many countries witnessed numerous anti-Semitic attacks, including the destruction of gravestones at a Jewish cemetery (Manchester) and vandalism at a Holocaust memorial in Budapest.[14] Anti-Semitism has risen to such levels that the German commissioner for anti-Semitism advised Jewish men against wearing the kippah in public.[15] Saudi Arabia limits the public expression of non-Wahhabi Islam, Christianity, and atheism.[16] Pakistan's government is unable or unwilling to remedy violence against Shiites and Christians by non-state actors. While the Islamic State's religiously motivated terrorism garnered much media attention due to its brutality, it is far from the only actor that prevented individuals from actively engaging with their deeply held religious beliefs.

---

[11] One can argue that they distorted the tenets of the faith while acknowledging that their views are still inspired by religion.

[12] Alissa Rubin, "French 'Burkini' Bans Provoke Backlash as Armed Police Confront Beachgoers," *New York Times*, August 24, 2016, https://www.nytimes.com/2016/08/25/world/europe/france-burkini.html. The ban on wearing a burkini in Nice was later overturned by the French judicial system.

[13] For example, four Jews were shot at a Jewish day school in Toulouse in March 2012. Katrina Lantos Swett, Testimony Before the House Committee on Foreign Affairs: Subcommittee on Africa, Global Health, Global Human Rights and International Organizations, February 27, 2013, Washington, D.C.

[14] Anti-Defamation League (ADL), "Global Anti-Semitism: Selected Incidents Around the World in 2016," December 31, 2016, https://www.adl.org/news/article/global-anti-semitism-selected-incidents-around-the-world-in-2016.

[15] British Broadcasting Corporation (BBC), "German Jews Warned Not to Wear Kippas after Rise in Anti-Semitism," May 26, 2019, https://www.bbc.com/news/world-europe-48411735?ocid=socialflow_twitter.

[16] Raif Badawi was charged with, among other things, "ridiculing religious figures" and has been imprisoned since 2012 for comments he posted to a blog. An appeals court sentenced him to ten years in prison and 1000 lashes. The state administered 50 lashes in 2015. For addition information, see USCIRF's 2017 Annual Report. Flogging was banned in 2020 as part of Crown Prince Mohammed bin Salem's reform project.

Many individuals, whether religious or secular, hide from government officials or non-state actors in the hope that their beliefs will not lead to discrimination, exile, imprisonment, or violence. Given the extensive numbers of people around the world who are denied the fundamental right of freedom of religion or belief codified in various state constitutions and the ICCPR, and the thousands who have been tortured or killed because of their beliefs, this problem warrants attention. How can an intolerant society become more tolerant and protect the basic right of religious freedom? Alternatively stated, how does a society move from religious intolerance to one where religious tolerance is guaranteed, and then ultimately where freedom of religion or belief is a basic right for all members of that society? The goal is religious freedom for all, even if religious tolerance may be a positive step in the short term.

What is the architecture or building blocks of a society that respects and protects this human right? If by architecture we think of the design and construction of a building, how can we build the infrastructure of freedom of religion or belief? This book articulates the necessary conditions by which the structure of freedom of religion or belief is designed to withstand pressure and endure. The materials or building blocks that are necessary for a stable and enduring religious freedom include political, legal, social, and normative aspects. The political system must not only create laws to establish freedom of religion or belief, but it must also develop institutions to protect this right without discrimination. The legal system, through the rule of law, must uphold legal protections for all aspects of freedom of religion or belief. This will also involve an effective education system. Citizens, including those in law enforcement, must internalize tolerant dispositions about others in society. Schools must teach these norms and ideas. In addition, national leaders and civil society organizations can contribute to the dissemination and acceptance of these ideas throughout the population. This study does not suggest that one specific blueprint will *guarantee* freedom of religion or belief. Just as different architectural designs depend on the cultural and environmental factors, different societies require specific policies depending on the history, culture, and political contexts. Some policies, as is the case with some building materials, are more helpful to create a lasting and sustainable environment.

To analyze the necessary components and building blocks, I explore how individual leaders, states (through domestic policies and foreign policy tools), and international actors contribute to this fundamental human right. At the international level, I survey elements of the international community's approach to freedom of religion or belief, focusing on international cooperation in international organizations and the development of multilateral approaches to this issue.

At the national level, I analyze educational reform, individual national leaders, and foreign policies to understand policies that further freedom of religion or belief. Civil society's role is also essential. When exploring domestic actors, such as religious organizations or national or international human rights organizations, we see how important non-state actors are to prod the development of the right to freedom of religion or belief. All these perspectives—international, domestic, individual—noted in Figure 1.1 are necessary to see Article 18 of the ICCPR fully implemented and protected.

Ultimately, studying these international, national, and individual factors results in a few important conclusions. There is not one simple path to achieve freedom of religion or belief. Instrumental arguments that revolve around the economic or security benefits of religious tolerance have not historically produced long-lasting religious freedom in a society. An enlightened leader who encourages a package of reforms can contribute to the successful development of religious freedom in a society. These reforms include strengthening the rule of law and limiting and confronting any negative depictions of the religious (or non-religious) Other in public discourse. Further reforms in the education curriculum and laws that enhance the ability of a wide range of civil society actors, including religious institutions and human rights organizations, to operate can contribute to a robust promotion of freedom of religion or belief. These reforms will not happen overnight. George Kennan suggested thinking about changes in global politics in terms of gardening. These reforms must be nurtured year after year.

Some argue that countries in the West, including the United States, should not attempt to promote freedom of religion around the world. Others have gone further and criticized efforts by Western actors as another example of Western imperialism.[17] In addition, some scholars in this tradition challenge the "universal" nature of religious freedom.[18] The argument and evidence presented in this book challenges this critical tradition. I argue throughout this book for the importance of and need for a coherent multilayered approach to the promotion of freedom of religion or belief around the world.[19]

---

[17] Elizabeth Shakman Hurd, *Beyond Religious Freedom: The New Global Politics of Religion* (Princeton, NJ: Princeton University Press, 2015). Saba Mahmood, "Religious Freedom, Minority Rights, and Geopolitics," in *Politics of Religious Freedom*, edited by Winnifred Fallers Sullivan, Elizabeth Shakman Hurd, Saba Mahmood, and Peter Danchin (Chicago: University of Chicago Press, 2015), pp. 142–8.

[18] Elizabeth Shakman Hurd, Testimony before the House Foreign Affairs Committee, Tom Lantos Human Rights Commission, July 13, 2021, Washington, D.C.

[19] Saiya also offers a summary of scholars critical of religious liberty in Chapter 5. Nilay Saiya, *Weapons of Peace* (Cambridge, UK: Cambridge University Press, 2018).

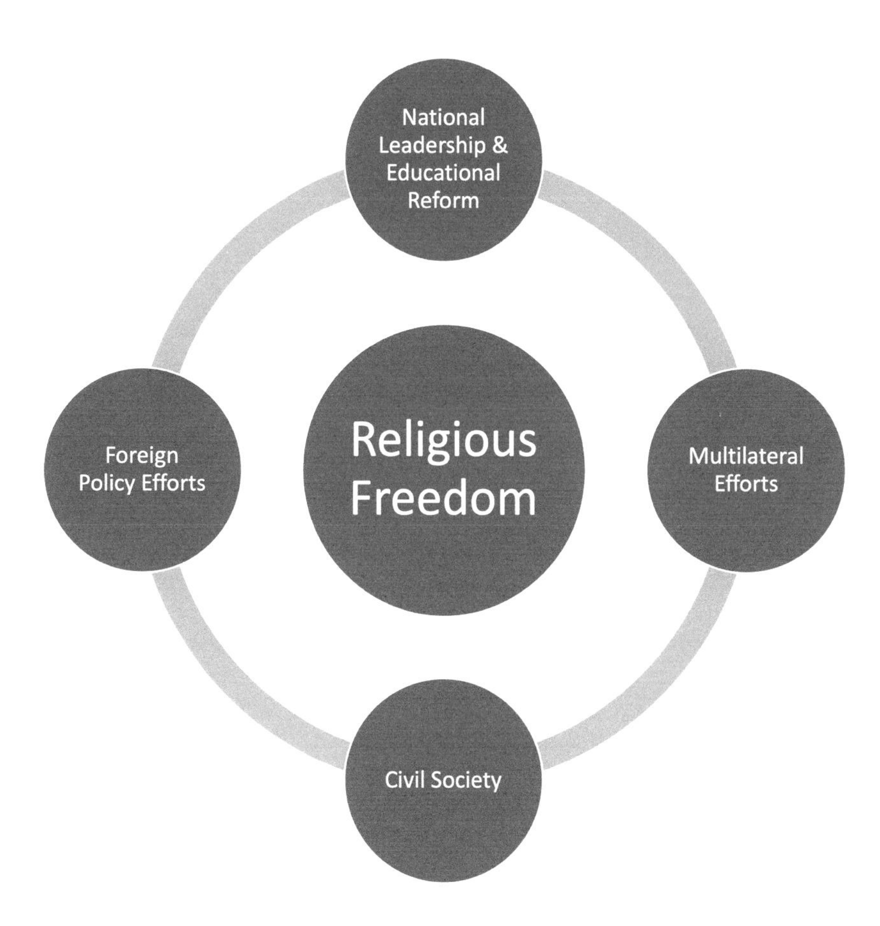

Figure 1.1 *Essential components to promote religious freedom*

UNDERSTANDING RELIGIOUS INTOLERANCE

As noted by various studies,[20] religious intolerance and persecution of some

[20] Pew Research Center, "In 2018, Government Restrictions Reach Highest Level Globally in More than a Decade," November 10, 2020, https://www.pewforum.org/2020/11/10/in-2018-government-restrictions-on-religion-reach-highest-level-globally-in-more-than-a-decade/; Brian Grim and Roger Finke, *The Price of Freedom Denied* (New York: Cambridge University Press, 2011); USCIRF, 2019 Annual Report, https://www.uscirf.gov/publications/2019-annual-report.

individuals because of religious identity, ideas, or practices is widespread. No region of the world is immune from religious repression. John Stuart Mill noted in the 19th century that while many will claim freedom of religion is a basic right of all, few societies have upheld this right:

> The great writers to whom the world owes what religious liberty it possesses, have mostly asserted freedom of conscience as an indefeasible right, and denied absolutely that a human being is accountable to others for his religious belief. Yet so natural to mankind is intolerance in whatever they really care about, that religious freedom has hardly anywhere been practically realized, except where religious indifference, which dislikes to have its peace disturbed by theological quarrels, has added its weight to the scale. In the minds of almost all religious persons, even in the most tolerant countries, the duty of toleration is admitted with tacit reserves.[21]

This continues to be true in the 21st century.

Understanding the diverse impulses that spur religious intolerance is the first step to encouraging religious tolerance. Theological disputes between key figures and different interpretations of sacred texts within one religious tradition resulted in numerous conflicts and intolerance dating back to ancient times. Doctrinal quarrels within Christianity in the 4th century over the nature of Jesus of Nazareth (divine, infinite, a finite being, etc.) and his relationship to God resulted in banishment and death for Arians. Some, such as Augustine, believed that religious intolerance was justified to save those in error. For Augustine, intolerance "is a righteous persecution, which the Church of Christ inflicts upon the impious" to save them from eternal damnation.[22] He provided a theological justification for repression against a dissenting group. Disagreements between Sunnis and Shiites over the legitimate successor to the prophet Muhammad precipitated fighting and massacres, including the Battle of Karbala in 680. These doctrinal disputes continue to the present day.

Disputes between communities of different faiths also result in intolerant policies. The tendency to favor members of one's own community—whether religious, ethnic, or tribal—can create tensions with the Other. Johnson and

---

[21] John Stuart Mill, *On Liberty*, edited by Stefan Collini (Cambridge, UK: Cambridge University Press, 1989), p. 11.

[22] Irwin Polishook, *Roger Williams, John Cotton and Religious Freedom* (Hoboken, NJ: Prentice Hall, 1967); Robert Louis Wilken, *Liberty in the Things of God: The Christian Origins of Religious Freedom*, (New Haven, CT: Yale University Press, 2019), pp. 31–2.

Koyama describe the demonization of the Other in their work *Persecution and Toleration*:

> with the rise of monotheism, outsiders who belonged to other religions came to be seen as cut off from the source of divine order and hence irredeemable. The ability to label outsiders as enemies is an effective strategy for building within-group trust and cooperation. But it comes at the cost of permanent conflict with those deemed outsiders.[23]

The religious Other may be viewed as dangerous, hostile, corrupt, or uncivilized. As such, the thoughts, practices, and in some cases individuals are a threat that cannot be allowed to contaminate one's own religious community.[24] For example, Huguenots in 16th-century France should not be tolerated according to some French Catholics because of their supposed erroneous beliefs, seditious acts, and rebellions.[25] Mack Holt also noted the perceived threat in *The French Wars of Religion*: "Viewed by Catholics as threats to the social and political order, Huguenots not only had to be exterminated—that is, killed—they also had to be humiliated, dishonored, and shamed as the inhumane beasts they were perceived to be."[26] Thus, fear and anxiety of the religious Other can lead to intolerance and persecution.[27]

When members of the religious Other are also perceived to be enjoying greater economic prosperity or societal benefits—access to better land, government contracts, or honors—anger and bitterness can contribute to social hostility and intolerance. In the 13th century, some Christians in Western Europe resented Jewish individuals in their towns. Some of this resentment stemmed from the perception that the Jewish community enjoyed economic

---

[23] Noel Johnson and Mark Koyama, *Persecution and Toleration: The Long Road to Religious Freedom* (Cambridge, UK: Cambridge University Press, 2019), p. 30.

[24] Fukuyama has argued, "human beings, in other words, are social animals by nature," and this universal aspect of human beings results in favoritism toward family and friends. "But their sociability takes the specific form of altruism towards family (genetic relatives) and friends (individuals with whom one has exchanged favors). This default form of sociability is universal to all cultural and historical periods." Favoring members of one's religious community can be seen as an extension of this practice of creating a religious Other. Francis Fukuyama, *Political Order and Political Decay* (New York: Farrar, Straus, and Giroux, 2014), p. 8.

[25] John Marshall, *John Locke, Toleration and Early Enlightenment Culture* (Cambridge, UK: Cambridge University Press, 2006), p. 544.

[26] Mack Holt, *The French Wars of Religion, 1562–1629* (New York: Cambridge University Press, 1995), p. 87.

[27] Nussbaum notes the role of fear in *The New Religious Intolerance* (Cambridge, MA: Belknap Press, 2012).

opportunities and benefits that they did not deserve.[28] This often resulted in pogroms, including in 1391 in Castile and Aragon. In contemporary times, Baha'is are one of the most persecuted religious groups in Iran due to the perception that they received favorable treatment from the Shah, as well as differences in theology with Shia Islam.[29] Often insecurity—physical or economic—and political disruption results in less tolerance.[30]

DIFFERENTIATING RELIGIOUS TOLERANCE FROM FREEDOM OF RELIGION OR BELIEF

Religious Tolerance

Ending religious persecution and encouraging religious toleration is an important and necessary step toward promoting freedom of religion or belief. However, religious tolerance is sometimes misunderstood and equated with religious freedom. It is important to distinguish and clearly define these concepts, not simply for intellectual clarity, but due to the real consequences that arise when these terms are mistakenly equated. Heiner Bielefeldt, UN Special Rapporteur on freedom of religion or belief, argued for a better understanding of religious freedom. He stated, "an urgent need exists for more conceptual clarity concerning freedom of religion or belief, not only in order to defend this right against inimical attacks from the outside, but also to strengthen the consensus about the significance of freedom of religion or belief within the human rights community itself."[31]

Studies that explore the global protection of freedom of religion or belief have struggled to articulate what freedom of religion or belief entails and

---

[28] Sara Lipton notes, "Jews in the early Middle Ages were legally free and their lives were considerably more prosperous, secure, and comfortable than those of most Christian peasants"; *Dark Mirror: The Medieval Origins of Anti-Jewish Iconography* (New York: Metropolitan Books/Henry Holt and Company, 2014), p. 5. Karen Armstrong, *Fields of Blood: Religion and the History of Violence* (New York: Alfred Knopf, 2015), pp. 223–4. Some Christians blamed the death of Jesus of Nazareth on Jews.

[29] Barbara Ann Rieffer-Flanagan, *Evolving Iran* (Washington, D.C.: Georgetown University Press, 2013).

[30] "Throughout Ottoman history deportations and conversions took place during periods of political and economic insecurity, especially during and after war when the state elite felt more vulnerable"; Karen Barkey, *Empire of Difference* (Cambridge, UK: Cambridge University Press, 2008), p. 113.

[31] Heiner Bielefeldt, "Misperceptions about Freedom of Religion or Belief," *Human Rights Quarterly*, Vol. 35 (2013), p. 35.

how it differs from religious tolerance. Michael Walzer explains that religious freedom in terms of separation. He notes that:

> The Wall between church and state creates a sphere of religious activity of public and private worship, congregations and consciences, into which politicians and bureaucrats may not intrude… Believers are set free from every sort of official or legal coercion. They can find their own way to salvation, privately or collectively; or they can fail to find their way; or they can refuse to look for a way. The decision is entirely their own; this is what we call freedom of conscience or religious liberty.[32]

While separation may provide the institutional framework for freedom of religion or belief to take hold, separation alone will not establish this basic human right. Separation may be an aspect of religious tolerance as it allows for freedom of worship or the ability to pray in a private building. However, this is not religious freedom. Not all societies that separate religion from the government enjoy religious tolerance, let alone freedom of religion or belief. In Cuba, the separation of religion and state has resulted in persecution and various violations of human rights.[33] Furthermore, maintaining a separation between politics and faith-based groups does not address the social hostilities that can arise between religious groups. Therefore, separation alone is inadequate as an understanding of religious tolerance or religious freedom.

Other studies have struggled to capture the essence of this concept.[34] Some have simply used the legal language in international treaties.[35] Some writers use the terms religious freedom and religious tolerance interchangeably.[36] If one cannot clearly define what this essential right entails, it will be more difficult for policy makers and human rights activists to promote and protect it in society.

---

[32] Michael Walzer, "Liberalism and the Art of Separation," *Political Theory*, Vol. 12, No. 3 (August 1984), p. 315.

[33] USCIRF, "Religious Freedom in Cuba in 2019," March 2020, https://www.uscirf.gov/sites/default/files/2020%20Cuba%20Policy%20Update.pdf.

[34] Jolanta Ambrosewicz-Jacobs, "Religious Tolerance, Freedom of Religion or Belief, and Education: Results of the 2001 UN Conference," in *Facilitating Freedom of Religion or Belief: A Deskbook*, edited by Tore Lindholm, W. Cole Durham, and Bahia G. Tahzib-Lie (Leiden: Martinus Nijhoff Publishers, 2004), Chapter 37. See also Jonathan Fox, "Religious Freedom in Theory and in Practice," *Human Rights Review*, Vol. 16, No. 1 (2015), pp. 1–22. Fox offers two definitions of religious freedom based on equality and free exercise, but he does not take a view on which is more substantive.

[35] Anat Scolnicov, *The Right of Religious Freedom in International Law* (New York: Routledge, 2010).

[36] "As I have assumed and often pointed out in this book, the ideas of tolerance and religious freedom are not separable"; Perez Zagorin, *How the Idea of Religious Toleration Came to the West* (Princeton, NJ: Princeton University Press, 2003), p. 311.

Neuser and Chilton, in their research on religious tolerance, explain that religious tolerance is "more than the capacity to live alongside a different religious tradition from one's own. It also refers to acceptance of attitudes and actions contrary to the morality to which one adheres."[37] This will involve the accommodation of a religious minority by the majority.[38] Green elaborates further: "the enduring and important question of religious tolerance" revolves around "the capacity of a religion to forbear another religion with which it disagrees."[39] Thus, one essential aspect of religious tolerance is the right to exist without being forced to change one's views.

Religious tolerance involves a willingness to endure and bear other individuals or groups with whom there is a significant difference in belief and practice. Religious tolerance encompasses living with others who hold dissimilar or objectionable beliefs and who engage in unfavorable practices without interference or persecution. The social aspect requires that citizens hold tolerant dispositions toward the religious (or non-religious) Other. This requires individuals to acknowledge and accept that while we may have different beliefs, practices, and worldviews, individuals in a different-faith community (or those who have no spiritual commitments) deserve respectful treatment with a recognition that we can coexist in society despite our differences.[40]

Arguments for Religious Tolerance

Understanding the arguments offered to encourage or justify religious toleration provides a tool for contemporary foreign policy makers as they attempt to limit discrimination and persecution and support the rights and freedoms that are necessary for human dignity. Historically, many of the arguments offered for religious tolerance stemmed from self-preservation. Members of a persecuted faith pleaded for religious tolerance to preserve their community and way of life. Anabaptists and Quakers were a few of the English religious

---

[37] *Religious Tolerance in World Religions*, edited by Jacob Neuser and Bruce Chilton (West Conshohocken, PA: Templeton Foundation Press, 2008), p. viii. While Neuser and Chilton's work presents an important discussion of religious tolerance, it should be distinguished from the fundamental right found in international law in Article 18 of the ICCPR.

[38] Neuser and Chilton, p. viii.

[39] William Scott Green, "The 'What' and 'Why' of Religious Toleration: Some Questions to Consider," in *Religious Tolerance in World Traditions*, p. 3.

[40] Anna Elisabetta Galeotti has emphasized toleration as recognition. The concerns she raises about the importance of toleration as recognition can be viewed through the lens of Pew's work that incorporates state policies (Government Restrictions Index, GRI) and attitudes (Social Hostilities Index, SHI); Galeotti, *Toleration as Recognition* (Cambridge, UK: Cambridge University Press, 2002).

minorities who sought the tolerance of the magistrate to practice their faith. King Charles II persecuted and incarcerated dissenting Protestants, and numerous Quakers died in prison in the early 1680s.[41]

The Quaker, William Penn, offered numerous justifications for tolerating Protestant dissenters and Catholics.[42] In *Considerations Moving to a Toleration* (1685), Penn noted the economic benefits of religious tolerance. In *Great and Popular Objection* (1687), he argued that providing liberty of conscience and religious tolerance to Catholics and dissenters would enhance the security of society.[43] Other thinkers offered pragmatic arguments. In *Leviathan,* Thomas Hobbes suggested that toleration was valuable because it could contribute to civil peace.[44] Religious tolerance was a means to secure peace between religious groups. These arguments placed limits on religious communities and the activities they could engage in. These interest-based arguments will resurface in contemporary times and in future chapters.

While tolerance was a means to avoid persecution, this did not stop some from rejecting tolerance when they moved from an embattled minority to the governing power. Calvin, once in power in Geneva, rejected tolerance and had Michael Servetus burned at the stake for his heretical views on the Trinity.[45] Martin Luther had no interest in promoting religious tolerance or freedom of religion, especially for Catholics. For Luther, "Heretics are not to be disputed with, but condemned unheard, and whilst they perish by fire, the faithful ought to pursue the evil to its source, and bathe their hands in the blood of Catholic bishops, and of the Pope, who is the devil in disguise."[46] Both men believed that they had religious truth on their side, and there were few limitations on what they were willing to do in the name of that righteous truth.

---

[41] Marshall (p. 112) notes that over 100 Protestant dissenters died in prison in 1683–4.

[42] Marshall, p. 72. See also Andrew Murphy, *Liberty, Conscious, and Toleration: The Political Thought of William Penn* (New York: Oxford University Press, 2016). William Penn sought to develop and protect these notions in his colony, Pennsylvania.

[43] William Penn's essay can be found at: http://quod.lib.umich.edu/e/eebo/A70777.0001.001/1:2?rgn=div1;view=fulltext. See especially page 22.

[44] Higgins notes, "it is important to realize that, for Hobbes, toleration is not an end of political life, rather it is a means to the broader goal of civil peace; and as such toleration is limited in application by its (perceived) ability to achieve peace"; see *Leviathan XVIII,* 9 on the sovereign's power to tolerate doctrines. Nicholas Higgins, "Hobbes's Paradoxical Toleration: Inter Regentes Tolerantia, Tolerans Intolerantia Inter Plebein," *Politics and Religion*, Vol. 9 (2016), p. 140.

[45] Coornhert condemned Calvin for his hypocrisy; he sought toleration until he gained the power to persecute others in *About the Constraint Upon Conscience Practiced in Holland* (1579). Marshall, p. 338.

[46] Polishook, p. 3.

Some philosophers, such as John Locke, argued for religious tolerance due to an epistemological skepticism:

> For every church is orthodox to itself; to others, erroneous or heretical. For whatsoever any church believes, it believes to be true and the contrary unto those things it pronounce to be error. So that the controversy between these churches about the truth of their doctrines and the purity of their worship is on both sides equal; nor is there any judge, either at Constantinople or elsewhere upon Earth, by whose sentence it can be determined. The decision of that question belongs only to the Supreme judge of all men, to whom also alone belongs the punishment of the erroneous.[47]

Since fallible humans lack epistemic certainty about the truth of various religious traditions, governments ought to treat diverse religious doctrines with equality and not persecution so long as they are not threatening the security of the state.[48]

Locke also noted in *A Letter Concerning Toleration* that the government cannot force beliefs on individuals:

> The care of souls cannot belong to the civil magistrate, because his power consists only in outward force; but true and saving religion consists in the inward persuasion of the mind, without which nothing can be acceptable to God. And such is the nature of the understanding that it cannot be compelled to the belief of anything by outward force. Confiscation of estate, imprisonment, torments, nothing of that nature can have any such efficacy as to make men change the inward judgement that they have framed of things.

A ruler can force an individual to attend a religious service or kneel during a prayer. However, no magistrate can force an individual to change the thoughts in their head or the loyalty in their heart. Further, Locke argued that people rebel and conspire against the government when oppressed:

> For if men enter into seditious conspiracies, tis not religion that inspires them to it in their meetings; but their sufferings and oppression that make them willing to ease themselves. Just and moderate Governments are every where quiet, every where safe. But Oppression raises Ferments, and makes men struggle to cut off an uneasie and tyrannical Yoke.[49]

---

[47] John Locke, *A Letter Concerning Toleration*, edited by James Tully (Indianapolis, IN: Hackett Publishing Company, 1983), p.32.

[48] It is also worth noting that Locke's friend, the Earl of Shaftesbury, was forced to seek exile in the Netherlands related to a religious dispute with the crown; Locke, p.46; Higgins, p.152.

[49] Locke, p.52. In their first chapter, Johnson and Koyama argue that arguments by philosophers such as Locke and Spinoza enjoyed a more hospitable environment due

Some grounded their arguments in a religion's theology. Some leaders used the theological tenets of the religion to ground the tolerance shown to minority groups. When Muslim rulers in al Andalusia or in the Ottoman Empire offered Jews and Christians some measure of acceptance and coexistence in their lands, they based their policies on protections established in the Qur'an for the People of the Book.[50]

Normative arguments were also articulated. During the Enlightenment, some argued that freedom of belief was an essential right that the government should not violate. The French Revolutionaries promoted religious tolerance in Article 10 of the French Declaration of the Rights of Man and of the Citizens (1789). It held that "no one is to be disquieted because of his opinions, even religious, provided their manifestation does not disturb the public order established by law." The revolutionary leaders also provided a more welcoming public space for France's Jewish citizens through civil emancipation and the opportunity to hold public office.[51] In contemporary times, human rights treaties codify normative arguments concerning the importance of a life with dignity.

These arguments contributed not only to theoretical justifications for religious tolerance, but more importantly to the empirical development of a space for individuals and groups to act in accordance with a commitment to their religious beliefs. Interest-based arguments influenced refugee policies in Malta in the 12th century and in the Dutch Republic in the 17th century.[52] Theological arguments affected religious policies in Andalusia. Numerous constitutions across Europe and North and South America incorporate normative arguments for the inherent dignity of the person.

Freedom of Religion or Belief

Embryonic notions of religious liberty developed during the Roman Empire. One of the earliest thinkers to discuss religious freedom was Tertullian. In a letter to Scapula, the proconsul in Africa, Tertullian argued for religious freedom and an end of the persecution of Christians. He explained that indi-

to stronger political systems. Monarchs developed stronger political institutions in their territory with greater capacity to tax their citizens.

[50] Barkey, *Empire*.

[51] Michele Ishay, *The History of Human Rights* (Berkeley: University of California Press, 2008), pp. 81–2.

[52] Dupertuis Bangs, "Dutch Contributions to Religious Toleration," *Church History*, Vol. 79, No. 3 (September 2010), p. 589. See also Evan Haefeli, *New Netherlands and the Dutch Origins of Religious Liberty* (Philadelphia: University of Pennsylvania, 2012).

viduals should have freedom in religious affairs because "it is a fundamental human right, a privilege of human nature that every man should worship according to his own convictions."[53] For Tertullian to be a moral agent, an individual must have the freedom to develop and act on their deeply held beliefs.[54] Tertullian influenced Lactantius, the Christian author and advisor to Constantine. Lactantius argued that religion cannot be coerced. The perception that beliefs and ideas cannot be forced is an essential and fundamental element of freedom of religion or belief. His influence was felt when Constantine issued the Edict of Milan in 313. This was a top-down effort by a leader to offer freedom of worship:

> We thought it fit to commend these things most fully to your care that you may know that we have given to those Christians free and unrestricted opportunity of worship. When you see that this has been granted to them by us, your worship will know that we have also conceded to other religions the right of open and free observance of their worship for the sake of the peace of our times, that each one may have the free opportunity to worship as he pleases; this regulation is made that we may not seem to detract from the dignity of any religion.[55]

Arguments by Tertullian and the Edict of Milan do not lay out a contemporary conception of freedom of religion or belief found in international law. They do include essential elements such as freedom of conscious and the freedom to practice and worship according to an individual's choice. While these early positive developments saw setbacks, these ideas would reemerge in later generations as a foundation for justifications for freedom of religion or belief.[56]

While religious tolerance is an initial step on the path to freedom of religion or belief, its minimal attributes are not the right articulated in Article 18 of the ICCPR. The essential elements of freedom of religion or belief go beyond the absence of persecution and require an active and comprehensive government policy to ensure respect for this fundamental right. This freedom requires the government to protect individuals and groups with divergent beliefs, practices, and activities (discussions, prayers, meditation, etc.). The individual aspects protect the internal aspects necessary for a life with dignity, including the ability to think, believe, and reject ideas according to one's conscience. This

---

[53] Geoffrey Dunn, *Tertullian* (New York: Psychology Press, 2004), p. 31.

[54] Wilken, p. 11.

[55] By 324, Constantine had issued another edit which offered religious tolerance as opposed to religious liberty for all. It is worth noting that the "Edict of Milan" was a letter that was limited in scope. The important aspect was that it reversed the anti-Christian legislation of previous emperors and Christianity was made legal.

[56] Peter Garnsey, "Religious Toleration in Classical Antiquity," in *Persecution and Toleration*, edited by W. J. Sheils (London: Basil Blackwell, 1984), p. 26.

right, like other rights articulated in treaties and covenants, is grounded in human dignity. The collective aspects of freedom of religion or belief require a safe and public space for a community of like-minded individuals to meet, discuss ideas, celebrate rituals,[57] and engage in other communal activities.[58] People, individually and collectively, must be able to engage in these activities without discrimination under the law. Thus, the legal system, as well as government policies, cannot adopt rules that produce inequalities or disabilities between individuals due to a divergent or disfavored set of beliefs.[59] An atheist, Hindu, Christian, or any other believer should suffer no legal burdens or bureaucratic harassment because they do not share the hegemonic religious community's views. Hence, this right goes further than merely reading a text in the privacy of one's home.

Citizens require government activities in several areas to safeguard their ability to engage with a belief system. For example, governments must guarantee the right to peaceful assembly. The government must not only *allow* individuals to assemble, but also protect them from hostility or violence from social actors. For example, the Swedish government has assisted its Jewish community to combat anti-Semitic attacks. The Egyptian government under President el-Sisi provided more security to Coptic Churches in response to a bombing at a Coptic Cathedral in Cairo in December 2016 and a church in Alexandria in 2017.[60]

The fundamental right of religious freedom also entails the right to change one's beliefs and to enter or leave a religious faith, as well as to discuss one's beliefs in public. To uphold this basic right, a state needs to ensure that laws protect an individual's right to association and speech. The state must also ensure that individuals and communities have a place to worship and are free from harassment—either from other religious groups or from sub-state actors.

Cultivating norms of respect and tolerance in education and the social environment (media, civil society, etc.) can address social hostility. When citizens hold tolerant dispositions, and social norms are embedded in society

---

[57] "Rituals are enactments—in song, story, visual representation, and gesture—of the narratives that inform a people's identity"; Harvey Cox, *The Future of Faith* (New York: Harper One, 2009), p. 39.

[58] Francesco Ruffini, *Religious Liberty* (New York: G. P. Putnam's Sons, 1912), p. 13. John Rawls, *The Laws of Peoples* (Cambridge, MA: Harvard University Press, 1999), p. 76.

[59] Ruffini, pp. 11–12.

[60] Declan Walsh and Nour Youseff, "Gunmen Attack Coptic Christian Convoy in Egypt Killing at Least 26," *New York Times*, May 26, 2017. For more information, see Tahrir Institute for Middle East Policy, "A Fragile Egypt in a Changing World: Six Years After the Revolution," 2017, https://timep.org/wp-content/uploads/2017/05/Fragile-Egypt-in-a-Changing-World.pdf

which respect the religious Other or non-religious Other, social hostility will decrease. When citizens believe that others deserve a place in the public square, social hostility, which can lead to religious persecution, will be less prevalent in society. When citizens internalize the notion that the Other, regardless of their beliefs, is worthy of being treated with dignity and habitually act in ways that respect the Other, there will be less need for government action to protect minorities because it will be ingrained in the citizens.

Individuals and groups must also have the freedom to produce and distribute materials related to their deeply held beliefs. These materials include printed literature, newsletters, webpages, blogs, social media accounts, and artwork. Furthermore, groups of individuals must be allowed to establish coursework, textbooks, and classes in the context of a freely chosen educational system. The ability to create and develop the infrastructure necessary to uphold individual beliefs, including charitable organizations, is also a basic aspect of freedom of religion or belief.[61] The government must also accommodate activities that individuals deem essential to their belief system, whether that involves specific attire (veil, kippah) or symbols (crosses, small dagger) or allowing some time for prayer or meditation. Thus, freedom of religion or belief is a positive right that goes beyond mere coexistence.

While religious tolerance is a necessary component of religious freedom, order and a capacity to govern are also important, albeit unacknowledged necessary conditions for freedom of religion or belief. While some states may deny religious freedom to some individuals because of theological disputes or perceived threats (e.g., Iran's treatment of the Baha'is and China's policies toward Tibetan Buddhists or Muslim Uyghurs), not all denials of religious freedom are the result of intentional state policies. A weak state or a failed state that does not have adequate control over all its territory may lack the capacity to provide a minimal level of religious tolerance or protect religious freedom. One scholar noted that a weak state that lacks bureaucratic efficacy might be unable to implement some basic human rights, including civil liberties.[62] In *Weapons of Peace*, Saiya also explained the connection to weak or failed states: "religious repression is especially dangerous in contexts where states that restrict religion are simultaneously too weak to provide security and basic services for all people living under their jurisdiction. In fragile and failing states, national and local authorities lack the capacity to prevent violence."[63]

---

[61] Bielefeldt and Michael Wiener refer to this as religious infrastructure; see *Religious Freedom Under Scrutiny* (Philadelphia: University of Pennsylvania Press, 2020), p. 54.

[62] Wade Cole, "Mind the Gap: State Capacity and the Implementation of Human Rights Treaties," *International Organization*, Vol. 69 (Spring 2015), pp. 405–41.

[63] Saiya, *Weapons of Peace*, p. 173.

Understanding this is important in constructing effective policies to first promote religious tolerance and then encourage the development of religious freedom. Punishment in the form of economic sanctions is unlikely to remedy the situation. Providing assistance to improve state capacity may produce better results. Thus, states such as Afghanistan under Presidents Karzai and Ghani had trouble governing their territory and the lack of governing capabilities contributed to the denial of religious freedom.

While an essential right to human flourishing,[64] this right is not without its limits. An individual's or group's freedom to believe does not extend to actions that violate the fundamental rights of others. The international community cannot tolerate groups who kill, torture, maim, and discriminate against or degrade others based on their beliefs. While non-state actors, such as al Qaeda, Boko Haram, and the Islamic State, may have deeply held beliefs, this does not entitle them to pursue their religious beliefs or practices when these violate the basic rights of others.

Furthermore, the fundamental right to religious freedom does not allow some members of a religious community to discriminate against or limit the freedoms of other members of that community in the name of religion. Unfortunately, this has occurred in numerous environments. The Special Rapporteur on freedom of religion or belief explained in a report how, throughout the world, he:

> identified laws enacted with the aim of mandating standards of conduct purportedly demanded by a particular religion that effectively deny women and other individuals the right to equality and non-discrimination on the basis of their sex, sexual orientation or gender identity… Governments in all regions of the world have also failed to uphold their obligation to protect people from gender-based violence and discrimination perpetrated against them by private individuals or entities claiming a religious justification for their actions and to sanction the perpetrators of such acts.

He noted various examples of this discrimination, including Saudi Arabia's laws that enshrine gender discrimination and fail to address gender-based violence. He also referenced how laws in numerous countries in Asia, the Middle East, and Africa prohibit homosexuality and are justified by tenets of Christianity or Islam.[65] Although some have claimed that their interpretation of

---

[64] "This is partly because of the widely shared assumption that religious freedom constitutes an inherent good that its realization is a key to individual emancipation and peaceful coexistence among different communities"; Lindkvist, p. ix.

[65] Ahmed Shaheed, "Gender-Based Violence and Discrimination in the Name of Religion or Belief," August 24, 2020, A/HRC/43/48, https://undocs.org/A/HRC/43/48. The UN Special Rapporteur in the field of cultural rights has also documented the misuse of "religious freedom" to deny some individuals their rights. See Karima

religion allows them to define the rights and opportunities of others based on religious tenets, this misuse of religious freedom should not be tolerated and is antithetical to the fundamental right articulated in Article 18 of the ICCPR.

Understanding the difference between religious tolerance and freedom of religion or belief is important, not simply for conceptual clarity but due to the policy implications that occur when tolerance—or mere coexistence—is confused with the fundamental human right. When a government allows a private prayer service or ignores an individual reading a text that is contrary to the hegemonic belief system in society, this amounts to religious tolerance. This does not allow for the full development of the individual and it does not uphold the individual's fundamental dignity. Therefore, policies that encourage a government, such as Saudi Arabia, to allow Christians to read a Bible at home does not fulfill the criteria of religious freedom. These policies may be the best that can be achieved at the current time, but they should not be confused with a fundamental right. Policies that encourage religious tolerance should be pursued in the short term to establish the foundation for religious freedom to develop over time.

OVERVIEW

This book is focused on the fundamental right of freedom of religion or belief. In the chapters that follow, I explore efforts to develop a religiously tolerant society and then ultimately one where the right to freedom of religion or belief is institutionalized in norms, dispositions, laws, and policies. The goal is to understand the various policies and institutions a society needs as it evolves from an intolerant society where persecution exists to one where individuals are recognized, respected, and protected. What are the best ways to promote freedom of religion or belief around the world? What are the social, legal, and educational policies developed in various countries to promote this right? Understanding the process and policies that move a society to freedom of religion or belief is key to improving domestic and foreign policy. To answer these questions, this work employs a multidimensional approach that explores how civil society, educational policies, domestic political leadership, international organizations, and foreign policy can make progress on this issue.

The Pew Research Center's analysis and empirical measures are employed throughout the chapters in this book. Specifically, I refer to Pew's Government Restrictions Index (GRI) and Social Hostilities Index (SHI) due to the reliability of Pew's research. Pew's indexes of every state in the world allow

---

Bennoune, "Report on Cultural Rights," July 17, 2017, Report No. A/72/155, https://undocs.org/en/A/72/155.

us to compare each state over time. Their indexes provide an objective and empirical measure of progress or setbacks in each state. Although no approach is perfect in its results, Pew provides consistent and quality research. The GRI and SHI are developed using double-blind coding and sound procedures for the evaluation of their data.[66] These empirical results offer evidence of violations of religious freedom or alternatively a religiously free environment.

Freedom of religion or belief does not have an eternal meaning. While some versions of it may be sought after in various centuries and across societies (most people do not want to be oppressed, tortured, or killed because of their beliefs), what freedom of religion or belief means has evolved over time. Article 18 of the UN Declaration of Human Rights (or in the ICCPR) articulates a universal goal or norm pronounced at a specific moment (mid-20th century). However, the instantiation (or actualization) of that right will depend on specific historical, social, and economic contexts. The context will be determined by the religious diversity in the society, how different religious groups interact at that moment, and how they have interacted over time. Understanding this reality means that policy proposals, as well as civil society initiatives, cannot be developed without a contextual understanding of the society if they are to succeed. Thus, there is no simple one-size-fits-all approach to this issue. What I do in various chapters is to explore what policies, approaches, and activities (education, civil society, etc.) helped allow individuals the political and social space to hold a set of beliefs freely and engage in activities related to those beliefs in a variety of countries and across religious (and non-religious) traditions.

The historical examples explored in the second chapter demonstrate that religious tolerance is possible in different social and cultural environments. For those who are willing to explore the details, history offers numerous societies that moved beyond religious persecution to religious tolerance and, in some cases, freedom of religion or belief. These cases indicate effective policies and actions that saw backsliding and reversals of religious tolerance. Promoting religious tolerance was often motivated by the perceived benefits that a religious minority could bring to society. These instrumental arguments, either for economic or security reasons, have echoes in contemporary times. One lesson of history is that instrumental arguments for religious tolerance can limit persecution and therefore should be pursued. However, we need to recognize the limitations of instrumental motivations for religious tolerance. Instrumental arguments for religious tolerance did not always result in freedom of religion

---

[66] Katherine Marshall, "Towards Enriching Understandings and Assessments of Freedom of Religion or Belief: Politics, Debates, Methodologies, and Practices," CREID Working Paper, Vol. 2021, No. 6, January 2021.

or belief. While history does not provide easy solutions, comprehending these different approaches would help Washington and human rights activists, civil society organizations, and international organizations, such as the United Nations (UN), to develop meaningful strategies in the future. The point of discussing these historical cases is to demonstrate a universal and timeless desire for, at a minimum, religious tolerance. This desire is not a creation of the West in the 20th century, Western realpolitik, or a form of Western imperialism.[67]

Chapter 3 explores how states working in multilateral forums and intergovernmental organizations, including the UN, developed norms, legal standards, and policies to further freedom of religion or belief. States codified this human right in Article 18 of the ICCPR (1976). In Europe, the Charter of Fundamental Rights of the European Union (2009) establishes this right in Article 10. Within the UN, the General Assembly 1981 Declaration on the Elimination of all Forms of Intolerance and Discrimination Based on Religion and Belief and Resolution 16/18: Combatting Religious Intolerance (2011) further strengthen the norms concerning religious freedom.

Beyond these norms, international organizations monitor the violation of this right and develop policies to combat religious intolerance. Specific positions created to protect this right include the UN Special Rapporteur on freedom of religion or belief and Special Envoy for the Promotion of Freedom of Religion and Belief outside the EU. This chapter traces the development of these initiatives and analyzes the efficacy of these efforts. It uses Myanmar as a case study. The UN and other international actors used various initiatives to address the plight of Rohingya Muslims. In 2017, Rohingya Muslims fled their homes due to attacks by Buddhist groups with military assistance. Over 700 000 refugees now live in Bangladesh. Thousands died at the hands of the military and Buddhists. While the UN distributed extensive humanitarian assistance to the Rohingya, the perpetrators of these crimes against humanity remain unpunished.

Religious freedom has foreign policy implications. Can a state, through its foreign policy, help a society evolve from religious intolerance to religious tolerance and then to freedom of religion or belief? The next chapter uses the United States to explore the role and impact of foreign policy on the promotion of religious tolerance and freedom of religion or belief. As one of the most powerful states on the world stage (i.e., economic and military power) and with its self-proclaimed belief in human rights, the United States has been an important actor on this issue. While Washington's rhetoric on human rights, including religious freedom, never matched the reality of its actions, this

---

[67] One aspect of the critical literature on religious freedom argues that promoting religious freedom is a form of Western imperialism. See Mahmood, pp. 142–8.

should not preclude an evaluation of American foreign policy as it pertains to freedom of religion or belief.

The United States was one of the first states to emphasize this right in its foreign policy and to encourage other states to join in these global efforts. Washington was motivated in the 1990s, and thereafter, by domestic factors, and those factors pushed this religious freedom agenda into the international realm. Washington used its diplomatic tool kit (military, quiet diplomacy, bilateral aid, and economic assistance) to promote this right and to encourage other international actors to do so as well. Washington's leadership contributed to the development of the Marrakesh Declaration, International Religious Freedom Alliance with 26 states, as well as the Parliamentarians for FoRB. This chapter examines some of the literature on efforts to promote religious freedom. After explaining why scholars such as Hurd and Mahmood are critical of these efforts, I offer a defense of diplomatic efforts to promote this right.

The fifth chapter explores the role that education plays in developing tolerant citizens. This chapter argues that more efforts are needed in education. It analyzes the domestic reforms that contribute to the dissemination of tolerant dispositions throughout a society. When schools teach children to hate and demonize those who are different, what are the consequences? Do societies that teach religious tolerance and respect for religious pluralism experience less social hostility, discrimination, and violence? Can educators help students to develop the skills that are needed to understand and respect different religious and non-religious values and perspectives? This chapter begins by exploring a country with decades of violent extremism and social hostility toward religious minorities. Saudi Arabia failed to develop a religiously tolerant society where all individuals are free to live according to their beliefs. While there are numerous factors that explain the religious persecution in this country, the education system in Saudi Arabia contributes to these problems. I discuss the classroom environment and educational materials used in Saudi classrooms. Given the intolerant lessons taught, educational reform could help to address some of the discrimination that individuals face in Saudi Arabia. Next, this chapter looks at two religiously tolerant societies—Oman and Sweden—to understand how the educational system aids in the development of tolerant citizens. While the educational systems in these countries are not the sole explanation for why there is less religious discrimination and hostility in these societies, neither promotes an intolerant environment.

Chapter 6 discusses the importance of individuals, specifically political leaders, to establish religious tolerance and the development of policies that would enhance freedom of religion or belief. While many democratic political systems established laws and policies to protect the beliefs and practices of religious (and non-religious) individuals and groups, religious tolerance can develop in a society without a democratically elected leader. Some authoritarian rulers ordered policies to promote religious tolerance because it was deemed essential to enhancing the empire's security or society's economic well-being. Regardless of motivation (whether social stability, economic prosperity, improved diplomatic ties, etc.), the perceived social benefits drove the policy, as opposed to a commitment to ethical principles or the fundamental rights and dignity of individuals in society. Can these instrumentally conceived policies for religious tolerance from above by an authoritarian leader last? What happens when an authoritarian or unelected leader decides to embrace religious tolerance? Can these policies evolve into a substantive protection of the right to freedom of religion or belief? The current political reforms in Uzbekistan offer a contemporary case study to explore these questions. This chapter charts the policies undertaken by President Mirziyoyev, as well as the additional changes that need to occur before the fundamental human right of freedom of religion or belief is instantiated in Uzbekistan.

While states are some of the most powerful actors in global affairs, non-state actors also engage in activities that further or limit freedom of religion or belief. Chapter 7 focuses on non-state actors in civil society working to promote religious tolerance and further the right of freedom of religion or belief. Civil society refers to private non-profit organizations, including non-governmental organizations (NGOs), human rights activists, and religious associations, to name a few, that peacefully seek policy changes at the local, national, or international level. Voluntary campaigners who advocate for a cause or attempt to advance specific values constitute civil society. These voluntary associations are motivated by principled ideas, morals, and values. They seek to improve society. These private actors engage in grassroots activities, such as lobbying public officials for political change, educating communities about a social concern, and providing services to a population in need. My approach in this chapter is actor centered. I seek to explain how one NGO, the Institute for Global Engagement (IGE), acts to influence the Vietnamese government and how the Vietnamese government has acted toward religious groups in its territory, as well as how it has responded to IGE's initiatives. IGE has worked to promote religious freedom for decades and demonstrates why a long-term, sustained commitment is needed to see progress on this human right.

In many countries around the world, the situation of citizens who seek to follow a specific set of beliefs is deplorable. Chapter 8 explores the difficult case of Egypt. In Egypt, Coptic Christians are treated as second-class citizens, while Shiites and other non-Sunni Muslims face legal discrimination from the government and social hostility from other Egyptians. What can be done in these societies where individuals have been killed for who they are and what they believe? This chapter applies the architecture and building blocks developed in previous chapters concerning educational reform, political leadership initiatives, and civil society organizations to this context to address what is necessary for Egypt to make progress on this fundamental right. It uses the diplomatic efforts and political reforms previously discussed to analyze how a comprehensive and multilayered approach could lead to improvements for Egyptians.

The conclusion emphasizes the following points. First, there is no one, simple guaranteed path to the development of freedom of religion or belief. The evolution from an intolerant society to a tolerant one that eventually protects the fundamental right of freedom of religion or belief will be based on environmental factors in the host society (demographic, cultural, and historical) and policy choices by political leaders. The diversity and dispositions of the population and the decisions made by political leaders will create the conditions for an oppressive society that lacks freedom or a rights-based one where religious freedom is guaranteed. Second, understanding the diverse paths that various societies took to achieve religious tolerance or religious freedom can guide policy choices in the future. The past does not offer a teleological approach to policy, but it can indicate some warning signs and policies that are worth pursuing. Third, instrumental arguments for religious tolerance and the policies based on them have limitations. They often do not lead to a long-lasting religious tolerance or freedom of religion or belief. A long-term strategy that combines international efforts, national reforms, and civil society has the greatest chance of success. Through improvements in the educational system focusing on teaching tolerant dispositions and respect for equality for others, and through civil discourse and the promotion of norms that respect rights via civil society, people can learn that religious freedom is a basic right of all members of society. Patient policies developed by national leaders and encouraged by international actors are needed, because many societies will take decades to move from religious intolerance to religious tolerance and ultimately to freedom of religion or belief.

2. History lessons on religious tolerance and religious freedom

INTRODUCTION

Many individuals throughout the world suffer persecution because of their religious beliefs and practices. Therefore, it is important for the United States and other actors in the international community to develop thoughtful, effective policies to address this problem. Religious tolerance involves putting up with disagreeable or erroneous ideas and beliefs. As one scholar noted, "For there to be a *practice* of toleration, one group must deem another differing group's beliefs or practices 'wrong, mistaken, or undesirable' and yet 'put up' with them nonetheless. That means that toleration is not at issue in cases where one group is *indifferent* to another."[1] Policy makers must understand that religious tolerance, the willingness to live with and accept individuals and groups who have dissimilar and, in some cases, disagreeable beliefs and practices, is not equivalent to religious freedom. As noted in Chapter 1, religious tolerance is an important initial stage on the way to ending religious oppression, but its minimal qualities fall short of upholding freedom of religion or belief.

The fundamental right of freedom of religion or belief as codified in international law includes the ability of an individual or group of individuals to engage in activities, whether prayers, fellowship, meditation, publishing literature, discussions, or ceremonies, deemed essential to their spiritual or intellectual well-being. To protect this crucial right, laws and policies must protect a public and private space for individuals and groups to engage with various ideas and practices. The government must ensure that the right to peaceful assembly is upheld and that individuals are not subjected to violence from other social actors within society. These measures go beyond mere coexistence or tolerance.

---

[1] Brian Leiter, *Why Tolerate Religion?* (Princeton, NJ: Princeton University Press, 2013), p. 8. Leiter argues in this work against the unique place of religious toleration. On page 133 he states, "Toleration may be a virtue, both in individuals and in states, but its selective application to the conscience of only religious believers is not morally defensible."

Understanding this distinction is necessary to craft policies that promote individual dignity. Thoughtful policies will also benefit from understanding examples from history that diverse societies took to promote religious tolerance and eventually religious freedom. For those who are willing to explore the details, history offers numerous societies that moved beyond religious persecution to religious tolerance and, in some cases, freedom of religion or belief. While no society upholds this right perfectly, there are lessons to be learned from exploring the evolution of these diverse societies. These cases can also alert policy makers to arguments and policies that were effective and, conversely, actions that saw backsliding and reversals of religious tolerance. This chapter explores some of the different historical experiences that produced religious tolerance and religious freedom to provide guideposts for future policy efforts. These examples demonstrate the motivations of diverse societies, as well as some of the limitations of instrumental impulses. The inclusion of examples from the non-West offers evidence that the desire for religious freedom is not simply a Western imposition forced on other societies. Efforts to secure freedom of religion in various regions over numerous centuries demonstrate a universal desire for human dignity to be respected.

First, this chapter explores top-down initiatives that furthered religious tolerance. Across diverse regions and religions, authoritarian emperors and monarchs instituted policies to protect religious minorities. These authoritarian and undemocratic rulers provided early examples of the importance of tolerant leadership. The benefits of a tolerant political leader, including those who do not rule over a democratic political system, will be revisited in Chapter 6 when I analyze the recent reforms in Uzbekistan. Next, I discuss self-interest. Religious tolerance was pursued in different historical contexts to end religious conflict or to encourage economic development or trade. Instrumental arguments concerning the economic or security benefits of religious tolerance will be further developed in Chapter 4. Then I document efforts where religious tenets and theological arguments coincided with self-interest. The final example details the evolution of a country from religious tolerance to the protection of freedom of religion or belief. This case demonstrates how civil society actors lobbied a government to adopt policies consistent with the fundamental right of freedom of religion or belief. The beneficial role that civil society can play is elaborated in a discussion of Vietnam in Chapter 7. Comprehending these cases would help Washington, human rights activists, and intergovernmental organizations (IGOs) develop meaningful strategies in the future.

THE IMPORTANCE OF TOLERANT LEADERSHIP[2]

The historical record documents strong leaders, in diverse regions, who enacted policies of religious tolerance due to personal inclinations or who identified religious tolerance as a strategic tool. Top-down initiatives by authoritarian leaders were not the result of a democratic process or an articulation of the fundamental dignity of the person. These efforts offer a temporary path to religious tolerance that can be the foundation for religious freedom in the future. Religious tolerance can develop out of a leader's perceived self-interest. If religious tolerance is thought to be a means to some other good—enhanced security, economic growth, or improved diplomatic ties—it will be pursued for the perceived benefits, and not due to some moral sentiment. In Cyrus the Great, Emperor Ashoka, and Napoleon, to name a few, we see authoritarian rulers who initiated policies that promoted religious tolerance.

Cyrus the Great (580–29 BCE), the founder of the Persian Empire, offered respect and tolerance to the religious minorities living within his realm.[3] After Cyrus conquered Babylon in 539 BCE, he issued the Cyrus Cylinder, which promised freedom of worship for the diverse communities in his empire.[4] One religious community was particularly grateful. Some of the political and economic elites from Jerusalem had been forced into exile in 586 BCE when Nebuchadnezzar destroyed the temple in Jerusalem. Cyrus went beyond freedom of worship and helped the Jewish population return to Jerusalem and offered financial support to rebuild the temple there.[5] This pragmatic policy, while beneficial to the new subjects, would serve the interests of the Persian Empire:

> The Persians' decision to allow the deportees to return home and rebuild their temples was enlightened and sensible: they believed it would strengthen their empire, since gods ought to be worshiped in their own countries, and it would win

---

[2] I am not suggesting that this is an exhaustive list of examples of religious tolerance or pleas from religious minorities. Many arguments made by persecuted groups for religious tolerance did not come to fruition. I am presenting a few examples from history to demonstrate that efforts to promote religious tolerance developed in various settings and not simply in the West. Furthermore, these examples present specific aspects, for example, the importance of a tolerant leader, that will be revisited in future chapters.

[3] Cyrus is praised numerous times in the Hebrew Bible for allowing the Jewish community to return to Jerusalem to rebuild the temple. Ezra 1:1–4 and Ezra 4:1–6.

[4] Bruce Rich, *To Uphold the World: A Call for a New Global Ethic from Ancient India* (Boston: Beacon Press, 2010), Chapter 2.

[5] Barbara Ferguson, "The Cyrus Cylinder—Often Referred to as the First Bill of Human Rights," *Washington Report on Middle East Affairs*, May 2013.

> the gratitude of the subject peoples. As a result of this benign policy, the Middle East enjoyed a period of relative stability for some two hundred years.[6]

Cyrus was not the only leader to offer his people the ability to practice their faith. Indian Emperor Ashoka issued a series of edicts after he came to power in 268 BCE. Ashoka's edicts, which explicitly assert a legal policy of religious tolerance, covered a diverse society.[7] One edict encouraged religious toleration of other faiths: "the faith of others all deserves to be honored for one reason or another. By honoring them, one exalts one's own faith and at the same time performs a service to the faith of others."[8] Indian history also offers a period of religious tolerance during the reign of Akbar in the 16th century. His openness to religious pluralism led him to invite individuals from various religious traditions to his royal court. He abolished the tax on non-Muslims—the *jizya*—in 1564.[9] He not only allowed religious tolerance for the People of the Book but extended this to Hindus as well.[10] Although these policies would not remain intact, they do demonstrate efforts in the non-West to promote religious tolerance.

Roger I's and Roger II's rule over Sicily and Malta (1091–1154) was also known for its religious tolerance. Roger de Hauteville invaded Sicily and took control from its Arab Muslim rulers at the end of the 11th century.[11] Roger I offered religious tolerance to the Muslims and Jews living there due to their administrative and economic skills. Administrators, scholars, and clerics were not expelled from the islands, but rather were encouraged to remain in their positions.[12] Further, they were not pressured to renounce their religious beliefs. It is also true that Muslims significantly outnumbered Roger I's Norman soldiers and followers.[13] Thus, it is understandable that he did not force the

---

6 Armstrong, p. 122.

7 Kristin Scheible, "Towards a Buddhist Policy of Tolerance: The Case of King Ashoka," in *Religious Tolerance in World Religions*, edited by Jacob Neuser and Bruce Chilton (West Conshohocken, PA: Templeton Foundation Press, 2008), p. 320.

8 Scheible, p. 323. See also Rich, Chapter 2; James Laine, *Meta-Religion: Religion and Power in World History* (Berkeley: University of California Press, 2015), Chapter 1; and Nussbaum, p. 60.

9 Shireen Moosvi, "Akbar's Enterprise of Religious Conciliation in the Early Phase, 1561–78: Spontaneous or Motivated," *Studies in People's History*, Vol. 4, No. 1 (2017), pp. 46–52.

10 Nussbaum, p. 60. See also http://www.columbia.edu/itc/mealac/pritchett/00islamlinks/ikram/part2_12.html.

11 Arab Muslims controlled Malta and Sicily from roughly 890 to 1090.

12 John Norwich, *The Kingdom in the Sun 1130–1194* (New York: Faber and Faber, 2010).

13 Hubert Houben, *Roger II of Sicily: A Ruler between East and West*, translated by Graham Loud and Diane Milburn (Cambridge, UK: Cambridge University Press, 2002), p. 16.

conversion of the Muslim population as that may have led to a rebellion. Roger II continued these inclusive and tolerant practices. Roger II's court was one of the most enlightened and intellectual courts in Europe at the time. The king spoke Arabic and welcomed scholars from all races and religions at his court. This is another example of a leader who developed tolerant policies while ruling over a religiously diverse population.

In the early 19th century, another powerful ruler of an empire instituted policies that offered some beleaguered religious minorities tolerance and a limited space in the public realm. Napoleon's rise to power in France and his subsequent military victories throughout the continent would improve the situation of Jewish communities in various parts of Europe. Jews who lived in Europe during the 15th, 16th, and 17th centuries were often subject to discriminatory policies, including being forced to wear distinctive clothing (including a Star of David). Some had to reside in ghettos. Two scholars described the situation of an emblematic Jewish community:

> The experience of members of the Jewish community of the Imperial Free City of Frankfurt-am-Main around 1600 is illustrative. From 1462 onward, Jews had been confined to the *Judengasse*—a single street, a quarter of a mile long and only twelve feet wide. They faced countless regulations that restricted their ability to leave the *Judengasse* (not during the night, on Sundays, or on Christian holidays). They were not allowed to bear arms, and their status was explicitly inferior to that of Christian members of the city.[14]

Jewish individuals fared far better under Muslim sultans in the Ottoman Empire than they did under Christian princes in many parts of Europe. Even in France where the French Revolution promised liberty, equality, and fraternity, and specifically asserted that "no one is to be disquieted because of his opinions, even religious," in Article 10 of the *Declaration of the Rights of Man and the Citizen* (1789), this was not always upheld in practice.[15] The revolutionaries' hostility toward religion, especially but not limited to the Catholic Church, and the Reign of Terror that followed, did little to promote religious toleration for Jews, Protestants, or Catholics.[16]

When Napoleon subdued the French political system and centralized power in his hands, he implemented measures to improve the Jewish community's situation in various parts of Europe. Napoleon made the Jewish faith one of the three official recognized religions in France. As Napoleon conquered vast ter-

---

14 Johnson and Koyama, p. 6.

15 Ishay, p. 81.

16 David Markham, "Was Napoleon an Anti-Semite? Napoleon, the Jews and Religious Freedom," Speech, Tel Aviv, Israel, May 31, 2007.

ritories from Italy to Central Europe, he liberated Jews living in ghettos.[17] On his 1798 campaign in Malta, the slave status of Jews was abolished and a synagogue was erected.[18] Additional legal efforts at promoting religious tolerance included the Concordat with the Vatican in 1801, the Napoleonic Code, and an 1807 edict granting Jewish individuals full citizenship rights in Westphalia.[19]

Napoleon was far from a liberal democrat, although he was influenced by the Enlightenment. Nor was he consistent in his toleration of his Jewish subjects. His anti-Semitic remarks or his restrictive decree (March 17, 1808—later withdrawn) should not be glossed over simply because anti-Semitism was quite common in 19th-century Europe. However, it would be a mistake to overlook his largely positive record regarding religious tolerance for Jews in Europe.[20] These brief examples of political rulers demonstrate the positive impact a leader can have on a society if they decide to promote religious tolerance in the realm.

INSTRUMENTAL MOTIVATIONS FOR RELIGIOUS TOLERANCE

History shows that tolerance of the religious Other was not always based on a noble philosophical truth or a moral imperative, but rather on the ugly reality of politics and power. One political regime may be unable to crush a religious minority without destroying much of the society in the process.[21] As Oliver

---

[17] Ibid.; Andrew Roberts, *Napoleon: A Life* (New York: Viking, 2014), pp. 96–7.

[18] Roberts, pp. 167–8.

[19] Roberts, p. 404. Napoleon's initiatives led to greater freedoms for some European Jews even after France lost conquered territories. For example, the Edict of June 10, 1813, "Regarding the Status of Persons of the Jewish Faith in the Kingdom of Bavaria" stated, "Persons of Jewish faith in the Kingdom are assured total freedom of conscience." For a translation of the document, see: http://www.rijo.homepage.t-online.de/pdf/EN_BY_JU_edikt_e.pdf.

[20] Markham (2007); Simon Schwarzfuchs, *Napoleon, the Jews and the Sanhedrin* (London: Routledge, 1979). There are different possible motives for Napoleon's policies. As a product of the Enlightenment, he had a secular outlook. He also told his soldiers in Egypt to respect Muslim leaders as "the Roman legions protected all religions" (Roberts, p. 168). It is also true to say that the campaigns in Egypt were brutal and Egyptians were hardly treated with dignity throughout Napoleon's time there. So, his religious tolerance may have stemmed from a desire to emulate those he respected in ancient times.

[21] "Much that has the appearance of principled toleration is nothing more than pragmatic or, we might say, 'Hobbesian' compromise: one group would gladly stamp out the others' beliefs and practices, but has reconciled itself to the practical reality that it can't get away with it—at least not without the intolerable cost of the proverbial 'war of all against all.'" See Leiter, p. 9.

Roy explained, "religious tolerance was not the fruit of liberalism and the Enlightenment. Rather, it was the product of grudging truces in savage wars of religion, from the Peace of Augsburg in 1555 to the Treaty of Westphalia in 1648. Politics played a bigger role than philosophy or theology."[22] This is a stark contrast to Cyrus the Great and Napoleon. Neither Cyrus the Great nor Napoleon extended religious tolerance to their respective Jewish subjects due to an inability to score a decisive military victory. Napoleon, in numerous instances, offered religious tolerance after he had conquered a territory. In contrast, Europe in the 16th and 17th centuries was convulsed by religious wars. Religious tolerance was viewed as an instrument to address a seemingly unending conflict. Hence religious tolerance was often motivated by the desire to end the bloodshed and was merely the instrument used to end the hostilities.[23] Isaiah Berlin echoed this when he stated that "toleration is historically the product of the realization of the irreconcilability of equally dogmatic faiths, and the practical improbability of complete victory of one over the other. Those who wished to survive realized that they had to tolerate error."[24]

In *Persecution and Toleration,* Johnson and Koyama discuss the less morally motivated development of what they refer to as conditional toleration. Conditional toleration was ubiquitous prior to the emergence of the modern state:

> Conditional toleration was ubiquitous because it reflected the political economy of late medieval and early modern Europe. Political authorities maintained social order by keeping groups with different beliefs legally, and often physically, separated. The maintenance of civil order through legislated separation and discrimination was part of the institutional structure of all European states, ingrained in law, politics and the economy.[25]

They further explain, "toleration today did not preclude religious persecution in the future."[26] This provides further support for one of the arguments of this

---

[22] Oliver Roy, "The Transformation of the Arab World," *Journal of Democracy*, Vol. 23, No. 3 (July 2012), p. 7.

[23] Butterfield argued that religious toleration developed in Europe due to military and political exhaustion from the religious conflicts between Catholics and Protestants. Hebert Butterfield, *Toleration in Religion and Politics* (New York: Council on Religion and International Affairs, 1980).

[24] Isaiah Berlin, "The Originality of Machiavelli," in *Against the Current: Essays in the History of Ideas* (New York: Viking Press, 1980), pp. 25–79.

[25] Johnson and Koyama, p. 7.

[26] Johnson and Koyama, p. 9. It is worth noting that Johnson and Koyama understand religious liberty as a commitment to individual freedom. "Toleration as part of a wider commitment to individual freedom. We call this form of toleration 'religious liberty.'" This does not capture all of the aspects established in international law in the

work. Freedom of religion or belief is needed because religious toleration is often limited in its duration and overall impact.

Edict of Nantes

In the 16th and 17th centuries, Europe was ravaged by conflicts, many of which concerned the "true" interpretation of Christianity. France was not immune to conflicts between Catholics and Protestants (Huguenots). Some 2 million French citizens were killed in the last 40 years of the 16th century. Henry IV sought to end the religious bloodshed when he became king in 1589. After he converted to Catholicism, he attempted to provide Huguenots with the means to maintain and adhere to their faith. To accomplish this, he issued the Edict of Nantes on April 13, 1598. The edict offered Protestants the ability to practice their faith in designated churches and to be unmolested in their affairs:

> And not to leave any occasion of trouble and difference among our Subjects, we have permitted and do permit to those of the Reformed Religion, to live and dwell in all the Cities and places of this our Kingdom and Countries under our obedience, without being inquired after, vexed, molested, or compelled to do anything in Religion, contrary to their Conscience, nor by reason of the same be searched after in houses or places where they live, they comporting themselves in other things as is contained in this our present Edict or Statute... We permit also to those of the said Religion to hold and continue the Exercise of the same in all the Cities and Places under our obedience, where it hath by them been Established and made public by many and diverse times, in the Year 1586, and in 1587, until the end of the Month of August, notwithstanding all Decrees and Judgments whatsoever to the contrary... To the end to reunite so much the better the minds and good will of our Subjects, as is our intention, and to take away all complaints for the future; We declare all those who make or shall make profession of the said Reformed Religion, to be capable of holding and exercising all Estates, Dignities, Offices, and public charges whatsoever, Royal, Signorial, or of Cities of our Kingdom, Countries, Lands, and Lordships under our obedience.[27]

While it did not allow proselytizing or other displays of their faith, the edict did offer Protestants a measure of tolerance in society.

Since years of indecisive warfare failed to settle the question of religion in France, Henry IV sought to end the bloodshed via a limited form of tolera-

ICCPR as articulated in Article 18. There are also collective aspects of freedom of religion or belief that have been established in international law.

[27] Martin I. Klauber (Ed.), "The Edict of Nantes," in *The Theology of the French Reformed Churches: From Henri IV to the Revocation of the Edict of Nantes* (Grand Rapids, MI: Reformation Heritage Books, 2014), Appendix A.

tion.[28] Although Henry hoped this cessation of hostilities would ease tensions with Huguenots, this was not the result.[29] Nor did the Edict of Nantes promote religious freedom for all. Huguenots were not won over or appeased. They protested and revolted, leading to the revocation of the edict in 1685 by Henry's grandson, Louis XIV.[30] The Edict of Fontainebleau (1685) stated:

> Be it known that for these causes and others us hereunto moving, and of our certain knowledge, full power, and royal authority, we have, by this present perpetual and irrevocable edict, suppressed and revoked, and do suppress and revoke, the edict of our said grandfather, given at Nantes in April, 1598, in its whole extent, together with the particular articles agreed upon in the month of May following, and the letters patent issued upon the same date; and also the edict given at Nimes in July, 1629; we declare them null and void, together with all concessions, of whatever nature they may be, made by them as well as by other edicts, declarations, and orders, in favor of the said persons of the R.P.R. ["the religion called the Reformed"], the which shall remain in like manner as if they had never been granted; and in consequence we desire, and it is our pleasure, that all the temples of those of the said R.P.R. situate in our kingdom, countries, territories, and the lordships under our crown, shall be demolished without delay.
>
> We forbid our subjects of the R.P.R. to meet any more for the exercise of the said religion in any place or private house, under any pretext whatever excuse it can be, even of real exercises or bailliages, even though the aforementioned exercises would have been maintained by the rulings of our council.
>
> We enjoin all ministers of the said R.P.R., who do not choose to become converts and to embrace the Catholic, apostolic, and Roman religion, to leave our kingdom and the territories subject to us within a fortnight of the publication of our present edict.[31]

This edict removed the civil and political freedoms of Protestants in France.[32] The resulting persecution of Huguenots took various forms, including coerced conversions and the destruction of Protestant churches.[33]

---

[28] Zagorin, pp. 10–11; Marshall, p. 76. Johnson and Koyama disagree with some historians on this. On page 140 they state, "Henri IV issued the Edict of Nantes in 1598 in an attempt to conciliate both the Catholics who remained suspicious of him and the Protestants whose faith he had abandoned. It was a compromise. Henri IV desired peace rather than toleration and the Edict envisioned religious concord and harmony without mentioning religious toleration explicitly."

[29] Armstrong, p. 253.

[30] Zagorin, p. 12. The Peace of Augsburg is another example of an effort to allow for toleration in order to stop a conflict between Catholics and Protestants. This effort failed as it did not result in a lasting peace or with religious freedom for all.

[31] The text of the Edict of Fontainebleau (1685) can be found at: https://clc-library-org-docs.angelfire.com/fontainbl.html.

[32] Ishay, p. 78. See also Holt, p. 187.

[33] Often, Catholic persecution of Protestants in France was used to justify Protestant intolerance and persecution of Catholics in England and Ireland; Marshall, p. 19.

The Treaties of Westphalia, which ended the religious wars between Catholics and Protestants in 1648, are another example in this mode. Between 1618 and 1648, much of Europe was convulsed by a series of religious conflicts between Catholics and Protestants. This bloodletting would come to an end with the two treaties making up the Peace of Westphalia. The Peace of Westphalia was the foundation of the modern state system and the principle of state sovereignty. State sovereignty gave the sovereign legal control over their territory. It also allowed the sovereign to determine the religion of the people living within the state's borders. It granted subjects of one state the right to emigrate to another state if they dissented from the religion of the king.[34] One of the goals of Westphalia was to stop the inter-state religious violence by determining the religion of the people within a state. While Westphalia did not end religious conflicts in Europe once and for all—as evidenced much later by the continued conflict between Catholics and Protestants in Northern Ireland, or the religious conflict in the former Yugoslavia—it did show the pragmatic value of religious tolerance. While this pragmatic approach has the benefit of ending the bloodshed, it can be temporary and reversible. As Lacorne notes, "the history of tolerance, examined over a long historical period, is a complex story of breaks and continuities, advances and regressions."[35] Still, it is a step in the right direction.

The instrumental value of religious tolerance can also be seen as a preemptive policy to blunt a violent uprising or as a means to promote trade and economic growth. Some large empires enacted policies that provided a minimal level of tolerance under certain conditions in an effort to maintain stability and prevent rebellions. Other polities tolerated the religious Other because it resulted in economic benefits. Again, these policies were not initiated due to the realization of the inherent value of the individual or the important role that freedom of conscience plays in the development of individual well-being. These policies were implemented due to the social goods they were thought to produce for society.

Dutch Republic

The Netherlands was the most tolerant polity in Western Europe.[36] In 1579, the northern provinces of the Netherlands were unified in the Union of Utrecht treaty. Article 13 offered individuals the freedom to pursue their religion:

---

34 Ishay, p. 78.

35 Denis Lacorne, *The Limits of Tolerance: Enlightenment Values and Religious Fanaticism* (New York: Columbia University Press, 2019), p. 7.

36 Zagorin, p. 147.

"every particular person shall remain free in his religion, and that no one will be pursued or investigated because of his religion."[37] While there were voices in society arguing for religious tolerance, including Spinoza and Dirck Volckertszoon,[38] these individuals had limited influence in society. Johnson and Koyama argue against the view that the ideas of John Locke, Baruch Spinoza, or other intellectuals led to the rise of religious freedom. Instead, they "propose that ideas played less a crucial role than did the changing incentives facing European rulers in the early modern period. The transformation of early modern economies and states led to the gradual recognition of the importance of religious freedom."[39] Political leaders, such as William of Orange, had the power to shape policies in ways that intellectuals and philosophers did not. Some Dutch leaders adopted pragmatic policies on religious tolerance due to the economic benefits that would ensue. Dutch authorities tolerated religious minorities in their domains in the 16th and 17th century: "The decision to allow the Jews to stay in New Netherland, despite the opposition of ministers, director general and council, and the colonists, was a consequence of the tolerant views of the directors in Amsterdam... The 'tolerant views' in Amsterdam were motivated by hope for economic advantage."[40] William of Orange echoed these instrumental arguments in 1578:

> [The] Reformed Religion is much followed and loved in this country not only because of the war, but also because we are necessarily host to merchants... of neighboring realms who adhere to this religion... [If] we do not grant it [Protestant faith] freedom of exercise by an amicable agreement and peace in the matter of religion... our common enemy will find it all easier to harm us.[41]

While Catholics and Jews did not enjoy the same rights as the members of the Dutch Reformed Church, they were tolerated in society and maintained the ability to live in accordance with some tenets of their faith.[42]

---

37 Bangs, p. 586. This freedom does not incorporate all aspects of Article 18 of the ICCPR but was offering individuals more tolerance than one could find in other parts of Europe.

38 Zagorin, Chapter 5.

39 Johnson and Koyama, p. 3.

40 Bangs, p. 589. See also George Smith, *Religion and Trade in New Netherlands: Dutch Origins and American Development* (Ithaca, NY: Cornell University Press, 1973); Haefeli (2012).

41 Herbert H. Rowen (Ed.), *The Low Countries in Early Modern Times: A Documentary History* (New York: Harper and Row, 1972), p. 65.

42 Zagorin, p. 150. Johnson and Koyama also categorize the Dutch Republic under conditional toleration (see pages 143–4). However, it is worth noting that within four decades, a military coup and the Synod of Dort rescinded Article 13, demonstrating some limits to instrumental approaches to religious tolerance.

As John Marshall explained in his magisterial work, *John Locke, Toleration and Early Enlightenment Culture*,

> Toleration as practiced in the Netherlands had largely evolved as the allowance alongside one public church of various private practices of worship, occurring in buildings which did not appear to be churches from the outside, and with processions disallowed or discouraged for Catholics and Jews. Sources of public enmity and disputation were thereby strongly discouraged or removed, and religion was increasingly rendered for the tolerated in the Netherlands what tolerationist writing often declared it to be, an essentially private matter between worshippers and their God.[43]

Individuals in the Netherlands, despite religious differences, were tolerated for pragmatic reasons, including the potential economic benefits from trade and peaceful coexistence. Some who were persecuted in other parts of Europe, such as Bayle and Locke, found refuge among the Dutch. This did not mean religious minorities enjoyed all the rights and opportunities of the Dutch Reformed Church. It did mean that they were tolerated and could live in a community of like-minded believers without the fear of being jailed or worse, as was the case in France and England at the time.

THEOLOGICAL JUSTIFICATIONS AND INTERESTS

While some societies, as noted above, pursued policies of religious tolerance out of self-interest, others also invoked theological justifications. In Medieval Spain, and under some Ottoman rulers, a pragmatic strategy of religious tolerance was justified by and was consistent with religious tenets. Thus, economic and security goals overlapped with theological justifications of tolerance for the religious Other. In these cases, toleration of religious minorities was defensible based on religious doctrines. Religious justifications that supported programs of religious tolerance sometimes helped to maintain peaceful, tolerant relations with religious minorities in society for decades or more.

Medieval Spain

Medieval Spain offers a society where religious minorities were not only tolerated but also offered a public space to flourish. Various Muslim rulers, including Rahman, accommodated the People of the Book in accordance with Islamic tenets. In her thoughtful book, *The Ornament of the World,* Menocal explained the coexistence and acceptance in al Andalusia: "This was the

[43] Marshall, p.358.

chapter of Europe's culture when Jews, Christians and Muslims lived side by side and despite their intractable differences and enduring hostilities, nourished a complex culture of tolerance."[44] Although numerous political leaders in Europe were concerned about the expansion of Islam out of Spain, Christians and Jews not only survived under Muslim rule, they were permitted to engage in economic and social activities and many thrived. While there were financial benefits to converting to Islam, Christians and Jews were not compelled to do so. Some have argued that Jewish individuals fared better under Muslim rule than under the Visigoths.[45] This is not to suggest that religious minorities enjoyed complete religious freedom. Limitations were placed on proselytization and public displays of religion:

> The Peoples of the Book were required to pay a special tax and to observe a number of restrictive regulations: Christians and Jews were prohibited from attempting to proselytize Muslims, from building new places of worship, from displaying crosses or ringing bells. In sum, they were forbidden most public displays of their religious rituals.[46]

These limitations should not detract from the tolerant culture that existed in al Andalusia. The willingness to tolerate non-Muslims was based on instrumental and theological motivations. When Rahman's rule began in 755, Muslims were a small minority in the midst of a large Catholic majority. In addition to numerical superiority, Christians (and Jews) possessed numerous economic skills (trade networks) and attributes that could aid a ruler. Muslim rulers, including Rahman, did not want or need continual conflict. Offering these subjects the ability to practice their faith encouraged an acquiescent population and preempted a large-scale conflict. In addition, the Qur'an encouraged tolerant treatment for the People of the Book since they had also received a revelation from God. According to Islamic law, the People of the Book would not only be protected (*dhimmi*), but also had the right to practice their faith and maintain

---

[44] Maria Rosa Menocal, *The Ornament of the World: How Muslims, Jews and Christians Created a Culture of Tolerance in Medieval Spain* (New York: Brown, 2003), p. 11. Johnson and Koyama consider Medieval Spain as an example of conditional toleration (see p. 154). While I agree with Johnson and Koyama that this is not a case of religious freedom, I follow scholars such as Menocal in acknowledging the positive aspects of the religious tolerance that was extended to religious minorities in Medieval Spain.

[45] "Having suffered severe discrimination at the hands of the Visigoths, Jewish communities under the Muslims enjoyed more freedom, affluence, and social standing than any Jewish community would until the 19th century"; Zachary Karabell, *Peace Be Upon You* (New York: Knopf, 2007), p. 71.

[46] Menocal, p. 73.

their autonomy and houses of worship.[47] This was the precedent established by Muhammad.[48] Additionally, there are prohibitions on religious coercion in Islam. The Qur'an is clear that "There is no compulsion in religion." God does not want people to engage in religious rituals due to compulsion, only by their own choice. Forced conversions carry no moral weight for either the agent or the victim of the process.[49]

The Ottoman Empire

Over a vast territory stretching from Central Europe throughout the Levant, Muslim Ottoman rulers, for over two centuries (starting in the 15th century), offered numerous religious communities tolerance in exchange for compliance with official policies.[50] These tolerant policies were known and discussed in Europe. Locke's *Letter Concerning Toleration* and Voltaire's writings on toleration note Ottoman rule. Not only did various sultans and viziers see the value of stability over the diverse religious communities within their borders, but offering religious toleration was consistent with Islamic doctrine. Islamic tenets argued that Muslims should show respect to other religious traditions, especially the People of the Book.

Sultans, such as Mehmed II in the 15th century, saw the merit of allowing non-Muslim communities a degree of autonomy and tolerance. These religious leaders and institutions could assist the sultan in executing his policies while

---

[47] Barkey, p. 120.

[48] Vincent Cornell, "Theologies of Difference and Ideologies of Intolerance in Islam," in *Religious Tolerance in World Religions*, edited by Jacob Neuser and Bruce Chilton (West Conshohocken, PA: Templeton Foundation Press, 2008), p. 289.

[49] The Qur'anic statement, "There is no compulsion in religion" (2:256), was not always upheld in Islamic realms. This does not distract from the theological underpinnings of religious tolerance, especially as it related to the dhimmi. Patricia Crone, *God's Rule – Government and Islam* (New York: Columbia University Press, 2004), p. 381. Ibrahim Kalim also discusses this in "Sources of Tolerance and Intolerance in Islam," in *Religious Tolerance in World Religions*, Chapter 11. Non-coercion is not limited to Islam. Christian thinkers made theological arguments against coercion as well. Lactantius, the Christian scholar who influenced Constantine's Edict of Milan in 313, offered theological arguments for why religion cannot be coerced. In the Divine Institutes, he states that religious sacrifice cannot be "extorted from a person against his will. For unless it is offered spontaneously, and from the soul, it is a curse: [this is the case] when men sacrifice, compelled by proscription, by injuries, by prison, by tortures"; quoted in E. Gregory Wallace, "Justifying Religious Freedom: The Western Tradition," *Penn State Law Review*, Vol. 114, No. 2 (2009), p. 507. The Edict of Milan (313) can be found at: https://sourcebooks.fordham.edu/source/edict-milan.asp.

[50] Johnson and Koyama refer to the millet system as another example of conditional toleration (p. 10). They do not stress the theological aspects of this relationship.

keeping these groups acquiescent. So long as these religious communities did not defy the ruling order and contributed to the peace of the empire, they would be left alone.[51] It was also true that Ottoman leaders understood that the non-Muslim communities within their territory could promote and enhance economic growth within the empire.[52] A prosperous empire offered various sultans the confidence to tolerate various religious minorities knowing that they were not only not a threat, but were contributing to the stability of the realm.

The self-governing system set up for religious minorities was known as the millet system.[53] The "millet" system was a loose and flexible (not a fully centralized standard) set of administrative rules and relationships between the Ottoman state and various religious communities (Greek Orthodox, Armenian, Jewish). This "bureaucratic tolerance" had benefits. According to one scholar,

> the millet system was clearly a novel form of bureaucratic tolerance that was designed to facilitate religious coexistence over a vast territory even if it did not create formal equality between all subjects. This system offered peace, prevented persecution for more than four centuries, and facilitated the incorporation of minority communities into the empire.[54]

It is worth recalling that in 1453 Mehmed demanded that Jews move to Constantinople not to convert them, but because he needed their skills.

---

[51] Barkey, p. 110. While there was always the possibility of a local leader acting aggressively toward a religious minority community, the policies developed by the Grand Vizier and other Ottoman officials in Constantinople opposed and limited intolerance. Sultan Beyazid III (1481–1512) pressured Jews to convert. Mehmed IV's rule (1648–1687) and specifically the period 1660–1680 were particularly intolerant times. "The great conflagration in Istanbul in the summer of 1660 was followed by a decree banning Jews from living in much of Istanbul and ordering them to sell their property and give their trusts to Muslims. In 1661, laws regarding the dress of Jews and Christians were redeployed; Jewish and Christian property was confiscated, and some churches and synagogues were destroyed. In 1662 seven churches were razed… During these years, Sufis were actively persecuted, some executed and their ceremonies banned, culminating in the destruction of the Shrine of Kanber Baba in 1667"; Barkey, p. 184.

[52] Barkey, p. 110.

[53] Karabell, p. 170. It is true that the *devshirme* policy of taking Christian boys from the Balkans to serve in the janissary was disruptive. Some parents tried to bribe officials not to take their kids, while others tried to get their sons into the *devshirme* because of the upward mobility that was possible. But this was not done to punish Christians.

[54] Lacorne, p. 82.

Offering non-Muslim religious leaders the autonomy to determine their community's religious affairs was also beneficial:

> The Ottomans had several goals: to ensure the loyalty of a growing Christian community with important economic skills, to increase legality and order, and to enable the administration to run smoothly and taxes to flow to the center while also reinforcing the wedge between the Orthodox and Catholic worlds of Europe.[55]

Religious minorities within the empire also coveted tolerance, not simply because it gave non-Muslim religious leaders the ability to control their communities, but also because it could enhance their reputations and status within society:

> The state institutionalized existing religious boundaries, and adapted its rule based on an understanding of Islamic domination over diverse non-Muslim communities, molded to its own interests in governance and legibility. Local community leadership entered negotiated agreements with Ottoman rulers based on their desire to maintain their religious autonomy and community existence free from interference.[56]

Thus, religious tolerance benefited both Ottoman leaders and the various religious communities spread throughout the domain. These pragmatic values were also in harmony with theological tenets of the faith.[57] In the Qur'an, the doctrine of the *dhimma*, established during the life of the Prophet establishes specific policies for non-Muslims. These policies offered the People of the Book protection, but not equal status with Muslims:

> From a theological point of view, the type of tolerance practiced in the Ottoman Empire has a distant source in the Qur'anic doctrine of the dhimma elaborated, according to tradition, by the prophet Muhammed and his lieutenants at the time of the conquest of Arabia. Dhimma designates accords or pacts signed between the conquering armies and conquered non-Muslims (dhimmis), extending privileges to the latter if they were Peoples of the Book—that is, Jewish and Christian readers of the Bible. These contractual agreements guaranteed freedom of movement, conscience, and religious practice; the right to own property; and the existence of a separate legal system with its own codes, courts, and methods for resolving conflicts. That said, peoples had to accept their status as subordinate individuals, treat Muslims with deference, and pay a person tax—the capitation, or jizya—or carry out tasks such as road maintenance.[58]

---

[55] Barkey, p. 130.
[56] Barkey, p. 114.
[57] Barkey puts less emphasis on the theological reasons than on the political and economic motivations.
[58] Lacorne, p. 71.

In fact, compared to its European counterparts, Ottoman lands were highly tolerant of religious difference:

> As the West banished its Jews, enclosed them in small and filthy ghettos, burned their heretics, unleashed its inquisitions among its own people, and tore apart the fabric of society in religious wars, the realms of the Ottomans were mostly peaceful, accepted diversity, and pursued policies of accommodation.[59]

The result of the millet system and the religious tolerance at its core was an empire that was largely stable for hundreds of years. This is not to suggest that there was no violence or persecution. But the overall record was one of tolerance, even though religious minorities did not enjoy full religious freedom.[60]

PROGRESSING FROM RELIGIOUS TOLERANCE TO FREEDOM OF RELIGION OR BELIEF

Some societies moved beyond religious tolerance to offer their citizens a more substantive protection of freedom of religion. In some cases, the development of religious freedom occurred due to efforts by civil society actors within a state. These efforts, whether by human rights activists or a religious organization representing a minority faith, originated from the position that an unequal or discriminatory policy ought to be changed. These civil society actors pursued changes in government policies from a grassroots or bottom-up approach. Sweden offers an example of this grassroots effort. The evolution of religious policy in Sweden moved from a state in the 16th century defined by the Lutheran tradition, to one where diverse religious communities are given the freedom and financial assistance to sustain their traditions within Swedish society.

In the 16th century (1593), the king decided to adopt the Lutheran faith as the national religion of Sweden.[61] In doing so, he turned away from the Catholic Church, and this impact would be felt in various territories in Scandinavia.[62]

---

[59] Barkey, p. 110.

[60] Barkey, p. 120.

[61] This religious transition was formally established in 1593 at the Uppsala Synod; Pirjo Markkola, "The Long History of Lutheranism in Scandinavia. From State Religion to the People's Church," *Perichoresis*, Vol. 13, No. 2 (2015), pp. 3–15.

[62] Christianity had been established between 800 ce and 1100 ce. Maarit Jantera-Jareborg, "Religion and the Secular State in Sweden," in *Religion and the Secular State: National Reports,* edited by Javier Martinez Torron and W. Cole Durham (Madrid: Servicio de Publicaciones de la Facultad de Derecho de la Universidad Complutense, 2015), pp. 670–71, https://www.iclrs.org/content/blurb/files/Sweden.1.pdf.

The connection between the king, country, and the Church of Sweden would remain strong until the 20th century when Free Churches would pressure the government for greater freedom and tolerance.[63]

In the 19th century, some Scandinavian countries experienced revivalist religious movements that sought to reinvigorate the faithful. In Sweden, revivalism resulted in the development of religious pluralism and active, Free Churches that sought autonomy from the Church of Sweden and the ability to govern their congregations.[64] They also sought to separate church and state.[65] In seeking self-governance, the Free Churches lobbied the government for religious tolerance. These organizations were part of a social network that continued to petition the government for greater rights pertaining to religious freedom.[66]

The development of religious tolerance in Sweden in the 19th century would progress into a robust form of religious freedom in the 20th century. This process occurred over a number of decades and demonstrates how long the road to freedom of religion or belief can be. In 1951, the Swedish government passed a law that dramatically changed the relationship between the state and various religious traditions within its borders: the Religious Freedom Act. The Church of Sweden was no longer a state institution, but rather a religious community, albeit a privileged one given its long history in Swedish society.[67] In the decades that followed, numerous reports and commissions studied the relationship between church and state.

As demographics changed and Sweden became more diverse, minority religious communities questioned whether freedom of religion or belief was being upheld and whether there was religious neutrality when the Church of Sweden enjoyed an advantageous position. Sweden has changed quite considerably over the last few decades. There are roughly 10 million inhabitants in Sweden and roughly "two million are of foreign origin." These changes have produced a multi-confessional society with Islam occupying a more public space: "This is demonstrated through newly built mosques (with minarets), religiously artic-

---

[63] Gunnar Edqvist, "Freedom of Religion and New Relations Between Church and State in Sweden," *Studia Theologica*, Vol. 54 (2000), pp. 35–41. Dag Thorkildsen, "West Nordic and East Nordic Religiousness and Secularity: Historical Unity and Diversity," in *Secular and Sacred? The Scandinavian Case of Religion in Human Rights, Law and Public Square*, edited by Rosemarie van den Breemer, Jose Casanova, and Trygve Wyller (Gottingen: Vandenhoeck and Ruprecht, 2014), p. 92.

[64] Thorkildsen, "West Nordic," p. 92.

[65] Per Pettersoon, "State and Religion in Sweden: Ambiguity between Disestablishment and Religious Control," *Nordic Journal of Religion and Society*, Vol. 24, No. 2 (2011), pp. 119–35.

[66] Thorkildsen, p. 95.

[67] Edqvist, p. 35.

ulated dressing codes, celebration of Ramadan, and increasingly, the founding of schools with a religious curriculum."[68] Some Swedes have not welcomed these demographic changes, as evidenced by Pew Research Center's Social Hostility Index in 2014.

Further legal changes ensued and resulted in the Act on Religious Communities (1998). This act, in conjunction with the 1974 constitution, establishes more robust protections for freedom of religion and belief.[69] It allows for the development of diverse religious communities, defined by their own beliefs and structure. If registered, these religious communities can seek financial support from the government so long as the community is upholding the fundamental values of society (hence, the community cannot promote racism or misogyny). It also establishes that citizens are not required to belong to a religious community.[70] The Swedish Commission for Government Support to Faith Communities (SST) provides grants to religious communities to build or renovate a building used for religious gatherings, religious education, or worship.[71] The SST also provides grants for traditional religious outreach and new activities.[72] Further, religious communities can apply for financial assistance from the Swedish government in order to maintain their faith and sustain their community. Sweden has a compulsory fee (or tax) that goes either to the Church of Sweden or to other registered religious communities.[73] This financial assistance has also been used to provide the Swedish Jewish Council with support to prevent anti-Semitic attacks.

Evidence of freedom of religion or belief is also found in policies that respect religious beliefs and attire. Jehovah's Witnesses are traditionally pacifists who refuse to use lethal force. They are not required to perform military service in Sweden on account of their beliefs. [74] The Swedish military also

---

[68] Jantera-Jareborg, p. 670.

[69] One section of the Swedish Constitution is the Ordinance of Government (also called the Instrument of Government). In it, the fundamental right of freedom of religion and belief is established in Chapter 2. Everyone has the right to free exercise of their religion without state interference and the right to disassociate with a religious tradition; Jantera-Jareborg, p. 675.

[70] Edqvist, pp. 38–9.

[71] See the commission's webpage for more information: http://www.sst.a.se/inenglish.

[72] Jantera-Jareborg, p. 682.

[73] Edqvist, p. 40. Some have questioned whether Sweden is truly neutral toward all religious (and non-religious) communities given the fact that the Church of Sweden is still a semi-official church with a special position in relation to the state (see Pettersoon, "State and Religion"). Whether or not the Swedish government is completely neutral is not my central concern. A state can protect religious freedom without being completely neutral.

[74] State Department (2015).

Table 2.1 Pew Research Center international religious freedom and restrictions scores

Sweden	2007	2014	2019
Government Regulations Index (GRI)	1.2	2.4	2.6
Social Hostilities Index (SHI)	0.7	4.6	1.5
Average of GRI and SHI	0.6	3.5	2.1

permits individuals to wear religious headwear that is consistent with their beliefs. In addition, individuals can wear religious symbols in public. Public schools also include curricula that teach students about various religious traditions in a comprehensive and tolerant manner.[75] We will return to the example of Sweden in Chapter 5 when we focus on the important role of educational policies.

According to the Pew Research Center's reports, Sweden is a religious free society with few government restrictions and some limited social animosity between religious groups. Sweden's scores are documented in Table 2.1. The Pew Research Center assesses government restrictions as follows: "The Government Restrictions Index measures government laws, policies and actions that restrict religious beliefs and practices. The GRI is comprised of 20 measures of restrictions, including efforts by government to ban particular faiths, prohibit conversion, limit preaching or give preferential treatment to one or more religious groups." The Social Hostilities Index explores ways in which social groups limit religious freedom: "The Social Hostilities Index measures acts of religious hostility by private individuals, organizations or groups in society. This includes religion-related armed conflict or terrorism, mob or sectarian violence, harassment over attire for religious reasons or other religion-related intimidation or abuse. The SHI includes 13 measures of social hostility." Pew uses a ten-point index, with higher scores indicating more government restrictions and social hostilities. A zero indicates low government and societal restrictions on religion and a ten represents the highest level of government and societal restrictions on religion.[76]

Thus, in Sweden we see that religious freedom evolved from religious tolerance in the 19th century to a right that is protected in various laws and policies. This was the result of various religious communities within civil

[75] Jantera-Jareborg, p. 684.

[76] Pew Research Center (2020). The criteria for how Pew develops its measures for government restrictions and social hostilities were discussed in Chapter 1.

society pushing for greater equality in the religious realm. We will return to the positive role civil society can play in Chapter 7.

The evolution of freedom of religion or belief in Sweden was also mirrored in other countries in Western Europe.[77] Some scholars have noted the role of civil society and Christian leaders in the development of religious freedom in the European Convention on Human Rights and the Universal Declaration of Human Rights after World War II.[78] These Christian leaders and groups (the World Council of Churches, for example) were concerned about the persecution of faith communities behind the Iron Curtain. For the scholar Samuel Moyn, the fear of communism and the threat to Christianity in Europe motivated civil society actors to develop freedom of religion or belief as a fundamental human right in regional and international law.

CONCLUSION

The different historical cases explored in this chapter demonstrate that religious tolerance is possible in different social and cultural environments. Promoting religious tolerance was developed by authoritarian leaders often motivated by the perceived benefits that a religious minority could bring to society. These instrumental arguments, either for economic or security reasons, have been echoed in contemporary times by numerous policy makers in the West.[79] History demonstrates that instrumental arguments for religious tolerance can limit persecution, and therefore should be pursued. However, we need to recognize the limitations of instrumental motivations for religious

---

[77] Markkola notes a similar pattern in Finland in the 20th century, as the Lutheran faith's role in society gradually changed.

[78] Samuel Moyn, "Religious Freedom and the Fate of Secularism," in *Religion, Secularism, and Constitutional Democracy*, edited by Jean Cohen and Cecile Laborde (New York: Columbia University Press, 2016), pp. 27–46.

[79] Eric Patterson, "What They Say and Do: Religious Freedom as a National Security Lens," *The Review of Faith and International Affairs*, Vol. 2, No. 1 (Spring 2013), pp. 22–30. State Department, Bureau of Democracy, Human Rights and Labor, *Religious Freedom and National Security*, August 17, 2011 (Washington, D.C.: US State Department); Malcom Evans, "Historical Analysis of Freedom of Religion or Belief as a Technique for Resolving Religious Conflict," in *Facilitating Freedom of Religion or Belief: A Deskbook*, edited by Tore Lindholm, W. Cole Durham, and Bahia G. Tahzib-Lie (Leiden: Martinus Nijhoff Publishers, 2004), pp. 11–14; Brian Grim, Greg Clark, and Robert Edward Synder, "Is Religious Freedom Good for Business? A Conceptual and Empirical Analysis," *Interdisciplinary Journal of Research on Religion*, Vol. 10, No. 4 (2014), https://www.religjournal.com/pdf/ijrr10004.pdf; Anthony Gill, "Religious Liberty and Economic Development: Exploring the Causal Connections," *The Review of Faith and International Affairs*, Vol. 2, No. 4 (2013), pp. 5–23.

tolerance. Instrumental arguments for religious tolerance have not always resulted in freedom of religion or belief. Therefore, it is important for the international community to develop policies and pursue diplomatic efforts that aim at the full realization of Article 18 of the ICCPR. The next chapter discusses international efforts to develop norms, legal standards, institutions, and policies to embed this fundamental human right across the globe.

3. Working collectively: multilateral approaches to the promotion of freedom of religion or belief

INTRODUCTION

On September 2, 2017, ten men were killed. These bound fishermen, students, and shopkeepers watched their neighbors dig a shallow grave that would soon hold their remains. Some of the Rohingya Muslim men were shot, while others were hacked to death by soldiers in the Burmese military and Buddhists in the village of Inn Din.[1] This is just one massacre in the genocide committed against the Rohingya Muslims of Myanmar. (In 1989, the military changed the country's name to Myanmar, although many continue to use Burma to refer to this state in Southeast Asia.) Soldiers and civilians burned villages, raped women and girls, and killed the Rohingya, whom they refer to as Bengalis. These clearance operations in 2017 took place in over 50 locations.[2] The Rohingya Muslims are considered illegal trespassers or migrants, but not fellow citizens to many Burmese. In a village approximately 40 miles to the north of Inn Din, Thar Nge indicated that the military burned a village with the help of local civilians: "The army invited us to burn the kalar village at Hpaw Ti Kaung." The military and local police forces sought to burn the property of the Rohingya so that they did not have a place to return to.[3] Over 6500 Rohingya were killed in approximately 30 days.[4] The military used Facebook

[1] Wa Lone, Kyaw Soe Oo, Simon Lewis, and Antoni Slodkowski, "How Myanmar Forces, Burned, Looted and Killed in a Remote Village," *Reuters*, February 8, 2018, https://www.reuters.com/article/us-myanmar-rakhine-events-specialreport/special-report-how-myanmar-forces-burned-looted-and-killed-in-a-remote-village-idUSKBN1FS3BH. This was not the first or only time the Rohingya were targeted; they were also violently attacked in 2012, 2013, and 2016.

[2] Yuzuki Nagakoshi, "The Scope and Implications of the International Criminal Court's [ICC's] Jurisdictional Decision over the Rohingya Crisis," *Human Rights Quarterly*, Vol. 43, No. 2 (2021), p. 264.

[3] Lone et al., "How Myanmar."

[4] Eleanor Albert and Lindsay Maizland, "The Rohingya Crisis," *Council on Foreign Affairs*, January 23, 2020, https://www.cfr.org/backgrounder/rohingya-crisis.

as a tool to promote hatred and encourage the killing of the Rohingya.[5] The fear of additional violence sent over 700 000 fleeing to Bangladesh and other countries in Southeast Asia.[6] The UN High Commissioner for Human Rights stated that "the situation seems a textbook example of ethnic cleansing."[7] Bangladesh and the UN High Commissioner for Refugees (UNHCR) estimated that more than 870 000 Rohingya refugees were living in Bangladesh at the beginning of 2021.[8]

This hatred and incitement of violence has been festering in a country where roughly 90 percent are Buddhists. Anti-Muslim sentiment and discourse were prevalent, and Buddhist nationalist groups such as Ma Ba Tha (the Committee for the Protection of Race and Religion) promoted it. One member of Ma Ba Tha explained his, and other Buddhists', fears that they would be eliminated by Muslims: "This country was founded with the Buddhist ideology. And if the Buddhist culture vanish, Yangon will become like Saudi and Mecca. Then, there wouldn't be the influence of peace and truth. There will be more discrimination and violence." He went on to say, "it can also be the fall of Buddhism. And our race will be eliminated."[9] Firebrand monks, such as Ashin Wirathu, promoted hatred toward the Rohingya Muslim population in speeches denouncing them as terrorists and criminals: "we are being raped in every town, being sexually harassed in every town, being ganged up on and bullied in every town… In every town, there is a crude and savage Muslim majority."[10] The expression of a threatening religious Other is similar to how

---

[5] Paul Mozur, "A Genocide Incited on Facebook, with Posts from Myanmar's Military," *New York Times*, October 15, 2018, https://www.nytimes.com/2018/10/15/technology/myanmar-facebook-genocide.html; Alexandra Stevenson, "Facebook Admits It Was Used to Incite Violence in Myanmar," *New York Times*, November 6, 2018, https://www.nytimes.com/2018/11/06/technology/myanmar-facebook.html.

[6] UN Human Rights Council, "Resolution 34/22, Situation on Human Rights in Myanmar," March 24, 2017, A/HRC/RES/34/22; Lone et al., "How Myanmar."

[7] Gert Rosenthal, "A Brief and Independent Inquiry into the Involvement of the United Nations in Myanmar from 2010 to 2018," May 29, 2019, https://www.un.org/sg/sites/www.un.org.sg/files/atoms/files/Myanmar%20Report%20-%20May%202019.pdf.

[8] Nagakoshi, p. 263.

[9] Francis Wade, *Myanmar's Enemy Within* (London: Zed Books, 2017), pp. 5–6. Christians in Myanmar also face discrimination and pressure to convert in Chin State, north of Rakhine.

[10] Nahal Toosi, "The Genocide the U.S. Didn't See Coming," *Politico*, March/April 2018, https://www.politico.com/magazine/story/2018/03/04/obama-rohingya-genocide-myanmar-burma-muslim-syu-kii-217214/.

Protestants and Catholics viewed each other in the 16th and 17th centuries, as noted in Chapter 1.[11]

Aung San Suu Kyi, the chair of the National League for Democracy (NLD) and Nobel Peace Prize laureate, used troubling language as well. She referred to the Rohingya as simply "Muslims" and claimed that "the loss of lives, injuries, burning of villages, and the displacement of peoples is the fault of armed Muslim groups," thus shielding the security forces and Tatmadaw (military) from responsibility for the massacres.[12] Regardless of these attempts to distract blame, the military was involved in the preparations for and organization of the operations. Senior General Min Aung Hlaing indicated his intentions in a Facebook post: "the Bengali problem was a long-standing one which has become an unfinished job despite the efforts of the previous governments to solve it. The government in office is taking great care in solving the problem."[13] Many criticized Aung San Suu Kyi and other political and military figures for these human rights violations. However, Myanmar demonstrates that the international community's multilateral efforts failed to address adequately this tragic situation. This was due to a lack of political will on behalf of key states and no coordinated campaign to pressure the government of Myanmar.

This chapter sets out some of the international architecture of religious freedom. To evaluate the events surrounding the Rohingya we need to understand the legal framework and the multilateral initiatives that can address this situation. While this chapter focuses on international institutions, including international law and international organizations, we need to recall that these are developed by and dependent on states. Various actors may try different measures to help promote and protect religious freedom, but states are sovereign. This chapter explains the laws and institutions that states created. It demonstrates what roadblocks develop when states decide that the violation of freedom of religion or belief is not a significant national concern.

One cannot analyze all the international laws or IGOs that address this topic. In this chapter, I offer a brief overview of some of the most prominent multilateral initiatives to promote and protect freedom of religion or belief, including the main aspects of international law and efforts by the UN to

---

[11] "Nationalist Rakhine leaders amplified the looming threat of further subordination, this time to Islam, and in the process created a narrative that centered on the need to purify the Rakhine identity and finally rid their land of any foreign contaminants"; Wade, p. 59.

[12] Lynn Kuok, "While the World Sleeps, Myanmar Burns," *Foreign Affairs*, September 28, 2017.

[13] UN Human Rights Council, "Human Rights Situations that Require the Council's Attention, Report of the Independent International Fact-Finding Mission on Myanmar," September 12, 2018, A/HRC/39/64.

promote this human right. The premise of this chapter is that the fundamental right to freedom of religion or belief is established in international law, and various multilateral initiatives seek to promote this right. Despite numerous multilateral actions undertaken on behalf of this human right, this has not produced a more tolerant or rights-protective global environment. Since states are the dominant actors in international relations, their efforts to promote religious freedom or their unwillingness to address religious persecution will determine whether a persecuted group will fend for itself in the state of nature or whether it will be protected. Myanmar shows that multilateral efforts, albeit with noble intentions, often fail to adequately address or remedy religious persecution, especially when powerful states lack the will to confront the bloodshed or are indifferent to human suffering. IGOs alone cannot protect this right established in international law. For the protection of freedom of religion or belief to take hold, IGOs need to convince states that the violation of this human right can harm their interests. IGOs also need to work with civil society actors to uphold international legal standards and produce thoughtful long-term policies to have a lasting impact. Future chapters will explore in detail how states and non-state actors are essential to furthering this fundamental human right.

INTERNATIONAL ORDER SINCE 1945

Given the anarchy of international relations, there is no overarching authority or global police force to respond to religious persecution or to end it. Thus, the failure to adequately address or protect the Rohingya Muslims is unsurprising. The international community, that is states, IGOs, NGOs, faith-based organizations (FBOs), and transnational companies, *can* engage in activities that advance or inhibit the human right to freedom of religion or belief. Without thoughtful policies that enjoy support from various stakeholders, especially powerful states, these efforts will result in many impotent and ineffective statements and resolutions with little impact on the ground. This will have tragic consequences for those facing persecution and extermination.

States dominate the global environment. There are numerous drawbacks to a state-centered international order. Nevertheless, this is the current reality. Many states guard their sovereignty and independent decision-making. States draft and ratify international legal documents. States create and join international courts and organizations. Even those states that relinquish some of their sovereignty to an international organization such as the European Union often do so with little enthusiasm. Further difficulties involve enforcement. International law is not self-enforcing. Policies created by international organizations do not implement themselves. International courts lack the power to enforce their rulings. Thus, for there to be successful outcomes in the realm of human rights or religious freedom, multilateral efforts require state efforts in coalition with international partners.

THE PROCESS OF PROTECTING HUMAN RIGHTS

The process to protect human rights, including freedom of religion or belief, begins by setting standards. States, in conjunction with other international actors, must discuss and then create standards and laws to identify what constitutes a human right. Once states ratify a treaty, policy makers and citizens need to be educated to ensure that others understand these legal standards. Some IGOs and civil society organizations will create programs to train law enforcement, judicial officials, and lawyers, and will help to draft national legislation that complies with international standards.

The next step in the process involves monitoring. Various international actors, including IGOs and NGOs, must track and monitor whether the human rights standards are respected or breached. Monitoring involves collecting accurate information. This occurs by witnessing first-hand the situation on the ground, collecting eyewitness accounts, analyzing media reports or social media accounts, and interviewing relevant stakeholders and affected individuals. Monitoring seeks to raise awareness and encourage states to comply with the legal commitments they undertook to protect human rights, including freedom of religion or belief.

IGOs, such as the UN or European Union (EU), can aid those in need. In a similar manner to a state's foreign policy (discussed in Chapter 4), IGOs can provide direct assistance to individuals who are suffering from discrimination or persecution due to their beliefs. This can take the form of legal aid for those imprisoned for their beliefs or financial support to renovate or rebuild a house of worship, religious school, or sacred space. If individuals have fled their country of origin due to violence, IGOs can offer immediate humanitarian relief (food, shelter, water, clothing) and then try to help repatriate them or persuade another state to give them asylum.

An additional part of the process requires enforcement mechanisms. To enforce these human rights standards, violators need to be held accountable. Punishing a violator can take various forms from publicly criticizing a violator, to withholding financial assistance, to implementing debilitating sanctions, to prosecution via court proceedings. Naming and shaming will be more effective if the violator cares about their international reputation and if the organization making the criticism is respected. An international organization that does not value human rights or does not have a history of speaking out about human rights violations will have less influence than those that consistently defended human rights, including freedom of religion or belief. IGOs can implement sanctions on a state or non-state actor that violates freedom of religion or belief by adopting resolutions that limit trade, or by imposing financial penalties on perpetrators. The use of force by IGOs is a tool rarely used to limit human rights violations, including freedom of religion or belief. More often, there is an attempt to prosecute individuals associated with atrocities and violations of international law through an international court.

In sum, states value their autonomy and independence, but they also seek to advance certain values including, at times, religious freedom. States create international rules and organizations to make international relations more orderly and systematic and to advance these values.

GLOBAL LEGAL STANDARDS OF FREEDOM OF RELIGION OR BELIEF

International norms and the treaties and covenants that constitute international law are the products of states. States engage in a variety of activities, including the creation of binding international legal standards and obligations. Some governments believe it is in their state's interest to do so. In other cases, a state may publicly accept legal norms or ratify a treaty for appearances or due to international pressure even if there is little intention to follow through on these legal commitments. Thus, states may make an insincere commitment in an effort to appease others in the international community.[14] States support resolutions and declarations, and sign these legal instruments, whether they intend to honor them or not, because they believe it is beneficial to do so. One of the most significant international documents to articulate the importance of freedom of religion or belief was the Universal Declaration.

Universal Declaration of Human Rights

The Universal Declaration of Human Rights was an aspirational document that prepared the way for two international treaties: the ICCPR and the International Covenant on Economic, Social, and Cultural Rights (ICESCR). While the Universal Declaration was not legally binding,[15] it did provide a foundation on which policy makers built legal obligations. The foundation

---

[14] Heather Smith-Cannoy, *Insincere Commitments: Human Rights Treaties, Abusive States, and Citizen Activism* (Washington, D.C.: Georgetown University Press, 2012). See also Giovanni Mantilla, *Lawmaking Under Pressure: International Humanitarian Law and Internal Armed Conflict* (Ithaca, NY: Cornell University Press, 2020).

[15] While the Universal Declaration was not legally binding, some aspects of the Declaration may be considered parts of customary international law and, hence, binding.

for the right to freedom of religion or belief and other rights established in the ICCPR and ICESCR is based on the inherent dignity of the person.

The preamble of the Declaration begins with: "Whereas recognition of the inherent dignity and of the equal and inalienable rights of all members of the human family is the foundation of freedom, justice and peace in the world."[16] Human dignity is a concept repeated in human rights treaties. It has been described as essential to human rights and as "a ground or feature of human rights."[17] Eleanor Roosevelt, the chair of the Human Rights Commission that drafted the Declaration, indicated, "the commission had decided to include it [human dignity] in order to emphasize the inherent dignity of all mankind."[18] They were universalizing human dignity by stating that everyone had it regardless of status.[19] Understanding how human dignity relates to or underpins human rights is important to understanding why freedom of religion or belief is necessary for human flourishing.

Scholars have offered different conceptualizations of the relationship between human dignity and human rights in terms of the intrinsic value of all human beings, the harm incurred when one's dignity is violated, and the diminishment of individual capacity to cite a few.[20] One prominent scholar of human rights explained that human dignity "requires autonomy, equality, societal respect, and recognition, as well as material security."[21] To live a life with dignity, individuals must have the capacity for self-determination; namely, an individual must have sovereignty and control over their thoughts, decisions, and life plan. Without the freedom to develop and carry out ideas about how to live, individuals lack the ability for self-direction and self-determination in the social, economic, and political realms. Without equality and respect from others in society, individuals cannot make meaningful decisions about how to structure their lives. Given our physical need for food, water, and shelter, if individuals are not consistently able to satisfy their basic needs (due to lack

---

[16] See https://www.un.org/en/universal-declaration-human-rights/. For an in-depth account of the development of Article 18 of the Universal Declaration of Human Rights, see Lindkvist, *Religious Freedom*.

[17] Charles Beitz, "Human Dignity in the Theory of Human Rights: Nothing but a Phrase?" *Philosophy and Public Affairs*, Vol. 41, No. 3 (Summer 2013), p. 268. Beitz also suggests that the drafters of the Universal Declaration did not have a clear view of what the concept of human dignity meant.

[18] Quoted in Beitz, p. 268.

[19] John Kleining and Nicholas Evans, "Human Flourishing, Human Dignity, and Human Rights," *Law and Philosophy*, Vol. 32, No. 5 (September 2013), pp. 539–64.

[20] Beitz details some of these discussions in his article.

[21] Rhoda Howard-Hassmann, *In Defense of Universal Human Rights* (Cambridge, UK: Polity Press, 2018), p. 11.

of access, climate degradation, or insufficient resources), their dignity is not being respected, recognized, or realized.

The right to freedom of religion or belief demonstrates the relationship and codependence between human dignity and human rights. When the state prevents an individual from freely organizing their life according to deeply held beliefs, that individual is denied their dignity and intrinsic worth as a member of the human family. If one experiences legal or political discrimination due to their beliefs (theistic or non-theistic) their dignity is disregarded. If one cannot secure a job due to the beliefs they hold and their material well-being is negatively affected, their capacity for self-determination and self-fulfillment is unobtainable and their dignity is violated.

The articles in the Universal Declaration articulate how individuals' dignity is established in a range of social, political, and economic activities and circumstances.[22] Article 18 of the Universal Declaration specifies how individuals ought to be treated with respect to their beliefs.[23] This was later expanded on in the ICCPR.

ICCPR

After the Universal Declaration of Human Rights, the ICCPR, which entered into force in 1976, is the most important international legal statement on the importance of the right to freedom of religion or belief. Article 18 of the ICCPR articulates the legal standard for freedom of religion and belief as follows:

1. Everyone shall have the right to freedom of thought, conscience, and religion. This right shall include freedom to have or to adopt a religion or belief of his choice, and freedom, either individually or in community with others and in public or private, to manifest his religion or belief in worship, observance, practice and teaching.
2. No one shall be subject to coercion which would impair his freedom to have or to adopt a religion or belief of his choice.
3. Freedom to manifest one's religion or beliefs may be subject only to such limitations as are prescribed by law and are necessary to protect public safety, order, health, or morals or the fundamental rights and freedoms of others.
4. The States Parties to the present Covenant undertake to have respect for the liberty of parents and, when applicable, legal guardians to ensure the religious and moral education of their children in conformity with their own convictions.[24]

---

[22] Bielefeldt and Wiener, p. 22.
[23] See https://www.un.org/en/universal-declaration-human-rights/index.html.
[24] See http://www.ohchr.org/en/professionalinterest/pages/ccpr.aspx.

The language in Article 18(2) of the ICCPR is important as it clearly states that no one can be coerced into accepting a belief system. Further, the freedom to believe or to maintain a belief system can never be subject to government restrictions. This protects the inner dimension (*forum internum*) and the internal integrity of every individual. The manifestations or demonstrations of those beliefs (*forum externum*) can be limited in a narrow set of circumstances when they are specifically "prescribed by law and are necessary to protect public safety, order, health, or morals or the fundamental rights and freedoms of others."

Article 18 protects the rights of individuals; it does not protect religion as a collective unit. Individuals can gather collectively, but they possess this fundamental right; it was not established as a right of a corporate entity. The UN Human Rights Committee monitors adherence to the treaty through a review process of state compliance with the treaty and through an individual complaint process. Over 170 states are party to this treaty.[25] Thus, the norm of freedom of religion or belief has been established and codified, even if this aspect of international law is weak and not always upheld in practice.

Declaration on the Elimination of All Forms of Intolerance and Discrimination Based on Religion or Belief

General Assembly Resolution 36/55: Declaration on the Elimination of All Forms of Intolerance and of Discrimination Based on Religion or Belief was adopted on November 25, 1981. Although it refers to and builds on the ICCPR, it does not have the status of legally binding international law.[26] The first articles of the resolution simply reiterate, almost word for word, the language of the ICCPR. It prohibits discrimination and intolerance in the second article. This article explains that "the expression 'intolerance and discrimination based on religion or belief' means any distinction, exclusion, restriction or

[25] W. Cole Durham and Brett Scharffs, *Law and Religion: National, International and Comparative Perspectives* (New York: Wolters Kluwer, 2019), p. 84. Myanmar is one of only a dozen states that have not ratified or acceded to this treaty.

[26] Additional declarations, both regional and religious, have been developed. The 2016 Marrakesh Declaration states that "cooperation must go beyond mutual tolerance and respect to providing full protection for the rights and liberties to all religious groups in a civilized manner that eschews coercion, bias and arrogance" (Executive Summary of the Marrakesh Declaration, January 27, 2016). This declaration was the outcome of a conference of over 300 Muslim scholars and political leaders in 2016. Susan Hayward, "Understanding and Extending the Marrakesh Declaration in Policy and Practice," US Institute of Peace, September 2016, https://www.usip.org/sites/default/files/SR392-Understanding-and-Extending-the-Marrakesh-Declaration-in-Policy-and-Practice.pdf.

preference based on religion or belief and having as its purpose or as its effect nullification or impairment of the recognition, enjoyment or exercise of human rights and fundamental freedoms on an equal basis."

The third article reaffirms that this right is grounded in human dignity. Further, it specifically explains in Article 6 what activities and freedoms are protected, including the right:

a. To worship or assemble in connection with a religion or belief, and to establish and maintain places for these purposes;
b. To establish and maintain appropriate charitable or humanitarian institutions;
c. To make, acquire, and use to an adequate extent the necessary articles and materials related to the rites or customs of a religion or belief;
d. To write, issue, and disseminate relevant publications in these areas;
e. To teach a religion or belief in places suitable for these purposes;
f. To solicit and receive voluntary financial and other contributions from individuals and institutions;
g. To train, appoint, elect, or designate by succession appropriate leaders called for by the requirements and standards of any religion or belief;
h. To observe days of rest and to celebrate holidays and ceremonies in accordance with the precepts of one's religion or belief; and
i. To establish and maintain communications with individuals and communities in matters of religion or belief at the national and international levels.[27]

Article 6, by elaborating on Article 18 of the ICCPR, presents concrete and empirically verifiable measures to evaluate whether the right to freedom of religion or belief is being violated or respected in a society.

There are also regional legal instruments that articulate concern for freedom of religion or belief. One regional treaty that built on the foundations of the Universal Declaration was the European Convention on Human Rights. This treaty, created after the horrors of World War II, entered into force in 1953. It applies to the 47 member states of the Council of Europe. Article 9 of the European Convention on Human Rights explain this freedom as:

1. Everyone has the right to freedom of thought, conscience, and religion; this right includes freedom to change his religion or belief and freedom, either alone or in community with others and in public or private, to manifest his religion or belief, in worship, teaching, practice, and observance.
2. Freedom to manifest one's religion or beliefs shall be subject only to such limitations as are prescribed by law and are necessary in a democratic society in the

[27] The resolution can be found at: https://www.un.org/en/genocideprevention/documents/atrocity-crimes/Doc.12_declaration%20elimination%20intolerance%20and%20discrimination.pdf.

> interests of public safety, for the protection of public order, health, or morals, or for the protection of the rights and freedoms of others.[28]

Individuals can petition the European Court of Human Rights if their rights under Article 9 are violated.

INTERGOVERNMENTAL ORGANIZATIONS: THE UN

IGOs are voluntary associations of states. States create these organizations to address collective problems and to further national interests. IGOs can bring multiple states together to work cooperatively to tackle issues in global affairs. While IGOs are far from perfect and have various limitations that impeded their effectiveness at times, they can provide opportunities and an institutional framework to further common goals. Some, such as the African Union, Association of Southeast Asian Nations (ASEAN), or EU,[29] are regional, while a few are global in orientation.[30]

United Nations

The UN, created in 1945, is the most prominent IGO due to its nearly universal membership and its global focus. The UN deals with almost every conceivable issue that arises in global affairs, including peace and security, human rights, sustainable development, and global health, to name a few. In terms of human rights, the UN Charter, Article 1(3), specifically states that one purpose of this organization is to promote and encourage "respect for human rights and for fundamental freedoms for all."[31] Thus, the UN Charter establishes obligations

---

[28] See http://www.coe.int/en/web/conventions/full-list/-/conventions/treaty/005.

[29] The EU developed a position dedicated to religious freedom: the EU Special Envoy for the Promotion of Freedom of Religion or Belief Outside of the EU. While the EU is one of the most developed and integrated regional organizations with 27 members, the Organization for Security and Co-operation in Europe (OSCE) is another that has paid attention to religious freedom. In the OSCE, there is an Office for Democratic Institutions and Human Rights. The OSCE has developed guidelines, provided expertise, and helped states that are drafting legislation.

[30] The European Court of Human Rights has adjudicated numerous cases related to freedom of religion. However, the Court's record has been inconsistent and uneven in its defense of this right. For a more detailed discussion, see Thiago Alves Pinto, "An Empirical Investigation of the Use of Limitations to Freedom of Religion or Belief at the European Court of Human Rights," *Religion and Human Rights*, Vol. 15, No. 1–2 (2020), pp. 96–133, https://brill.com/view/journals/rhrs/15/1-2/article-p96_7.xml?language=en.

[31] The United Nations Charter can be found at https://www.un.org/en/about-us/un-charter/full-text.

for all member states to respect human rights, including the right to freedom of religion. However, it is only as effective as its member states allow it to be. As one observer noted:

> The United Nations is armed with its moral authority, its values and principles, and its ample range of capabilities, but it has limited political space in countries whose Governments forcefully invoke sovereignty and non-intervention in their internal affairs as a cover for not meeting their commitments to abide by international humanitarian and human rights laws and norms. The conundrum, then, is how the United Nations can maintain some type of constructive engagement with individual member states where human rights abuses are systematically taking place, while at the same time pressing for those states to uphold their international commitments.[32]

The most prominent institutions within the UN are the Security Council, General Assembly, International Court of Justice, and Secretariat. Although the Security Council has the greatest authority within the UN due to its ability to respond to threats to peace and security, it has not consistently addressed religious persecution. Its binding resolutions are often reactive rather than proactive, and are often stymied by veto-wielding members such as China and Russia. Neither Beijing nor Moscow has demonstrated a commitment to human rights in general or freedom of religion or belief in particular. Both are reluctant to sign on to binding Security Council resolutions pertaining to human rights given their own domestic records, their attachment to autonomous action, and protection of state sovereignty.

Within the UN, the UN Human Rights Committee monitors state compliance with the ICCPR including Article 18. The Human Rights Council and the UN Office of the High Commissioner for Human Rights (OHCHR) are also institutional aspects of the UN that monitor and attempt to promote human rights. Their ability to fulfill their mandate and effectively protect individuals from human rights violations is furthered or stymied by the member states of the UN.

Human Rights Committee

The Human Rights Committee is the body of experts that oversees the protection and implementation of the ICCPR.[33] It has provided guidance on how to interpret and understand aspects of the ICCPR. It can also review state policies to evaluate a state's adherence to treaty obligations. The Committee's General

---

[32] Rosenthal, "A Brief."

[33] Gehan Gunatilleke, "Criteria and Constraints: The Human Rights Committee's Test on Limiting the Freedom of Religion or Belief," *Religion and Human Rights*, Vol. 15 (2020), p. 21.

Comments "provide authoritative legal analysis" on the treaty.[34] The Human Rights Committee produced General Comment No. 22 in 1993 to analyze and clarify aspects of Article 18 (Box 3.1). In General Comment No. 22, the Committee explained how morals can limit the manifestation of freedom of religion or belief and argued that states cannot rely on one single moral or religious tradition.[35] The Committee also indicated that states ought to act in a non-discriminatory manner, and policies or laws that are discriminatory in nature violate Article 18.

BOX 3.1 HUMAN RIGHTS COMMITTEE, GENERAL COMMENT 22, ARTICLE 18 (FORTY-EIGHTH SESSION, 1993)[36]

1. The right to freedom of thought, conscience and religion (which includes the freedom to hold beliefs) in Article 18.1 is far-reaching and profound; it encompasses freedom of thought on all matters, personal conviction and the commitment to religion or belief, whether manifested individually or in community with others... The fundamental character of these freedoms is also reflected in the fact that this provision cannot be derogated from, even in time of public emergency, as stated in article 4.2 of the Covenant.
2. Article 18 protects theistic, non-theistic, and atheistic beliefs, as well as the right not to profess any religion or belief. The terms "belief" and "religion" are to be broadly construed. Article 18 is not limited in its application to traditional religions or to religions and beliefs with institutional characteristics or practices analogous to those of traditional religions. The Committee therefore views with concern any tendency to discriminate against any religion or belief for any reason, including the fact that they are newly established, or represent religious minorities that may be the subject of hostility on the part of a predominant religious community.
3. Article 18 distinguishes the freedom of thought, conscience, religion, or belief from the freedom to manifest religion or belief. It does not permit any limitations whatsoever on the freedom of thought and conscience

[34] Gunatilleke, p. 26.

[35] Human Rights Committee, General Comment No. 22 on Article 18 of the ICCPR, CCPR/C/21/Rev.1/Add. 4, July 30, 1993.

[36] U.N. Doc. HRI/GEN/1/Rev.1. This document can be found at: https://undocs.org/HRI/GEN/1/Rev.1.

or on the freedom to have or adopt a religion or belief of one's choice. These freedoms are protected unconditionally…

4. The freedom to manifest religion or belief may be exercised "either individually or in community with others and in public or private." The freedom to manifest religion or belief in worship, observance, practice, and teaching encompasses a broad range of acts. The concept of worship extends to ritual and ceremonial acts giving direct expression to belief, as well as various practices integral to such acts, including the building of places of worship, the use of ritual formulae and objects, the display of symbols, and the observance of holidays and days of rest. The observance and practice of religion or belief may include not only ceremonial acts but also such customs as the observance of dietary regulations, the wearing of distinctive clothing or headcoverings, participation in rituals associated with certain stages of life, and the use of a particular language customarily spoken by a group. In addition, the practice and teaching of religion or belief includes acts integral to the conduct by religious groups of their basic affairs, such as the freedom to choose their religious leaders, priests and teachers, the freedom to establish seminaries or religious schools, and the freedom to prepare and distribute religious texts or publications.
5. The Committee observes that the freedom to "have or to adopt" a religion or belief necessarily entails the freedom to choose a religion or belief, including the right to replace one's current religion or belief with another or to adopt atheistic views, as well as the right to retain one's religion or belief. Article 18.2 bars coercion that would impair the right to have or adopt a religion or belief, including the use of threat of physical force or penal sanctions to compel believers or non-believers to adhere to their religious beliefs and congregations, to recant their religion or belief or to convert… The same protection is enjoyed by holders of all beliefs of a non-religious nature…
8. Article 18.3 permits restrictions on the freedom to manifest religion or belief only if limitations are prescribed by law and are necessary to protect public safety, order, health or morals, or the fundamental rights and freedoms of others. The freedom from coercion to have or to adopt a religion or belief and the liberty of parents and guardians to ensure religious and moral education cannot be restricted.

Human Rights Council

The UN General Assembly oversees the Human Rights Council, constituted by 47 member states. While the Security Council may take up emergencies with massive human rights violations that threaten peace and security, the Human Rights Council often handles routine human rights diplomacy. The purpose of the Human Rights Council is to encourage respect for the protection of the fundamental human rights of all individuals. This has included developing resolutions to address religious intolerance. For example, Resolution 16/18 seeks to combat "intolerance, negative stereotyping, and stigmatization of, and discrimination, incitement to violence, and violence against persons based on religion or belief."[37] Despite its mandate, the Human Rights Council's reputation suffered from the authoritarian and rights-violating members (for example, China and Russia) that have diminished its effectiveness. The Council oversees the work of the Special Rapporteur on freedom of religion or belief.

UN Special Rapporteur on Freedom of Religion or Belief

At the international level, the UN's Special Rapporteur on freedom of religion or belief is one of the central actors who focus on this human right. Initially created in 1986, the Special Rapporteur on freedom of religion or belief's mandate involves promoting policies and measures to protect freedom of religion or belief, identifying obstacles to the enjoyment of this right, and offering remedies for violations of freedom of religion or belief.[38] To fulfill this mandate, the Special Rapporteur conducts fact-finding visits to states, presents reports based on those visits, and presents annual thematic reports, general summaries, and analysis concerning the protection of this fundamental right to the Human Rights Council and the General Assembly of the UN.[39]

One thematic report focused on anti-Semitism. In this report, the Special Rapporteur examined how "anti-Semitism manifests itself" and why it was so pervasive throughout the world.[40] In this report, he recommended the UN Secretary-General develop a senior position to address anti-Semitism.[41] Other

---

[37] UN Human Rights Council, "Resolution 16/18, Combating Intolerance, Negative Stereotyping and Stigmatization of, and Discrimination, Incitement to Violence, and Violence Against Persons Based on Religion or Belief," March 24, 2011, A/HRC/RES/16/18, https://www2.ohchr.org.A.HRC.RES.16.18_en.pdf.

[38] See https://www.ohchr.org/EN/Issues/FreedomReligion/Pages/Mandate.aspx.

[39] Ibid.

[40] Ahmed Shaheed, "The United Nations Addresses Antisemitism as a Human Rights Issue: A Historic Achievement," September 19, 2019, https://www.ajc.org/the-united-nations-addresses-antisemitism-as-a-human-rights-issue-a-historic-achievement. His report (A/74/358) was transmitted to the General Assembly on September 20, 2019.

[41] Given the rise in anti-Semitism, in February 2020, Secretary-General Guterres appointed Miguel Moratinos to be the focal point at the UN to monitor such acts.

thematic reports focused on Islamophobia and Anti-Muslim hatred (2021) and gender-based violence and discrimination in the name of religion or belief (2020). In the report on Islamophobia, there were numerous references to Myanmar and hostility against Muslims spread on social media.[42]

Ahmed Shaheed, who became the Special Rapporteur in 2016, explained that his mandate is "to advance the adoption of measures that promote freedom of religion or belief for all, and focus on... states as duty bearers; to identify and report on existing and emerging challenges to the enjoyment of religious freedom by all."[43] He also stated that mass atrocities related to freedom of religion or belief and the impunity of those who commit those atrocities is the most serious global challenge he had to address.[44]

Thus, the Special Rapporteur encourages states to adopt and comply with international legal standards on freedom of religion or belief and monitors the protection of this right. In doing so, the Special Rapporteur recognizes the power and agency of states as a primary actor to advance religious freedom. The goal is to "mobilize national and international public opinion to nudge the government towards adopting a policy more closely in keeping with international human rights norms."[45] He, like many other defenders of freedom of religion or belief, offered instrumental arguments for this right saying, "it is vital to underline the urgent need for states to implement the internal commitments to respect religious freedom... the right [not] only protects the dignity

---

Moratinos explained that his mandate includes monitoring the growth of anti-Semitism around the globe as well as providing assistance within the United Nations. These activities will include educating and training members at the United Nations about what anti-Semitism entails and encouraging countries to honor Holocaust Remembrance Day; Miguel Moratinos, "The UN's First Anti-Semitism Envoy: A Conversation with High Representative for the UN Alliance," August 13, 2020, https://www.ajc.org/news/the-uns-increased-focus-on-antisemitism-a-conversation-with-high-representative-miguel.

[42] "In Myanmar, inflammatory statements shared on social media by prominent Buddhist monks have alleged that Muslims generally are responsible for sexual crimes against Buddhist women." Report of the Special Rapporteur on freedom of religion or belief to the Human Rights Council, "Countering Islamophobia/Anti-Muslim Hatred to Eliminate Discrimination and Intolerance Based on Religion or Belief," February 25, 2021, A/HRC/46/30.

[43] Ahmed Shaheed, "Conversation with the Council on Foreign Relations Religion and Foreign Policy Webinar Series," September 22, 2020.

[44] Ahmed Shaheed, "Conversation with USCIRF Spotlight Podcast," June 11, 2021, https://www.uscirf.gov/news-room/uscirf-spotlight/top-priorities-un-special-rapporteur-freedom-religion-or-belief.

[45] Surya Subedi, "Protection of Human Rights through the Mechanism of UN Special Rapporteurs," *Human Rights Quarterly*, Vol. 33, No. 1 (February 2011), p. 215.

of all human beings, but also is closely linked to sustaining peace, security, and human development."[46]

The UN Special Rapporteur's country visits, based on an invitation from the host country, and reports raise awareness about this issue. These visits allow the Special Rapporteur to access the situation of freedom of religion or belief within the country and offer suggestions for improving the protection of this right. The Special Rapporteur can observe the environment, interact with witnesses and civil society, and potentially facilitate a dialogue with the government to improve the situation in the country. One of the strengths of this position is the inclusive mandate. The Special Rapporteur does not focus on one religious minority or show favoritism to believers over non-believers. This universal approach provides legitimacy for the position. Shaheed also noted that joint statements from multiple mandate holders at the UN can be powerful and bring more international attention to the situation. Further, it is "more likely a state will respond" when a joint statement is issued.[47]

Despite these valiant efforts, the UN Special Rapporteur has limited resources in which to carry out the mandate of the office. The position does not come with a salary. Further difficulties arise from the fact that some states simply refuse to allow the Special Rapporteur to visit and report about freedom of religion or belief in their country. The Special Rapporteur can make recommendations and suggest specific measures that would be consistent with international religious freedom standards, but cannot require a state to act in a specific manner or to follow through on these recommendations.

The Office of the High Commissioner for Human Rights

The High Commissioner for Human Rights is another figure at the UN who seeks to promote and protect the broad range of human rights articulated in the Universal Declaration. This position and its associated office were established in 1993 by General Assembly resolution 48/141.[48] The High Commissioner monitors and advances the protection of human rights worldwide through a range of activities. They seek to educate and spread awareness about human rights. Furthermore, visits to states and field operations provide support for those who are at risk or who have had their human rights violated.[49] One significant attempt by the OHCHR to advance freedom of religion or belief was the Rabat Plan.

46 Ahmed Shaheed, September 22, 2020.
47 Ahmed Shaheed, June 11, 2021.
48 See https://www.un.org/ga/search/view_doc.asp?symbol=A/RES/48/141.
49 See https://www.ohchr.org/EN/AboutUs/Pages/WhoWeAre.aspx.

The Rabat Plan

The OHCHR organized five workshops between 2011 and 2012. These workshops brought together experts to discuss the incitement of national, racial, or religious hatred.[50] The result was the Rabat Plan of Action on the prohibition of advocacy of national, racial, or religious hatred that constitutes incitement to discrimination, hostility, or violence.

The Rabat Plan called on media organizations and religious and community leaders to act in a responsible manner: "Political and religious leaders should refrain from using messages of intolerance or expressions which may incite violence, hostility or discrimination; but they also have a crucial role to play in speaking out firmly and promptly against intolerance, discriminatory stereotyping and instance of hate speech."[51] The Rabat Plan states clearly that religious leaders have a role to play in addressing religious hatred. They need to clearly articulate their opposition to hate speech and the use of violence.[52]

This is also true of the media. For example, digital platforms such as Facebook, Twitter, and Instagram were criticized at various times for being the vehicle used for hatred and religious intolerance. Ahmed Shaheed has repeatedly spoken of the need for digital platforms and social media companies to do more to combat hate. Moratinos also indicated that social media companies (Twitter, Facebook) need to do more to remove anti-Semitic content on their platforms and that he would engage with various social media companies to address this harmful content.[53]

AD HOC MULTILATERAL EFFORTS

International Panel of Parliamentarians for FoRB

In recent years, there have been some efforts to develop new networks and collective approaches to promoting freedom of religion or belief. One example

---

[50] UN Human Rights Council, "Annual Report of the High Commissioner for Human Rights," January 11, 2013, A/HRC/22/17/add.4.

[51] Ibid.

[52] Bielefeldt and Wiener, p. 178.

[53] We will "continue to engage and collaborate with social media companies including Facebook, Twitter, and YouTube—which have recently taken steps to remove egregious anti-Semitic content and close their authors' accounts. However, there has been other cases of inconsistencies and we need to continue this engagement and identify the red lines within the framework of international human rights law"; Miguel Moratinos, "Remarks at the WJC International Meeting of the Special Envoys and Coordinators Combating Anti-Semitism," November 19, 2020, https://www.unaoc.org/2020/11/remarks-international-meeting-of-the-special-envoys-and-coordinators-combating-anti-semitism/.

is the International Religious Freedom or Belief Alliance. The International Religious Freedom or Belief Alliance has over 30 countries participating in various activities. It consists of senior government officials who engage in collective efforts to promote religious freedom, including joint advocacy of religious groups, protection of cultural heritage and places of worship, and responding to mass atrocities targeting religious minorities.[54] Some multilateral efforts exist outside of any regional or global IGO. One prominent effort is the International Panel of Parliamentarians for Freedom of Religion or Belief (IPPFoRB). A member of the British House of Lords developed the idea for the IPPFoRB in 2014. This initiative brings parliamentarians who are interested in freedom of religion or belief across the world together to further this human right. The IPPFoRB was formally established in Norway in November 2014. Thirty legislators from over a dozen countries signed the founding charter—the Oslo Charter for Freedom of Religion or Belief.[55] There are currently some 100 countries represented at the IPPFoRB who are committed to ending religious persecution.

The IPPFoRB employs various initiatives to further this basic human right. They host training sessions, conferences, as well as the IPPFoRB Academy to teach legislators about the situation of freedom of religion or belief around the world. Further, the Academy offers case studies and tools to address religious persecution in various locations.[56] These meetings allow parliamentarians from diverse regions to network and interact with civil society organizations to share ideas and successful programs to further freedom of religion or belief.

The IPPFoRB also monitors violations of this right by organizing fact-finding trips to specific countries. These visits "provide the opportunity for rapid response and strategic intervention, as well as an opportunity to build the capacity of local parliamentarians to FoRB by introducing them to a wider network of parliamentarians."[57] Traveling to a country of concern encourages a dialogue that can contribute to promoting a more tolerant society.

---

[54] Joint Statement, "A Shared Vision for Advancing Freedom of Religion or Belief for All," November 17, 2020, https://www.state.gov/a-shared-vision-for-advancing-freedom-of-religion-or-belief-for-all/. It is worth noting that while the Trump administration played a prominent role in establishing the International Religious Freedom or Belief Alliance, Donald Trump often failed to articulate a consistent message of religious freedom for all. He began his administration with a travel ban on Muslims entering the United States and often expressed hostility to those of the Muslim faith. He did not demonstrate a commitment to a broad range of human rights over the course of his four years as president.

[55] See https://www.ippforb.com/about/oslo-charter.

[56] See https://www.ippforb.com/our-work.

[57] Ibid.

Fact-finding missions investigated the situations in Myanmar, Nepal, and Malaysia.

The IPPFoRB network has advocated for various prisoners of conscience and policies to further freedom of religion or belief. In the first five years, over 30 letters have been sent to heads of state, including to the prime ministers of Vietnam, Pakistan, India, Malaysia, as well as to the presidents of Myanmar, Cuba, Egypt, and Sudan, to name a few. In some instances, multiple letters went out to the same foreign leader to express concern about religious discrimination.[58] Over 60 parliamentarians, including some from Asia, signed the letter to express their concerns over the environment in Vietnam.[59] The IPPFoRB is important not simply because of its diverse membership, but also because of the infrastructure that it developed to advance this right. Liv Kvanvig, the Director of the IPPFoRB, noted that they "have various ways of engaging, both trying to build capacity of our parliamentarians, but also providing network and platforms where they can engage with each other and also other relevant actors."[60] This global infrastructure can remind repressive governments that their policies are being scrutinized. It also has more flexibility and fewer institutional constraints than an IGO such as the EU or UN.

IMPACT

Assessing the impact of international law and multilateral efforts by IGOs to promote freedom of religion or belief is complicated and challenging in a complex global environment. It is possible to state that there have been more multilateral actions and cooperation in the last few decades. Fact-finding trips and reporting on religious persecution is a necessary element to address these violations. More attention and resources directed to this problem and more actors attempting to address religious persecution around the world is a positive development in a fraught global world. States may hesitate to persecute believers if they know that the international community is watching. Occasionally a state does make significant changes due to multilateral efforts. Shaheed indicated that his visit to Uzbekistan led to the closure of a notorious prison and a road map to improve laws and policies in Uzbekistan.[61] Chapter 6 discusses the positive reforms undertaken in Uzbekistan.

---

[58] See https://www.ippforb.com/our-work/advocacy-letters.

[59] Shaheed, September 22, 2020.

[60] Ibid.

[61] Ahmed Shaheed, "UN Special Rapporteur for Freedom of Religion or Belief, Ahmed Shaheed's Message to UCC SoR Students," *Study of Religions, UCC, Ireland*, February 11, 2021, https://www.youtube.com/watch?v=uRFUv2rR5dE.

These good intentions and actions do not change the reality that there is still much persecution and repression felt by believers in every region of the world. In many circumstances, multilateral efforts do not produce immediate tangible results in a country due to the unwillingness of a government to commit to a recommendation. For example, the Special Rapporteur for freedom of religion or belief has no ability to enforce his recommendations.[62] It remains difficult to hold violators accountable, whether the violator is a state or a non-state actor. If a state has a strong economy and significant military power, it will be very difficult to sanction or persuade them to change their behavior, especially if they decide the religious group is a threat to national security or the government's grip on power. This is why we see there has been little to no progress on the Uyghur Muslims detained in camps in China. Special Rapporteur Shaheed criticized China saying, "China has sought to justify its coercive detention of over a million Muslim Uyghurs, Kazakhs and other predominately Muslim ethnic minorities in state-run 'reeducation' camps as part of de-extremism regulations." However, the campaign against the Uyghurs "is illustrative of broader ill-treatment by China of minority religion or belief communities such as Falun Gong and Tibetan Buddhists."[63] A powerful state such as China, with its veto at the Security Council and its economic tentacles throughout the world, has yet to be held accountable for the extensive human rights violations of its Uyghur citizens. Unfortunately, given China's economic interests in Myanmar and its vocal support for state sovereignty, meaningful protection of the Rohingya Muslim community has yet to develop.

Many in the international community, including the UN in its various offices and councils, issued numerous statements on the plight of the Rohingya Muslims in Myanmar. In one statement, the Security Council "strongly condemns the widespread violence that has taken place in Rakhine State, Myanmar, since August 25, which has led to the mass displacement of more than 607 000 individuals, the vast majority belonging to the Rohingya community." It went on to say:

> The Security Council further expresses grave concern over reports of human rights violations and abuses in Rakhine State, including by the Myanmar security forces, in particular against persons belonging to the Rohingya community, including those involving the systematic use of force and intimidation, killing of men, women, and

[62] Surya Subedi, "Protection of Human Rights through the Mechanism of UN Special Rapporteurs," *Human Rights Quarterly*, Vol. 33, No. 1 (February 2011), pp. 201–28.

[63] Edith Lederer, "UN Investigator: Rights of Minorities to Worship Undermined," *Associated Press*, November 4, 2020, https://apnews.com/article/religion-maldives-freedom-of-religion-discrimination-north-korea-16c8581a5a00b5d4f0887e803e8c40dc.

children, sexual violence, and including the destruction and burning of homes and property.[64]

The Security Council was not alone in voicing concerns about the situation in Myanmar. Adama Dieng, the Special Advisor on the Prevention of Genocide, was scathing in his criticism: "All the information I have received indicated that the intent of the perpetrators was to cleanse the northern Rakhine State of their existence, possibly even to destroy the Rohingya as such, which, if proven, would constitute the crime of genocide." He went on to say, "the scorched earth campaign carried out by the Myanmar security forces since August 2017 against the Rohingya population was predictable and preventable," and that "the international community has buried its head in the sand."[65] The UN High Commissioner for Human Rights consistently called on political and military leaders in Myanmar to address the human rights violations in the country.[66]

The UN Human Rights Council had previously created a special rapporteur on human rights in Myanmar to address prior atrocities. Yanghee Lee made her fifth visit in January 2017 and noted her concerns about the citizenship law (1982), the discriminatory race and religion laws from 2015, and condemned the violence against minorities.[67] She was not allowed to visit the country in December 2017, and the Myanmar government suspended cooperation with her, preventing any further assessment of the situation or the conditions of the Rohingya.[68] She noted her fears about the violence in August and September of 2017: "The humanitarian situation is deteriorating rapidly and I am concerned that many thousands of people are increasingly at risk of grave violations of their human rights." The UN Special Rapporteur on the human rights situation in Myanmar went on to say: "The worsening cycle of violence is of grave concern and must be broken urgently."[69]

The UN Human Rights Council adopted Resolution 34/22. This resolution established the Independent International Fact-Finding Mission on Myanmar

---

[64] UN Security Council, Statement, November 6, 2017, S/PRST/2017/22, https://www.un.org/press/en/2017/sc13055.doc.htm.

[65] UN News, "Rohingyas Could Face Further Violence if They Return to Myanmar, UN Adviser Warns," March 13, 2018, https://news.un.org/en/story/2018/03/1004842.

[66] Rosenthal, "A Brief."

[67] UN Human Rights Council, "Report of the Special Rapporteur on the situation of human rights in Myanmar," March 14 2017, A/HRC/34/67.

[68] Albert and Maizland (2020).

[69] UN Human Rights Council, Press Release, "Myanmar: Worsening Cycle of Violence in Rakhine Must Be Broken Urgently, UN Expert Warns," August 31, 2017, https://www.ohchr.org/EN/NewsEvents/Pages/DisplayNews.aspx?NewsID=22018. Shaheed endorsed the statement by Yanghee Lee.

(IIFFMM) to ascertain if security forces committed human rights violations in Rakhine State.[70] This mission found widespread human rights violations, including crimes against humanity, by Myanmar's military and security forces:

> The mission finds that crimes against humanity have been committed in Kachin, Rakhine, and Shan States, principally by the Tatmadaw. In the case of Kachin and Shan States, the crimes include murder, imprisonment, enforced disappearance, torture, rape, sexual slavery, and other forms of sexual violence, persecution, and enslavement. In Rakhine State, these and other crimes against humanity have been committed. The elements of extermination and deportation are also present, while the systematic oppression and discrimination not only supports a finding of persecution but may also amount to the crime of apartheid.[71]

The IIFFMM recommended that the Security Council refer the situation to the ICC or establish an independent ad hoc court to address these horrific violations of human rights perpetrated based on religion and ethnicity.

The Human Rights Council created the Independent Investigative Mechanism for Myanmar (IIMM) after IIFFMM ended in September 2019. The IIMM was given the following instructions:

> To collect, consolidate, preserve, and analyze evidence of the most serious international crimes and violations of international law committed in Myanmar since 2011, and to prepare files in order to facilitate and expediate fair and independent criminal proceedings, in accordance with international law standards, in national, regional, or international courts or tribunals that have or may in the future have jurisdiction over these crimes, in accordance with international law.[72]

The government, including Aung San Suu Kyi, downplayed or dismissed the allegations of widespread and intentional human rights violations. The government did not cooperate with the IIFFMM,[73] nor has it assisted the hundreds of thousands of Rohingya Muslims who fled to other countries. However, the work of the IIFFMM and IIMM is important and can be essential to see justice in the future. Collected and preserved evidence can be transferred to an independent judicial mechanism (court, tribunal, ICC) and used later. The IIMM preserves the possibility of accountability or, at a minimum, an accurate record for the future. This may be the most that can be accomplished at the present

---

[70] UN Human Rights Council, "Resolution 34/22, Situation on Human Rights in Myanmar," March 24, 2017, A/HRC/RES/34/22.

[71] Human Rights Council, "Report of the Independent International Fact-Finding Mission on Myanmar," September 28, 2018, A/HRC/39/64.

[72] Quoted in Nagakoshi, p. 266.

[73] Human Rights Council, September 28, 2018.

time. While inadequate, it may allow for a future judicial proceeding and some limited measure of justice.

In 2019, Gambia, acting on behalf of the Organization of Islamic Cooperation, filed a case against Myanmar for violating the Convention on the Prevention and Punishment of the Crime of Genocide in the International Court of Justice.[74] The International Court of Justice is the judicial arm of the UN. Gambia also sought immediate action to prevent a deterioration of the Rohingya Muslims' situation. The court said that the government of Myanmar should protect the Rohingya and submit additional reports. The court offered these initial statements despite Aung San Suu Kyi's direct involvement as the head of Myanmar's legal team and her denial that "the government had genocidal intent."[75]

Other offices of the UN have tried to alleviate the plight of the Rohingya. The UNHCR has aided over a million people in Myanmar, including internally displaced people and stateless individuals.[76] In addition, it has helped hundreds of thousands of Rohingya who fled to Bangladesh. There are over 870 000 refugees in Cox's Bazar District. The UNHCR has sought close to $300 million for those refugees in Bangladesh alone.[77] Although assisting refugees after mass atrocities is far from ideal, it provides for some of the Rohingyas' immediate and basic needs. These efforts help to preserve the possibility of a future return to their homes. While a proactive global response would have been preferable, this may be the most that can be accomplished at the present time.

Despite these activities, various problems with how the UN approached Myanmar are worth noting. In addition to the unwillingness of the Security Council to take decisive action due to some of the permanent-five members (China and Russia), there was no common strategy to deal with the vast challenges that Myanmar faced in the years prior to 2017. In 2017, the Security Council waited two weeks before discussing the situation in Rakhine State. There were disagreements within various offices at the UN as to how to

---

[74] There is also an ongoing investigation at the ICC focused on the crime of deportation. The crime of deportation is a subcategory of Article 7, Crimes Against Humanity. The ICC has stated it has jurisdiction because Bangladesh signed the Rome Statute. See Nagakoshi for a discussion of the jurisdiction basis for the ICC to investigate this situation.

[75] Richard Paddock, "U.N. Court Orders Myanmar to Protect Rohingya Muslims," *New York Times*, January 23, 2020, https://www.nytimes.com/2020/01/23/world/asia/myanmar-rohingya-genocide.html; Nagakoshi, p. 266.

[76] UNHCR, "General Overview," https://reporting.unhcr.org/sites/default/files/Myanmar%20factsheet%20August%202021.pdf.

[77] Only about half of this amount has been funded; UNHCR, "Bangladesh Operational Update," July 2021, https://reporting.unhcr.org/sites/default/files/Bangladesh_Operational%20Update_July%202021.pdf.

approach the government. Some advocated for private diplomacy, while others wanted a more robust form of public advocacy and attention to human rights violations. A consultant asked to review the situation concluded:

> without question serious errors were committed and opportunities were lost in the UN system following a fragmented strategy rather than a common plan of action. It goes beyond the scope of this review to try and adjudicate responsibilities to entities or personalities (they are, after all, accountable for their actions), but the consultant was left with the impression that the over-all responsibility was of a collective character; in other words, it truly can be characterized as a systemic failure of the United Nations.[78]

CONCLUSION

There are a lot of multilateral initiatives,[79] declarations, and meetings to promote this fundamental human right. These multilateral activities do not always translate into a genuine protection of freedom of religion or belief. More coordination among the various initiatives and actors would be beneficial for many of the persecuted around the globe.

Unfortunately, the international community has been unwilling to take decisive action to punish military and political leaders for the extensive human rights violations and crimes against humanity that targeted the Rohingya Muslims. To date there have been few penalties for those who committed crimes against humanity. This situation demonstrates the weaknesses of some multilateral efforts, especially when powerful states are indifferent or have more pressing national interests. This was again repeated in 2021. The religious persecution of the Rohingya occurred during the democratic phase when Aung San Suu Kyi's National League for Democracy shared power with the military after elections in 2016. (The military continued to control the ministries of Defense, Home Affairs, and Border Affairs.) In February 2021, Myanmar's democratic transition came to a halt when the military, led by Min Aung Hlaing, assumed power. The military arrested thousands of protestors and NLD members, including Aung San Suu Kyi, in the months following the coup and killed over

---

[78] Rosenthal, "A Brief."

[79] Another example is the International Contact Group on FoRB. This was developed in 2015 and has approximately 30 members. It is an early warning system to raise awareness about potential problems and to coordinate activities among its members. For more information, see: https://www.international.gc.ca/world-monde/issues_development-enjeux_developpement/human_rights-droits_homme/freedom-religion-liberte-group_groupe.aspx?lang=eng

a thousand.[80] In response to the coup and harsh crackdown, ethnic minorities and prodemocracy supporters used violence against the military. We should hardly expect a military coup to improve the situation of religious minorities. Conditions for many in Myanmar deteriorated especially with the spread of COVID-19. Reports suggests that the Tatmadaw prevented the Rohingya from obtaining a COVID vaccine. Furthermore, houses of worship, both Christian and Muslim, have been attacked since February 2021.[81]

IGOs need to work collectively with a range of states and non-state actors, including NGOs, to educate citizens and political leaders on tolerance, counter hate speech, and encourage indigenous civil society organizations to address intolerance and to promote economic co-development. Understanding and mobilizing the power and interests of states is necessary to have any chance of success in the battle against religious persecution. Multilateral approaches must be undertaken in conjunction with state foreign policy, as well as domestic reforms. These topics are the subject of the next few chapters.

---

[80] Thank Myint-U, "Myanmar's Coming Revolution," *Foreign Affairs*, Vol. 100, No. 4 (July/August 2021), pp. 132–45.

[81] USCIRF, "Spotlight Podcast with Nadine Maenza," August 25, 2021, https://www.uscirf.gov/news-room/uscirf-spotlight/fourth-anniversary-rohingya-genocide.

4. Protecting the faithful in foreign policy: Washington's efforts on freedom of religion or belief

INTRODUCTION

Jewher Ilham pleaded for her father's release. "My father and all the other people in the camps should be released… Please demand that China release all the people who have been taken to the camps for false crimes." Ilham Tohti, a Uyghur economist, was jailed in 2014 by the Chinese government. Jewher Ilham argued, "his fight for the Uyghurs to be treated equally could not be tolerated by the Chinese. The Chinese are threatened by religious freedom because free, faithful people are a threat to them… The Chinese government decided to eliminate our culture. They do this by suppressing our religious rights." She made this plea at the 2019 Ministerial to Advance Religious Freedom. The State Department, which criticized Beijing repeatedly for its denial of religious freedom, gave her a platform to speak. Former Secretary of State Michael Pompeo specifically chastised Beijing: "China is home to one of the worst human rights crises of our time. It is truly the stain of the century."[1] This was the second ministerial hosted by the US State Department. Convening this conference was just one of numerous foreign policy activities Washington developed to promote freedom of religion or belief.[2]

In Chapter 2 I documented the diverse motivations that propelled states such as the Ottoman Empire to pursue domestic policies of religious tolerance and, in the case of Sweden, freedom of religion or belief. States choose, for intrinsic or instrumental reasons, to adopt policies that protect religious tolerance and encourage freedom of religion within their borders. In addition, states via their

---

[1] Keynote Address at the Ministerial to Advance Religious Freedom, July 18, 2019, Washington, D.C., https://2017-2021.state.gov/secretary-of-state-michael-r-pompeo-keynote-address-at-the-ministerial-to-advance-religious-freedom/index.html.

[2] State Department, "Ministerial on Religious Freedom," July 2019, https://www.state.gov/ministerial-to-advance-religious-freedom-schedule-of-events/. See also: https://www.youtube.com/watch?v=KsgWzQ2jTxw and https://uhrp.org/news-commentary/jailed-uighur-scholars-daughter-pleads-his-freedom.

foreign policies, messaging, and other activities can help other countries that seek to protect religious freedom. Intolerant states can be prodded and cajoled to commit to freedom of religion or belief. Sanctioning a violator of freedom of religion, by limiting trade, withholding bilateral aid, or naming and shaming via public diplomacy, can pressure a state that persecutes individuals for their beliefs to change their laws and policies.

This chapter explores the role and impact of US foreign policy on the promotion of religious freedom. I selected the United States as a case study and example of foreign policy efforts because of its early attention to this issue. This chapter begins with a brief review of American history. The early experiences in the colonies and the polity created after the revolution is important as freedom of religion is one of the country's enduring values. This history helps to explain the bipartisan support for freedom of religion or belief in contemporary foreign policy.

As one of the most powerful states on the world stage (i.e., economic and military power) and with its self-proclaimed belief in human rights, the United States *can be* an important actor on this issue. While Washington's rhetoric on human rights, including religious freedom, has never matched the reality of its actions, this should not preclude an evaluation of American foreign policy as it pertains to freedom of religion or belief. While some officials in the Trump administration made this issue a priority (Secretary of State Pompeo and Ambassador Brownback), the former president mostly offered rhetorical support, apparently with an eye toward his base of evangelical voters. The Biden administration offered support for this right in the context of protecting a broad range of human rights. Secretary Blinken noted, "Religious freedom is a key element of an open and stable society. Without it, people aren't able to make their fullest contribution to their country's success."[3]

Although Washington has a unique and large footprint around the world, its effective policies can be replicated elsewhere to improve the lives of many. Conversely, ineffective, poorly conceived, or poorly implemented policies contribute to harm experienced throughout the world. This chapter traces efforts by Washington over the last few decades to fight religious persecution and promote Article 18 of the ICCPR. I highlight these efforts to demonstrate how states can use their foreign policy tools to advance this fundamental human right.

[3] Tweet, July 16, 2021, https://twitter.com/statedept/status/1419353000133505026?lang=en.

FOREIGN POLICY

Foreign policy involves encouraging international actors to behave in acceptable ways. States employ various tools to influence other states and non-state actors. States engage in diplomacy. Private diplomacy, or quiet diplomacy between two states, articulates foreign policy goals or requests for action. These quiet conversations conducted outside of the media spotlight offer a government the opportunity to change a policy without appearing to cave in to pressure. Public diplomacy involves acts that range from a public comment to a social media post, to a government report or withdrawal of an ambassador. All are public demonstrations of goals and interests. These actions indicate what is or is not considered a vital interest.

Beyond these verbal or written signals, states also engage in economic and military activities to demonstrate policy preferences. Providing financial assistance (a loan or grant) or signing a trade deal can indicate happiness with the policies of another country. Conversely, states use visa bans, asset freezes, and economic embargos to indicate consternation with another country's policies and actions. If none of these actions alters the behavior of the targeted state, military action can be undertaken to force a change in policy. Next, this chapter explores the diplomatic, economic, and military tools employed by Washington to limit religious intolerance and to further freedom of religion or belief.

FREEDOM OF RELIGION IN AMERICAN HISTORY

The origins of the colonies and their quest for religious liberty is a familiar and often repeated narrative. Former Secretary of State John Kerry explained, "Freedom of religion is a core American value. It's one that helped to create our country. It's been at the core of our national consciousness since the 1600s, when the Pilgrims fled religious persecution and landed in my home state of Massachusetts."[4] The complicated history of the United States goes beyond the uplifting story of Pilgrims in search of a peaceful environment in which they could abide by their faith. Despite the simplicity of the creation stories of the colonists, many sought distant shores in the hopes of practicing their faith without harassment. The history of religious freedom in the United States is a long and complicated one. However, freedom of religion is cemented in the American tradition.

---

[4] John Kerry, "Remarks on the Release of the International Religious Freedom Report," May 20, 2013, Washington, D.C.

Colonial America

From its earliest days, the American colonists valued religion and the ability to freely follow one's conscience. Many Europeans journeyed to North America not only as part of what they took to be a religious obligation, but also to escape religious persecution. In 1630 English Puritans, who previously fled to the Low Countries, sailed across the Atlantic in search of the freedom to practice their faith without government interference.[5] Although many Americans applaud the early colonists' desire for religious freedom, the reality of the early history was far more complex. The early colonies sought religious freedom from the dictates of Rome and the Anglican Church. Their understanding of religious freedom did not entail tolerating those who disagreed with majority sentiment.[6]

Some individuals journeyed across the Atlantic to create a society that promoted the common good and upheld God's vision and religious rules.[7] Their desire to create a society that protected their religious beliefs often came at the expense of religious dissent. Hence, dissenters faced persecution and expulsion in the Massachusetts Bay Colony. As Gottshalk notes for the Puritans, "their pursuit of religious freedom was rooted in the effort to realize rigid ideals of community identity and doctrinal cohesion that necessarily came at the cost of the freedom of others to dissent."[8]

Puritan leaders feared that free individuals following their conscience would veer away from the "true faith" and that the community would disintegrate. The result would be moral decay. Simply put, dissenters posed a danger to society: "The Puritans believed that God held them to far higher standards than other, less godly people, that they reaped precious benefits and bore extraordinary burdens in New England because they had entered into a close and particular contract, a 'covenant,' with God."[9] John Winthrop noted this in 1630: "for we must consider that we shall be as a city upon a hill, the eyes of all people are upon us; so that if we shall deal falsely with our God in this work we have undertaken, and so cause Him to withdraw his present help from us."[10]

---

[5] Jon Meacham, *American Gospel* (New York: Random House, 2007), p. 37.

[6] Walter McDougall, *Promised Land, Crusader State: The American Encounter with the World Since 1776* (New York: Mariner Books, 1998), p. 18.

[7] Andrew Preston, *Sword of the Spirit, Shield of Faith* (New York: Anchor Books, 2012), p. 25.

[8] Peter Gottschalk, *American Heretics* (New York: Palgrave Macmillan, 2013), p. 13.

[9] Alan Taylor, *American Colonies* (New York: Penguin, 2001), pp. 178–9.

[10] Meacham, pp. 46–7. Chris Seiple, "The Essence of Exceptionalism: Roger Williams and the Birth of Religious Freedom in America," *The Review of Faith and International Affairs*, Vol. 10, No. 2 (Summer 2012), p. 85. Of course it is also true that

Other colonies were more tolerant and provided a haven for people of different faiths.[11] Lord Baltimore established Maryland as a refuge for his fellow Catholics.[12] William Penn founded Pennsylvania as a refuge for religious dissenters. Colonies, such as Rhode Island where Roger Williams and Anne Hutchinson went after being expelled from Massachusetts, were established to give religious minorities a hospitable environment to practice their faith.[13]

The Revolution and the Influence of the Founding Fathers

The American Revolution forged these distinct colonies, with a diversity of religious faiths, into a new federal state. The new constitution established the importance of religious liberty in the First Amendment: "Congress shall make no law respecting an establishment of religion, nor prohibiting the free exercise thereof."

Williams and Locke influenced the doctrine of religious freedom articulated in the Bill of Rights.[14] In 1644, Roger Williams, a settler living in the British colonies in North America, published *The Bloudy Tenent of Persecution.* He argued that religious freedom was a God-given right that the state could not abrogate.[15] Locke, writing four decades after Williams, influenced the political system and rights articulated in the founding documents. The *Second Treatise on Government* offered a justification for revolution when citizens were denied their basic rights. Locke's *Letter Concerning Toleration* defended religious tolerance and warned of the detrimental consequences of persecution. As noted in the first chapter, Locke believed that religious tolerance contributed to peace in the realm. Many founders, including Jefferson and Madison, accepted and amplified Locke's arguments.

The basis of the First Amendment would be known as the Wall of Separation. Roger Williams articulated the notion of a "wall" separating religion from politics when he called for a "hedge or wall of separation between the Garden of the Church and the Wilderness of the World."[16] Jefferson also advocated for freedom of conscious and a wall of separation, both in Virginia's

---

some came to North America in search of wealth. The Charter for Virginia encouraged the settlers to dig for silver and gold, among other raw materials. Meacham, p. 41.

[11] Taylor, *American Colonies*, pp. 265–6.

[12] "As a Catholic sympathizer, King Charles I favored Lord Baltimore's plan to demonstrate that a policy of religious toleration could permit Protestants and Catholics to live together in harmony." Taylor, *American Colonies*, p. 137.

[13] "Roger Williams was banished from Massachusetts in 1636 and founded Rhode Island later that year." Seiple, "The Essence of Exceptionalism," p. 84.

[14] Meacham, p. 69.

[15] Edwin Gaustad, *Roger Williams* (Oxford: Oxford University Press, 2005), p. 95.

[16] Meacham, p. 54.

state constitution and in the federal framework.[17] He wanted to keep the Church separate from the state because of his fear of the violent consequences of this interaction.[18]

Another Virginian, James Madison, voiced his concerns about the intertwining of religion and government in his 1785 essay *Memorial and Remonstrance*.[19] Madison echoed what others had observed, namely, the negative consequences of government interference in religious matters. Thus, to avoid these problems, the government must protect the beliefs and practices of the faithful. The struggle to obtain, first, religious tolerance, and then freedom of religion or belief for all citizens in the United States took time. At various points, this right was violated due to government interference or societal discrimination. The incomplete protection of religious freedom at home did not preclude efforts to promote this right abroad.

In sum, while the early experiences of disparate colonies saw diverse approaches to the place of religion in society, there was agreement on the value of religious freedom. It was unwise for the federal government to establish and elevate a particular religion. In this regard, the founders learned from the religious wars of 17th-century Europe. Ultimately, this is not an obscure, foreign right or one that is alien to Americans. Rather, it is one that has deep roots in American soil. These values would be a basis for promoting religious freedom abroad and they influenced foreign policy in future decades.

AMERICAN FOREIGN POLICY EFFORTS TO PROMOTE RELIGIOUS FREEDOM

Given the importance of religious freedom during the colonial period and America's self-image as a shining city on a hill, one may be surprised to learn that promoting this basic right in foreign policy was not always a priority for the US government. For much of the country's first hundred years, the United States was preoccupied with establishing and enlarging the territory. A power deficit explains the lack of emphasis on religious freedom. This new polity was not powerful enough to actively promote religious liberty abroad.[20] The situation changed in the 20th century.

---

[17] Thomas Jefferson, *Notes on the State of Virginia*, edited by William Peden (Chapel Hill: University of North Carolina Press, 1955), p. 159.

[18] "As a student of history Jefferson knew Europe had fought wars and led crusades over faith and that the first English colonies in North American had harsh models of religious freedom." Meacham, p. 4.

[19] Quoted in Meacham, p. 86.

[20] "It is not that past presidents had not cared about religious freedom, but that the United States did not previously have the ability or interest in projecting power and

Prominent voices articulated the necessity of this right for individuals around the world in the last few decades. George W. Bush proclaimed before the United Nations, "freedom is God's gift to every man, woman, and child—and that freedom includes the right of all people to worship as they see fit."[21] Barack Obama unequivocally articulated support for freedom of religion or belief, saying "promoting religious freedom is a key objective of US foreign policy. And I'm proud that no nation on Earth does more to stand up for freedom of religion around the world than the United States of America."[22] Pompeo noted that "religious freedom is embedded deeply in the American character."[23] Promoting freedom of religion was also included in the Trump administration's National Security Strategy: "The United States also remains committed to supporting and advancing religious freedom—America's first freedom. Our founders understood religious freedom not as the state's creation, but as the gift of God to every person and a fundamental right for our flourishing society."[24] John Barsa, the acting Administrator for USAID, stated clearly, "For Americans, religious freedom is grounded in our founding documents and has always been a bipartisan issue."[25] Evidence of the bipartisan support can be seen in the 85–5 Senate vote to confirm Rashad Hussain as Ambassador at Large for International Religious Freedom on December 16, 2021. In these pronouncements, one can see bipartisan support for the fundamental rights of freedom of religion or belief even if the rhetoric did not always match the policies of various administrations.[26] One former member of Congress told me that no one is opposed to religious freedom.

---

influence abroad." William Inboden, "Promoting Religious Freedom from the Oval Office," February 19, 2015. Berkeley Center, https://berkleycenter.georgetown.edu/essays/promoting-religious-freedom-from-the-oval-office.

[21] Patrick Worsnip, "Bush Promotes Religious Freedom at UN Gathering," *Reuters*, November 13, 2008, http://www.reuters.com/article/us-un-interfaith-idUSTRE4AC75Y20081113.

[22] David Hudson, "President Obama Praises Freedom of Religion at the National Prayer Breakfast," February 6, 2014, https://obamawhitehouse.archives.gov/blog/2014/02/06/president-obama-praises-freedom-religion-national-prayer-breakfast.

[23] Pompeo, July 18, 2019.

[24] Trump White House, *National Security Strategy of the United States of America*, December 18, 2017, p.41, https://trumpwhitehouse.archives.gov/wp-content/uploads/2017/12/NSS-Final-12-18-2017-0905.pdf.

[25] John Barsa, "Remarks on USAID Advancing Religious Freedom," August 17, 2020, https://www.usaid.gov/news-information/speeches/aug-17-2020-u.

[26] One can also see that this has not been a priority by the absence for long stretches of an Ambassador for Religious Freedom. John Handford served as Ambassador from 2002 to 2009. The next ambassador was Suzan Johnson Cook, who served from 2011 to 2013 after a two-year vacancy. When Johnson Cook left the position in 2013, it was vacant until David Saperstein became Ambassador in 2014.

Beyond the soaring rhetoric, some policy makers offered instrumental arguments touting the positive consequences of freedom of religion or belief. The State Department's International Religious Freedom Report argued, "while the violation of religious freedom contributes to instability and economic stagnation, respect for religious freedom paves the way for a more secure, peaceful, and prosperous world."[27] President Obama's Deputy National Security Advisor, Denis McDonough, explained that freedom of religion was tied to national security: "History bears us out in demonstrating that a lack of religious freedom weakens social cohesion and alienates citizens from their government, fomenting internal unrest, breeding extremism, and inhibiting national unity and progress."[28] USAID Administrator Samantha Power explained, "We know that when countries promote religious freedom and protect religious minorities, democracy is more stable, communities are more likely to develop equitably and prosper, the rights of women and girls are more likely to be protected, and overall quality of life improve."[29]

These arguments echo some of the instrumental reasons given in prior centuries. Contemporary scholars also advanced these arguments for making freedom of religion or belief a foreign policy priority.[30] Eric Patterson explained that promoting religious freedom would advance our national security because religious persecution is a threat to US security interests.[31] Other scholars noted that oppressing religious minorities can create instability within a country which can then lead to instability in various regions of the world.[32] In sum, many scholars and policy makers made the point that the denial of religious freedom often leads to violence and instability, therefore Washington ought to place greater emphasis on protecting this fundamental right globally because it is in America's national interest.

These arguments and the rhetoric employed by some politicians offer some of the motivations for the development of the laws and policy initiatives relating to religious freedom. Systematic efforts to place greater emphasis on this human right gained momentum in the 1990s. Many Christian activists and

---

[27] State Department, "Executive Summary."

[28] Denis McDonough, "International Religious Freedom: A Human Right, a National Security Issue, a Foreign Policy Priority," July 31, 2012, https://obamawhitehouse.archives.gov/blog/2012/07/31/international-religious-freedom-human-right-national-security-issue-foreign-policy-p.

[29] USAID Administrator Samantha Power, "Remarks at the 2021 International Religious Freedom Summit," July 14, 2021.

[30] Monica Duffy Toft, Daniel Philpott, and Timothy Samuel Shah, *God's Century: Resurgent Religion and Global Politics* (New York: W. W. Norton and Company, 2011), p. 222.

[31] Patterson, pp. 22–30.

[32] Grim and Finke, *The Price*.

academics believed that freedom of religion or belief was a right neglected by the State Department and American foreign policy more generally, and demanded changes.[33]

International Religious Freedom Act

These lobbying efforts eventually resulted in legislation that would frame American foreign policy efforts for decades. The International Religious Freedom Act (IRFA), passed in 1998, required policy makers to focus more attention on freedom of religion or belief. One important aspect of IRFA was that it put religious freedom on the international agenda and brought more attention to the issue.[34] As Katrina Lantos Swett, former chair of the USCIRF, noted, "the Act was a response to the growing concern about religious persecution worldwide and the perception that religious freedom was an orphan human right that the US government was not adequately focused on."[35] IRFA articulated what freedom of religion entails:[36]

(i) assembling for peaceful religious activities such as worship, preaching, and prayer…
(ii) speaking freely about one's religious beliefs;
(iii) changing one's religious beliefs and affiliation;
(iv) possession and distribution of religious literature, including Bibles; or
(v) raising one's children in the religious teachings and practices of one's choice.

IRFA then defines (section 3) particularly severe violations of religious freedom as "systematic, ongoing, egregious violations of religious freedom, including violations such as torture or cruel, inhuman, or degrading treatment or punishment as well as prolonged detention without charges."

The legislation empowers the Secretary of State to designate a country that allows severe violations of religious freedom as a Country of Particular Concern (CPC). A CPC designation enables the President to punish a state

---

[33] Nina Shea was one activist who sought to bring more attention to religious freedom. According to one human rights activist, Shea referred to freedom of religion as "the red-headed stepchild of human rights." Interview, June 23, 2017.

[34] The issue received little attention from policy makers in the 1990s. Since IRFA, the issue has been given more attention at the OSCE and in other countries. I am indebted to T. Jeremy Gunn for his insights on this point.

[35] Katrina Lantos Swett, Testimony Before the National Security Subcommittee of the House Committee on Oversight and Government Reform, June 13, 2013, Washington, D.C.

[36] The right codified in IRFA is a narrower conception of religious freedom than Article 18 of the ICCPR, which emphasizes both freedom of religion *and belief*; https://www.congress.gov/bill/105th-congress/house-bill/2431/text.

for these violations through several means including economic sanctions.[37] In addition to providing the executive branch with the tools to encourage freedom of religion or belief, IRFA also created a new office in the State Department—the Office of International Religious Freedom—an Ambassador at Large for Religious Freedom, and a new commission—USCIRF. USCIRF is "an independent, bipartisan US government advisory board that monitors religious freedom worldwide and makes policy recommendations."[38] Both USCIRF and the Office for International Religious Freedom produce reports on the status of religious freedom of all faiths and extensively document religious persecution around the globe.

IRFA required greater diplomatic focus on freedom of religion or belief. Some of these diplomatic efforts involve discussions conducted behind closed doors between diplomats. Quiet diplomacy can encourage progress on human rights without a foreign leader publicly appearing to cave in to pressure from Washington. Some policy makers noted that efforts to allow private worship for Christians in Saudi Arabia or quietly securing the release of a prisoner of conscience were the result of private diplomacy.[39]

Public diplomacy, including naming and shaming, typically receives more attention. US public diplomacy for greater respect for religious freedom takes many forms, including public statements,[40] social media posts, and public reports. Many policy makers argued forcefully for this human right. Former Ambassador for International Religious Freedom Saperstein traveled widely and advocated for the victims of the genocide carried out by the Islamic State in Iraq and Syria. One NGO activist praised Saperstein, saying "He brought

---

[37] IRFA gives the authority to designate a state as a CPC to the president. However, the president has delegated this power to the Secretary of State. USCIRF makes recommendations to the Secretary of State as to which countries should receive a CPC designation. It also gives the president much leeway in how and when to punish a CPC. In 2018, the State Department announced that the Secretary of State had redesignated Burma, China, Eritrea, Iran, North Korea, Sudan, Saudi Arabia, Tajikistan, Turkmenistan, and Uzbekistan as CPCs; see Heather Nauert, Press Release, "Designations Under the International Religious Freedom Act of 1998," January 4, 2018, Washington, D.C. In 2021, Secretary Blinken designated Burma, China, Eritrea, Iran, North Korea, Pakistan, Russia, Saudi Arabia, Tajikistan, and Turkmenistan as CPCs; see Antony Blinken, Press Release, "Religious Freedom Designations," November 14, 2021.

[38] USCIRF, Annual Report of the US Commission on International Religious Freedom, April 2013.

[39] Interview, December 13, 2012, Washington, D.C.

[40] Statements by a spokesperson can also indicate that this is an issue of concern. "I am deeply concerned about the fate of US citizen Saeed Abedini, who has been detained for nearly six months and was sentenced to eight years in prison in Iran on charges related to his religious beliefs." John Kerry, Press Statement, March 22, 2013.

energy to the position and credibility."[41] The two most prominent acts of public diplomacy are the annual reports produced by the State Department and USCIRF. Both reports highlight violations of this right in multiple countries. The International Religious Freedom Report is an attempt to "bear witness and speak out."[42] The State Department does not gloss over violations by long-term allies. The 2011 International Religious Freedom Report recorded that some French laws limited the ability of Muslim women to dress according to their deeply held beliefs. It also criticized strategically important countries including Saudi Arabia and China. Despite the economic and security relationships that Washington had with Riyadh and Beijing, both were designated as CPCs by consecutive administrations.[43]

USCIRF's annual report differs from the State Department's in that it does not describe the situation of religious freedom or religious persecution in every country. Rather, these reports emphasize states that are of greatest concern. USCIRF also established a watchlist for countries moving in a troubling direction. Unfortunately, several countries are highlighted every year, indicating little progress on religious freedom (Myanmar, North Korea, Iran, Eritrea, China, Pakistan, Saudi Arabia, Sudan, Turkmenistan).

IRFA empowers the executive branch with several tools to address violations in various countries. These tools include economic rewards (loans) and punishments (sanctions). Section 405 of IRFA obliges the president to engage in at least one of the following measures if a state has been designated as a CPC: submit a private statement or issue a public censure to the government, limit or revoke financial assistance in the form of developmental aid or security cooperation. In egregious cases of religious persecution, the law allows for the use of force as a last resort. The law (section 407) also offers the executive substantial leeway to forgo all penalties if it is deemed to be in the country's national interests:

> (a) IN GENERAL.—Subject to subsection (b), the President may waive the application of any of the actions described in paragraphs (9) through (15) of

---

[41] Interview, June 23, 2017. This activist also noted that Knox Thames, the Special Advisor for Religious Minorities in the Near East and South/Central Asia, also traveled a lot and was very engaged on social media. Saperstein's office had a budget of roughly $20 million—a minuscule amount by Washington's standards. Kelsey Dallas, "What Does the International Religious Freedom Ambassador Do?" *Desert News*, July 30, 2017.

[42] State Department, *International Religious Freedom Report for 2011*. Washington, D.C.: US State Department.

[43] Ibid. One State Department official told me that she had never been pressured to change a report or downplay a violation in the name of good relations. Interviews, December 2012, Washington, D.C.

section 405(a) (or commensurate action in substitution thereto) with respect to a country, if the President determines and so reports to the appropriate congressional committees that—

(1) the respective foreign government has ceased the violations giving rise to the Presidential action;

(2) the exercise of such waiver authority would further the purposes of this Act; or

(3) the important national interest of the United States requires the exercise of such waiver authority.

In 2016, Congress passed the Frank R. Wolf International Religious Freedom Act, which amended IRFA and provided more tools to policy makers to promote religious freedom. It also articulated the instrumental justifications and the social benefits of freedom of religion or belief: "Because the promotion of international religious freedom protects human rights, advances democracy abroad, and advances United States interests in stability, security, and development globally, the promotion of international religious freedom requires new and evolving policies and diplomatic responses."[44] The law established a broader and more inclusive understanding of this right: "The freedom of thought, conscience, and religion is understood to protect theistic and non-theistic beliefs and the right not to profess or practice any religion."[45] This law requires all foreign service officers to receive training on religious freedom prior to being posted abroad. In addition, it compels the president to designate non-state actors who engage in "particularly severe violations of religious freedom." This was a necessary update to IRFA as many of the perpetrators of religious persecution are groups such as the Islamic State, Boko Haram, and al Qaeda. This act also encouraged Congress to provide sufficient appropriations for grants to groups who monitor violations of freedom of religion, promote "norms of international religious freedom," and "seek to address and mitigate religiously motivated and sectarian violence."[46]

Since IRFA was codified as law, and updated in 2016, presidents from both parties have resisted using many of the economic tools at their disposal to address religious persecution abroad. Over the course of multiple administrations, various states designated as CPCs saw no new sanctions or other penalties imposed on them. Numerous administrations choose to employ sanctions previously applied or waive sanctions entirely in the name of national interests and priorities. Two states—China and Saudi Arabia—demonstrate how a pres-

[44] Frank R. Wolf International Religious Freedom Act, Public Law 114-281, December 16, 2016.

[45] Ibid.

[46] Ibid.

ident can ignore or avoid sanctioning a government with an egregious record of religious persecution.

China was designated a CPC in 1999; Saudi Arabia was designated five years later. Since that time, neither country has demonstrated any significant improvements in their treatment of religious minorities (or atheists, in the case of Saudi Arabia). In fact, the annual International Religious Freedom Report often noted the deterioration of freedom of religion or belief in both countries.[47] One International Religious Freedom Report's section on China noted:

> the government continued to exercise control over religion and restrict the activities and personal freedom of religious adherents that it perceived as threatening state or CCP [Chinese Communist Party] interests, according to religious groups, nongovernmental organizations (NGOs), and international media reports… There continued to be reports of deaths in custody and that the government tortured, physically abused, arrested, detained, sentenced to prison, subjected to forced indoctrination in CCP ideology, or harassed adherents of both registered and unregistered religious groups for activities related to their religious beliefs and practices.

There were numerous reports that authorities closed or destroyed Islamic, Christian, Buddhist, Taoist, Jewish, and other houses of worship and destroyed public displays of religious symbols throughout the country:

> The US government estimates that since April 2017, the PRC [People's Republic of China] government arbitrarily detained more than one million Uighurs, ethnic Kazakhs, Hui, and members of other Muslim groups, as well as Uighur Christians, in specially built or converted internment camps in Xinjiang and subjected them to forced disappearance, political indoctrination, torture, physical and psychological abuse, including forced sterilization and sexual abuse, forced labor, and prolonged detention without trial because of their religion and ethnicity.[48]

Similarly, Washington repeatedly criticized Saudi Arabia for the lack of religious freedom or even a minimal level of religious tolerance in the realm.

---

[47] State Department, *International Religious Freedom Report*, 2010. According to Human Rights Watch, the Saudi government sent a letter to the US government promising to allow private worship without interference. They said they would "guarantee and protect the right to private worship for all, including non-Muslims who gather in homes for religious practice," and "ensure that members of the [religious police] do not detain or conduct investigations of suspects, implement punishment, [or] violate the sanctity of the private home." This, unfortunately, did not occur. Human Rights Watch, "Saudi Arabia: Christians Arrested at Private Prayer," January 30, 2012.

[48] State Department, *2019 International Religious Freedom Report*, June 10, 2020, https://www.state.gov/wp-content/uploads/2020/06/CHINA-INCLUDES-TIBET-XINJIANG-HONG-KONG-AND-MACAU-2019-INTERNATIONAL-RELIGIOUS-FREEDOM-REPORT.pdf.

USCIRF noted the "government of Saudi Arabia engages in systematic, ongoing and egregious violations of the right to freedom of thought, conscience, religion or belief."[49] The 2019 State Department report stated:

> According to the 1992 Basic Law of Governance, the country's official religion is Islam and the constitution is the Quran and Sunna… Freedom of religion is not provided under the law. The government does not allow the public practice of any non-Muslim religion. The law criminalizes "anyone who challenges, either directly or indirectly, the religion or justice of the King or Crown Prince." The law criminalizes "the promotion of atheistic ideologies in any form," "any attempt to cast doubt on the fundamentals of Islam..."[50]

Washington issued an indefinite waiver to Riyadh starting in 2009, and various administrations used long-standing sanctions unrelated to religious freedom for Beijing.[51] More troubling, the Trump administration elevated a potential trade deal with China over the human rights violations of the Uyghurs.[52] Despite the lack of freedom of religion or belief in both countries, there were few penalties for the violation of this fundamental right. American economic interests (trade with China and access to oil with Saudi Arabia) and security cooperation with Riyadh meant religious freedom was not a diplomatic priority in either bilateral relation.[53]

Military actions were even less frequently employed than economic sanctions. The Yazidis in Iraq were a notable exception to this pattern. The Obama administration deployed military strikes to protect Yazidis in Northern Iraq. This limited military campaign sought to provide food and supplies to individuals who escaped to Mount Sinjar to avoid slaughter at the hands of the Islamic State in 2014. President Obama explained his motivations: "We've begun operations to help save Iraqi civilians stranded on the mountain. As ISIL has

---

[49] USCIRF, Annual Report, May 2004. See also USCIRF, 2021 Annual Report, https://www.uscirf.gov/sites/default/files/2021-05/Saudi%20Arabia%20Chapter%20AR2021.pdf.

See https://www.state.gov/reports/2019-report-on-international-religious-freedom/saudi-arabia/.

[50] Ibid.

[51] Actions taken under the Foreign Relations Authorization Act FY 1990 and FY 1991 restrict exports of crime control and detection instruments and equipment.

[52] Michael Crowley, "Trump Says He Avoided Punishing China Over Uighur Camps to Protect Trade Talks," *New York Times*, June 21, 2020, https://www.nytimes.com/2020/06/21/us/politics/trump-uighurs-china-trade.html.

[53] Barbara Ann Rieffer-Flanagan, "Rhetoric versus Reality: American Foreign Policy and Religious Freedom in the Middle East," in *Routledge Handbook on Human Rights and the Middle East and North Africa*, edited by Anthony Tirado Chase (New York: Routledge, 2017), pp. 317–29.

marched across Iraq, it has waged a ruthless campaign against innocent Iraqis. And these terrorists have been especially barbaric towards religious minorities, including Christian and Yezidis, a small and ancient religious sect."[54] This military campaign was a rare example of the use of hard power to halt religious persecution. These efforts, while praiseworthy, were not motivated for simply humanitarian reasons. The Islamic State's control over parts of Iraqi territory and its oil resources were detrimental to American national interests in Iraq and in the region.[55]

The Trump administration, especially Secretary of State Pompeo and Ambassador Brownback, took an aggressive and outspoken approach to the defense of religious freedom. Under the guidance of these two officials, the United States convened the Ministerial to Advance Religious Freedom in July 2018. Over 80 governments attended this gathering. This first ministerial sought to empower civil society organizations to actively promote religious freedom. Further, it brought together like-minded governments to identify, strategize, and respond to religious persecution worldwide.[56] The State Department hosted this event again in 2019. These conferences brought together policy makers, religious leaders, and civil society organizations to raise awareness and to develop practical responses to religious discrimination and persecution around the world. Additional policies were articulated by the White House.

On June 2, 2020, the White House issued an executive order to advance religious freedom. Given the continuing protests of systemic racism and the incompetent handling of COVID-19, which had killed over 100 000 Americans by June 1, the executive order appeared to be a distraction from the multiple crises facing the country. This order was not groundbreaking. It expanded mandatory training on religious freedom for foreign officers and increased foreign assistance to $50 million annually. It encouraged the Secretary of the Treasury to use economic tools to promote religious freedom where possible (section 6) and states that religious freedom is a priority (section 1).[57] While

---

[54] Barack Obama, Statement, August 7, 2014, Washington, D.C., https://obamawhitehouse.archives.gov/the-press-office/2014/08/07/statement-president.

[55] A senior official in the Obama administration said the airstrikes were based not simply on humanitarian concerns, but rather "to protect our personnel and facilities specifically in Erbil." Office of the Press Secretary, "Background Briefing by Senior Administration Officials on Iraq," August 8, 2014, https://obamawhitehouse.archives.gov/the-press-office/2014/08/08/background-briefing-senior-administration-officials-iraq.

[56] See https://2017-2021.state.gov/ministerial-to-advance-religious-freedom/about-the-ministerial-to-advance-religious-freedom/index.html.

[57] See https://trumpwhitehouse.archives.gov/presidential-actions/executive-order-advancing-international-religious-freedom/.

the additional funding can further religious freedom goals, other aspects of policy did not change. Trump did not press China on the internment camps in Xinjiang. He was unwilling to sanction Beijing because he did not want to jeopardize a trade deal.

ASSESSING AMERICAN FOREIGN POLICY

Despite the legislative requirement to actively pursue freedom of religion or belief, Washington continued to see millions persecuted for their beliefs and practices across the globe. Some have questioned whether the US government should be engaged in this type of religious stewardship at all.[58] These scholars argued that Washington should not attempt to promote freedom of religion around the world. Some suggested that foreign policy efforts in this realm are a form of Western imperialism.[59] Others questioned whether religious freedom is a universal right.[60]

Some individuals within the bureaucracy voiced different concerns. One State Department official expressed his frustration: "To be frank, more of the world is moving in a negative direction."[61] Annual reports by the State Department and USCIRF often found that year after year the same countries violated this human right. Myanmar, China, Eritrea, Iran, North Korea, Pakistan, Saudi Arabia, Tajikistan, and Turkmenistan were again designated as CPCs in December 2019. Most of these countries consistently appeared on the CPC list for the last 15 years.[62] While Washington had some limited successes, including the Defamation Resolution at the United Nations,[63] and prisoner releases, few societies evolved from religious intolerance and persecution to religious tolerance, let alone freedom of religion or belief.[64] Uzbekistan is one of the few countries that made demonstrable progress on religious tolerance. I document Uzbekistan's progress in Chapter 6.

---

[58] See Hurd, *Beyond Religious Freedom*, p. 16.

[59] Mahmood, "Religious Freedom," p. 142–8.

[60] Hurd, "Testimony."

[61] Interview, October 13, 2017.

[62] Secretary of State Michael Pompeo, Press Statement, "United States Takes Action Against Violations of Religious Freedom," December 20, 2019, Washington, D.C.

[63] UN Human Rights Council, "Resolution 16/18."

[64] When I asked one official who has been working on religious freedom issues for over a decade for success stories he said, "Nothing jumps to mind." He went on to add, "Europe over decades in the Thirty Years War. You had a religious ideology and these religious conflicts had to exhaust themselves. That is a discouraging model." Interview, September 2017. Many of the officials I interviewed struggled to identify concrete accomplishments.

What accounts for Washington's limited impact? To begin, the scale of societal transformation required to move from intolerance of the Other (religious or non-religious) to religious tolerance and then religious freedom is quite large in many societies. The evolution of a society from hostility and hatred of different-faith communities to one of forbearance or grudging accommodation and eventually one of mutual respect and genuine participation in society requires time and patient policies. National political leaders and civil society actors must develop respectful dispositions about diverse religious (or non-religious) individuals. Further, laws, policies (e.g., educational reforms), and institutions (rule of law upheld by an independent judiciary) to protect an open space for individuals and communities to practice essential activities require time to become embedded in society. Knox Thames, the US Special Advisor for Religious Minorities in the Near East and South/Central Asia, explained, "This is the work of generations. This is not meant to be discouraging. There have been incremental changes that give us hope. Getting laws and policies right is important because this works out ten or twenty or thirty years from now."[65] A State Department official also echoed this and said, "solving the problem of violent extremism" associated with religious persecution by Boko Haram and other groups "is a long-term project."[66] Another added, our "broad policy work involves moving governments towards Article 18. We want governments to protect all people's rights under Article 18. That is the generational struggle."[67] Given the decades-long nature of efforts to promote religious freedom, we should not expect to see immediate results.

The second reason for the absence of a global transformation on religious freedom stems from Washington's tendency to elevate perceived national interests over many human rights issues including religious freedom. While various administrations strongly articulated their support for freedom of religion or belief around the world, the reality was far different.[68] A USCIRF official noted the elevation of economic interests over religious freedom: "the State Department's administrative policy is still episodic. It is pushed down the list of concerns. It is outweighed by economic interests, other interests." She went on to say, "I would like to see a more consistent focus, though this has not happened in any of the last few administrations. This is not a foreign policy priority. Sometimes it is raised… even though a lot like to say they are interested in religious freedom, they don't follow through."[69] Some in Congress argued that the US needs to work with el-Sisi in Egypt, Xi Jinping in China,

---

[65] Interview, September 29, 2017.
[66] Interview, November 2017.
[67] Interview, October 13, 2017.
[68] Rieffer-Flanagan, "Rhetoric versus Reality."
[69] Interview, July 2017.

or the monarchy in Saudi Arabia to address more pressing issues, including Islamic terrorism and the nuclear threat from North Korea. This is also evident in Washington's bilateral relations with Pakistan.

The USCIRF and the State Department's annual reports consistently criticized Pakistan over the persecution and violence suffered by religious minorities. One International Religious Freedom Report noted, "members of religious minority communities continued to raise concerns regarding the government's inconsistency in safeguarding minority rights, and official discrimination against religious minorities persisted."[70] USCIRF went further: "During the past year, the Pakistani government continued to perpetrate and tolerate systematic, ongoing and egregious religious freedom violations."[71] These criticisms have been repeated over the last 15 years. These egregious violations did not prevent the US government from giving billions of dollars in aid to Islamabad due to its strategic importance in the war on terrorism and in the efforts to stabilize Afghanistan. In the 15 years between 2002 and 2017, Pakistan received over $33 billion in aid from the United States, with little attention paid to freedom of religion or belief.[72]

In addition, some officials fail to appreciate the conceptual difference between religious tolerance and religious freedom and use these terms interchangeably. In discussions with officials at the State Department, some discussed conflict resolution programs, religious engagement programs, and interfaith dialogue under the heading of religious freedom programs.[73] One individual who served on the National Security Council noted that he tried to promote religious freedom in the Middle East and convinced the Saudis to allow Christians to worship in private house churches.[74] Washington should encourage the Saudi government to allow non-Sunni Muslims, including atheists, greater freedom to pursue ideas and religious tenets to further religious tolerance. This, however, does not provide an individual with the ability to

---

[70] State Department, *International Religious Freedom Report for 2016*, Washington, D.C.: US State Department.

[71] State Department, *International Religious Freedom Report for 2017*, Washington, D.C.: US State Department.

[72] Mark Landler and Adam Goldman, "U.S. Will Withhold Security Aid from Pakistan," *New York Times*, January 4, 2018, https://www.nytimes.com/2018/01/04/us/politics/trump-pakistan-aid.html?action=Click&contentCollection=BreakingNews&contentID=66316241&pgtype=Homepage&_r=0. See also Susan Epstein and K. Alan Kronstradt, "Pakistan: US Foreign Assistance," Congressional Research Service, October 4, 2012.

[73] Interview with State Department official, December 14, 2012. Interview with State Department official, July 10, 2013. Interview with former State Department official, February 27, 2014.

[74] Interview, December 13, 2012.

freely engage in public and in private with a set of deeply held beliefs and therefore ought not to be confused with freedom of religion or belief.[75]

Policy makers also stressed their efforts at religious engagement.[76] A State Department official highlighted some of the department's successful efforts as follows: "There is good news in terms of positive US engagement. For example, due to steady engagement, and despite the severe religious freedom problems that the Secretary mentioned, Sudan this year released some people who were imprisoned for their religious beliefs."[77] Engagement, either with a foreign government or with diverse religious groups, should be understood as a tool, not the realization of the right established in the ICCPR.

While the State Department refers to Article 18 of the ICCPR, many of their actions and policies are efforts to promote religious engagement or religious tolerance. These efforts fall short of the legal right of freedom of religion or belief. For example, the American embassy in Tunisia "hosted several key speakers to engage Tunisian youth, women's groups, and civil society about mainstream views and practices of Islam in American society as a way to promote religious freedom."[78] One speaker, Joycelyne Cesari, a professor from Harvard, delivered lectures on Islam in America in an effort to promote interfaith dialogue and "to foster cultural and religious exchanges."[79] Attempts to foster interfaith dialogue can encourage tolerance of the religious Other. However, they do not address the essence of the right of freedom of religion or belief.

---

[75] While many of the individuals I spoke with used the terms religious freedom and religious tolerance interchangeably, and while some documents use the terms without distinction, there are some policy makers who understand the difference. One explained, "I do not love the word tolerance… You can tolerate someone [of a different faith] by not killing them." "We focus on inclusion. We are aiming at full inclusion in society. Tolerance is a step on the road towards full inclusion." Interview, October 13, 2017.

[76] "The White House launched the Interagency Working Group on Religion and Global Affairs in February 2010… Our first task was a massive survey, commissioned by the president, of how the federal government was engaging religious groups and faith-based groups overseas." Judd Birdsall, "Obama and the Drama Over International Religious Freedom Policy: An Insider's Perspective," *The Review of Faith and International Affairs*, Vol. 10, No. 3 (Fall 2012), p. 35.

[77] Ambassador Mike Kozak, Bureau of Democracy, Human Rights, and Labor, Special Briefing, August 15, 2017, Washington, D.C.

[78] American Embassy, Tunis, "Tunisia Religious Engagement Report," June 16, 2010, EO 12958.

[79] Ibid.

The executive branch also mentioned their efforts to free religious minorities in numerous countries.[80] They noted their public criticisms of Pakistan's blasphemy laws and Myanmar's discrimination of Rohingya.[81] Kozak specifically highlighted the release of religious prisoners in Uzbekistan and Sudan in his briefing in 2017. If a government continues to arrest citizens, freeing one or two individuals has not stopped the violation of this human right. A cynical observer might suggest that releasing a prisoner or two here and there is actually a method a government can use to appear to be working with Washington and addressing Washington's human rights concerns. Efforts by policy makers to free a religious dissident, encourage interfaith dialogue, and criticize discrimination against religious minorities are meaningful activities and should be continued.[82] However, they should not be misinterpreted as promoting freedom of religion or belief. They are valuable efforts to encourage religious tolerance and limit religious persecution, but they are limited.

Consistent Strategies

The absence of a consistent and coherent strategy to promote freedom of religion or belief continues to limit the impact of American foreign policy. One former State Department official complained about the lack of an overarching strategy to guide American foreign policy on religious freedom.[83] An NGO activist working on this issue echoed this sentiment, saying there is "no strategy in the DoS [Department of State] or White House today" on religious freedom and "no strategy in place on human rights generally."[84] A USCIRF official indicated that there was not much evidence of a strategy at the State Department. This official went on to say, "it is hard to come up with a strategy.

---

[80] Under Secretary of State Burns urged the government of Uzbekistan in 2009 to offer amnesty to some prisoners of conscience explaining, "such actions by the GOU would demonstrate our shared objective to promote religious freedom, renew our religious freedom dialogue, and provide a firm foundation for continued improvement in our bilateral relationship." Unclassified email from SecState to American Embassy, Tashkent, Uzbekistan, June 8, 2009. UNCLAS State 058954. State Department, "Executive Summary."

[81] President Obama publicly criticized the government for its treatment of this religious minority during a visit in 2014. State Department, "Executive Summary."

[82] USCIRF, "Vietnam: Religious Prisoner of Conscience Pastor Nguyen Cong Chinh Released," July 31, 2017. Pastor Nguyen Cong Chinh was released from prison, and he and his family were allowed to leave the country.

[83] Thomas F. Farr, "Examining the Government's Record on Implementing the International Religious Freedom Act," Testimony before the Subcommittee on National Security of the House Committee on Oversight and Government Reform, June 13, 2013, pp. 12–15.

[84] Interview, February 22, 2014.

You need a bunch of different strategies… but it is not easy."[85] This is related to the confusion between religious tolerance and religious freedom and in some cases religious engagement.

The deficiencies in US foreign policy are important because individuals are being tortured and killed for their beliefs. If one reads the various reports from USCIRF and the State Department, one will see similar violations in countless countries every year. Some State Department officials will admit this privately.[86] A former director of the Office of International Religious Freedom echoed this: "in Iraq, Afghanistan, Pakistan, Egypt, Saudi Arabia, and Russia, levels of religious freedom are declining and religious persecution is rising."[87] It is difficult to identify a significant number of countries where American religious freedom policy has helped to reduce religious persecution or increase religious freedom in any substantial way. Even Vietnam, a country removed from the CPC designation, does not fully protect religious freedom.[88] Given the limited progress seen around the world, Washington should focus on a specific set of issues going forward. This is also true for other countries that seek to promote Article 18 in their respective foreign policies.

FOREIGN POLICY GOING FORWARD

Foreign policy makers need to correctly identify the situation in the country. Is there religious persecution based on government policies (government restrictions, discriminatory regulations), or do the problems stem from social actors within society encouraging violence and discrimination against the religious (or non-religious) Other? Understanding the source of the religious intolerance is the first step toward rectifying it.

If religious tolerance does not exist, the United States and other governments should deploy various foreign policy tools to address religious persecution. At minimum, policy makers should criticize religious persecution. The individuals responsible for the persecution should face sanctions. Individuals can be sanctioned under the US Global Magnitsky Act. Officials responsible

---

85 Interview, July 2017.

86 Interviews, State Department, December 2012.

87 Farr, "Examining."

88 USCIRF, "Vietnam," https://www.uscirf.gov/sites/default/files/Vietnam.pdf. "The government continued to enforce the Law on Belief and Religion, which requires religious organizations to register with the state, and to harass unregistered religious groups… Applications were often pending with no formal decision for months or even years. Throughout the year, authorities interrogated, harassed, or physically assaulted individuals affiliated with unregistered religious groups… when they attempted to attend religious ceremonies."

for flagrant denials of religious freedom should be denied visas to travel abroad either alone or with their families. For example, on December 10, 2021, the Treasury Department employed the Global Magnitsky Sanctions program against officials in the Chinese Communist Party, Shohrat Zakir and Erken Tuniyaz, for their repressive action against Muslim Uyghurs in Xinjiang.[89]

Policy makers can encourage a foreign leader to maintain a minimal level of religious tolerance by using instrumental arguments concerning either the economic or security benefits of religious tolerance. This must be done with the understanding that these interest-based arguments will not immediately produce freedom of religion or belief. In some countries, a minimal level of religious tolerance may be the best outcome that can be achieved in the short term. Washington and other like-minded governments must also be aware of the possibility of backsliding. An enlightened leader who undertakes reform may be followed by one who is intolerant or less capable of producing positive change. There is no guarantee that an enlightened leader, such as Uzbek President Mirziyoyev or King Mohammed VI of Morocco, will be replaced by another tolerant ruler.[90]

Governments can also encourage institutional changes through their foreign policies. They can help a government to establish a complaint mechanism or develop training programs for police and security forces and work on legal reforms. If a country lacks the capacity or the institutions to protect religious tolerance, states can provide aid (loans, grants, technical expertise) in these areas. Programs ought to be developed with clear strategies and consistent goals. For FY 2016/2017 the Bureau of Democracy, Human Rights, and Labor offered funding of $3.4 million for Global Religious Freedom Programs. This was distributed to Europe ($450 000), Malaysia, Indonesia, Vietnam, and Laos ($1.5 million), Sri Lanka and Bangladesh ($1 million), and global parliamentary training programs ($500 000) in Pakistan, Egypt, Nigeria, Burma, Malaysia, and Indonesia. The following year, $2.4 million was made available for the Near East ($1.2 million), Malaysia ($500 000 related to the rule of law), and Nigeria ($700 000).[91] These programming opportunities have the potential

---

[89] Antony Blinken, Press Release, "The United States Promotes Accountability for Human Rights Violations and Abuses," December 10, 2021.

[90] Morocco, while not a religiously free society, does offer religious minorities religious tolerance. Christians and Jews can engage in religious activities, including running religious schools. So long as there are no efforts to proselytize, Christians and Jews are allowed to practice their faith. The government also financially supports the study of Jewish culture and heritage at some universities. State Department, *International Religious Freedom Report for 2014*.

[91] Democracy, Human Rights, and Labor: Notice of Funding Opportunity: DRL Global Religious Programs (FY 17/18) September 25, 2017, DRLA-DRLAQM-18-010;

to contribute to progress on religious freedom, but only if they are part of a systematic approach to protecting this human right and not random programming with little connection to a coherent global policy.

Furthermore, Washington and other states should commit more resources to this task. One State Department official was encouraged by an increase in funding ($20 million) for international religious freedom in FY 2017.[92] However, the executive order in June 2020 establishing $50 million for religious freedom is a meager amount by Washington standards. In 2016, the military bands maintained by the Department of Defense alone cost the American taxpayer approximately $500 million dollars.[93] If Washington genuinely wants to support freedom of religion or belief, it ought to put more resources into the protection of this human right.

Foreign policy should focus on addressing the root causes of religious intolerance—social hostility to the religious (or non-religious) Other. While religious persecution can be a result of laws and government policies, it is also a result of the hatred and intolerance some citizens feel about their neighbors. In Pakistan, hostility and violence against Christians, Ahmadi, and Shiites often stems from groups within society. To stem the social hostility, programs need to be developed that humanize the Other to counter the demonization some citizens hear on television, social media, in schools, and elsewhere. Reforming school curricula can help to develop tolerant citizens. Nelson Mandela noted that "no one is born hating another person because of the color of his skin, or his background, or his religion. People must learn to hate, and if they can learn to hate, they can be taught to love, for love comes more naturally to the human heart than its opposite." It is possible to teach people to respect other individuals despite differences. Teaching citizens, especially in their formative years, to tolerate and respect others can go a long way toward preventing social hostilities. These efforts are discussed further in Chapter 5.

Thus, states should work with foreign governments to encourage educational reform (reform of textbooks, lesson plans, and other educational materials). Policy makers in the United States and elsewhere can also work in tandem with grassroots activists and indigenous NGOs to encourage tolerant messages in society. The more citizens are exposed to messages of tolerance and the need to respect all individuals, the less likely it will be that hateful messages will resonate. In this vein, grants to civil society actors to combat and address intolerance in the media, as have been supported in Central and

---

Democracy, Human Rights, and Labor: Notice of Funding Opportunity: DRL Global Religious Programs, September 14, 2016, DRLA-DRLAQM-17-006.

[92] Interview, October 13, 2017.

[93] Jessica Mathews, "America's Indefensible Defense Budget," *The New York Review of Books*, July 18, 2019.

Eastern Europe, should be expanded.[94] With more financial support, these programs could monitor and combat intolerance on a greater scale. The US and other countries should encourage civil society and education reform via a bottom-up approach with the understanding that it may take decades to move from religious intolerance to freedom of religion and belief.

CONCLUSION

Religious freedom is an important aspect of American history. It is a valued part of American political culture. This establishes the cultural foundation for contemporary foreign policy. It is this entrenched value that helps to explain why policy makers passed legislation to promote freedom of religion or belief abroad more than 200 years after the founding of the political system.

Furthering freedom of religion or belief is a worthwhile goal in American foreign policy. Not only is it a fundamental human right codified in international law, but it also has the potential to reduce one source of violence and conflict in global affairs. While instrumental arguments for the economic or security benefits of religious freedom may be a strategic means to convince a foreign leader to undertake reforms, more is needed to uphold all aspects of this essential human right.

States need a coherent, consistent, and comprehensive strategy to promote freedom of religion or belief if they want to have a significant impact on the ground. A comprehensive strategy begins with a clear understanding of the difference between religious tolerance and freedom of religion or belief. Religious engagement, conflict resolution programs, and interfaith dialogue meetings may be helpful initiatives to fostering religious tolerance, but they do not provide the essentials of religious freedom for individuals. A comprehensive strategy should emphasize the rule of law, education reform, multilateral efforts with IGOs and like-minded states, as well as support for independent actors in civil society. Without a comprehensive strategy in foreign policy, there is little hope for significant global improvement on freedom of religion or belief.

---

[94] The State Department developed a grant to support NGOs in Eastern and Central Europe to monitor anti-Semitism in the media. Office of the Press Secretary, "Promoting and Protecting Religious Freedom Around the Globe," August, 10, 2016, https://obamawhitehouse.archives.gov/the-press-office/2016/08/10/fact-sheet-promoting-and-protecting-religious-freedom-around-globe. The State Department's Bureau of Democracy, Human Rights, and Labor has offered grants to combat anti-Semitism and anti-Muslim intolerance in Europe. In 2016, DRL allocated $450 000 for this purpose. Bureau of Democracy, Human Rights, and Labor, Notice of Funding Opportunity: DRL Global Religious Freedom Programs, DRLA-DRLAQM-17-006, September 14, 2016.

This is not to suggest that global change will occur overnight. There are limits to what a state can accomplish via its foreign policy. In some cases, there is very little that can be done to improve the lives of religious minorities beyond admitting refugees who are fleeing religious persecution. Unfortunately, this is the reality of the global environment.

In the short term, policy makers should seek a minimal level of religious tolerance and plant the seeds for the further development of freedom of religion or belief. In the long term, the United States and other governments need to engage in what Kennan referred to as gardening. States can pass legislation at home and establish offices to address religious persecution and the promotion of this human right. This is the policy making infrastructure that can help further freedom of religion or belief in other parts of the world. Programs and initiatives developed in conjunction with indigenous civil society actors can help encourage mutual respect, tolerant dispositions, and social norms of acceptance for the Other in society. Educational reforms and strengthening the rule of law will contribute to progress over time. But these efforts must be consistently cultivated over the years to see these efforts bloom. Furthermore, foreign policy makers should combine top-down leadership to promote religious tolerance with a long-term strategy that helps to develop and encourage grassroots efforts to have an extensive impact around the world. I am not suggesting that this will be easy, or that progress will be evident overnight. However, it will only be through the development of a long-term, thoughtful strategy that Washington and like-minded states will be able to plant the seeds that may allow freedom of religion or belief to germinate over time. Over the next few chapters, efforts to encourage political leaders to reform the judicial and educational systems will be explored in diverse countries and social environments.

5. Reforming education: teaching narratives of religious tolerance

INTRODUCTION

Religious intolerance is not indigenous to any society or individual. No one arrives in this world reflexively hating another. Hatred and intolerance are learned. Understanding how intolerance develops involves understanding how societies teach their members to disrespect and alienate some individuals and groups. Until governments, international organizations, and civil society activists confront and combat the root causes of religious intolerance, the basic right to freedom of religion or belief will remain an unrealized aspiration.

As noted in Figure 5.1, there are various ways to influence the beliefs of children. In some societies, intolerance is bred and nurtured in families, religious institutions, and via the media. In others, the government foments hatred across society through a drumbeat of propaganda and repeated public declarations. Another major source of this intolerance resides in the educational systems of numerous countries. While school systems are often assessed on whether students have acquired critical skills to succeed in a globalized world (reading comprehension, qualitative and quantitative reasoning, etc.), rarely are they evaluated on the development and attainment of tolerant dispositions and respect for others.

Young minds are impressionable, which is why the content of classrooms and the educational environment children experience are important not only for the development of productive individuals who contribute to a nation's gross domestic product, but also tolerant citizens. The importance of the positive role that education plays was recognized in Article 26 of the Universal Declaration of Human Rights. The article states: "Education shall be directed to the full development of the human personality and to the strengthening of respect for human rights and fundamental freedoms. It shall promote understanding, tolerance, and friendship among all nations, racial or religious groups." Countries can prosper and advance when they produce highly qualified, educated citizens. Conversely, societies can be destroyed by intolerant citizens who are taught to hate the Other or to hold demeaning and unequal views of the Other. Numerous studies have documented that religiously intolerant societies face

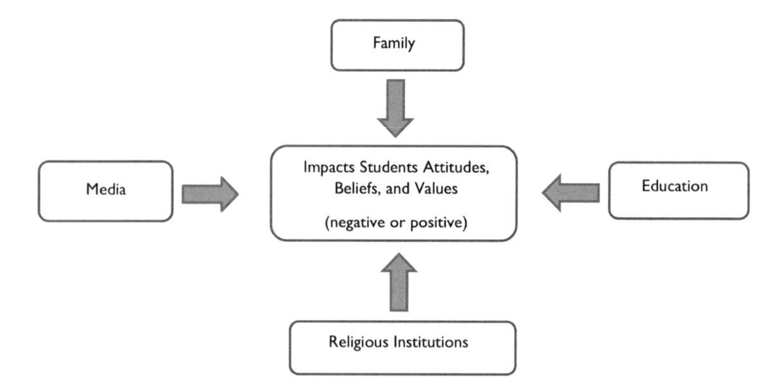

To cultivate tolerant youths and ultimately citizens who respect Freedom of Religion or Belief, an education system must create a learning environment where tolerant values are developed and nurtured. The classroom environment is shaped by teachers, educational materials (including textbooks) and other students.

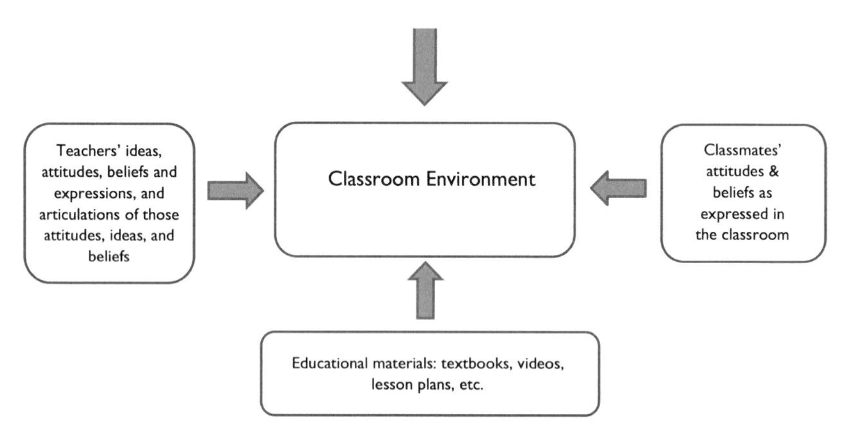

Figure 5.1 Influences on children's attitudes and beliefs

civil unrest and conflict.[1] When encouraged, prejudices can result in limited acts of violence against minorities, or in more extreme cases, civil unrest and ethno-religious cleansing, as we saw in Myanmar, when government troops carried out atrocities against the Rohingya Muslim community in 2017.

---

[1] Grim and Finke, *The Price*. Daniel Philpott, "Religious Freedom and Peacebuilding: May I Introduce You Two?" *The Review of Faith and International Affairs*, Vol. 11, No. 1 (2013), pp. 31–7.

Human rights activists and scholars documented the societal benefits of teaching children about tolerance and the value of diversity.[2] The long-term consequences of teaching tolerance to a generation of young people can be quite significant.[3] The former UN Special Rapporteur on freedom of religion or belief noted the impact:

> Besides providing students with the necessary knowledge and information in different disciplines, school education can facilitate a daily exchange between people from different ethnic, economic, social, cultural and religious backgrounds. The possibility of having face-to-face interaction of students on a regular basis is not less important than the development of intellectual skills, because such regular interaction can promote a sense of community that goes hand in hand with appreciation of diversity, including diversity in questions of religion or belief.[4]

Policy makers are aware of the devastating consequences of intolerant messages and lessons. "We realize that the messages these individuals are exposed to can change the course of their lives and push them to carry out heinous crimes of their own in their own communities, and in those communities they may have never known, but their actions have led to dehumanization."[5] Stuart Levey, the former Under Secretary for Terrorism and Financial Intelligence, argued:

> Even more important, however, is preventing people from embracing violent extremism in the first place. Among other things, we must focus on educational reform in key locations to ensure that intolerance has no place in curricula and textbooks. There is still much to be done in this area, but unless the next generation of children is taught to reject violent extremism, we will forever be faced with the challenge of disrupting the next group of terrorist facilitators and supporters.[6]

---

[2] Kenneth Bush and Diana Saltarelli, "The Two Faces of Education in Ethnic Conflict: Towards a Peacebuilding Education for Children," UNICEF, Florence, Italy, 2000. In their study, the authors incorporate religion in their understanding of ethnicity. "An ethnic group is a community of people who engage in shared social practices that reinforce their sense of identity: examples would include religious, linguistic, and cultural communities" (p. 2).

[3] USCIRF, "Connecting the Dots: Education and Religious Discrimination in Pakistan," November 2011, https://www.uscirf.gov/sites/default/files/resources/Pakistan-ConnectingTheDots-Email(3).pdf.

[4] Heiner Bielefeldt, Report of the Special Rapporteur on freedom of religion or belief, UN Human Rights Council, December 15, 2010, A/HRC/16/53, p. 8.

[5] Representative Ted Poe, Opening Statement, "Saudi Arabia's Troubling Educational Curriculum," House of Representatives, Subcommittee on Terrorism, Nonproliferation and Trade, July 19, 2017, Washington, D.C.

[6] Stuart Levey, "Loss of Moneyman a Big Blow for al-Qaeda," *Washington Post*, June 6, 2010, http://www.washingtonpost.com/wp-dyn/content/article/2010/06/04/AR2010060404271_pf.html

One scholar explained the impact of intolerant views taking hold in future citizens:

> Why are misguided, bigoted, or intolerant views problematic? The vast majority of those who hold such views will not turn toward violent extremism… the most extreme or radical attitudes, even when not violent themselves, can create an enabling environment for militants, who need shelter and operational, logistical, and financial support from sympathizers to survive in any context.[7]

Understanding how intolerance develops and which strategies counteract such intolerance is one piece of this puzzle. This chapter explores the role that education can play in developing tolerant citizens. When schools teach kids to hate and demonize those who are different, what are the consequences? Do societies that teach religious tolerance and respect for religious pluralism experience less social hostility, discrimination, and violence? Can educators help students to develop the skills necessary to understand and respect different religious and non-religious values and perspectives? Can educators create a safe and open environment in which students can ask questions and learn about difference?

This chapter begins by exploring Saudi Arabia. Saudi Arabia has dealt with social hostility toward religious minorities and terrorism perpetrated by religiously motivated groups. It has failed to develop a religiously tolerant society where all individuals are free to live according to their beliefs. While there are numerous factors that contribute to religious persecution in this country, the education system in Saudi Arabia augments these problems. After a brief discussion of the religious intolerance in the country, I discuss the classroom environment and educational materials used in Saudi classrooms. Given the intolerant lessons taught in various classrooms, educational reform could help to address some of the discrimination that individuals face. Next, this chapter looks at two religiously tolerant societies, Oman and Sweden, to understand how the educational system aids in the development of tolerant citizens. While the educational systems in these countries are not the sole explanation for why there is less religious discrimination and hostility in these societies, neither promotes an intolerant environment.

---

[7] Madiha Afzal, "Education and Attitudes in Pakistan," US Institute of Peace, Special Report 367, April 2015.

EDUCATION AND ATTITUDES, OR THE ROLE OF THE EDUCATION SYSTEM[8]

A country's education system is often the foundation for building successful and productive citizens. Teaching children to read and write, to communicate effectively, and to think critically can produce citizens who innovate, create jobs, build businesses, and address and solve societal problems. Or it can fail to create thoughtful citizens that contribute to society. As Postman noted, "It [public education] creates a public. The question is, what kind of public does it create? A conglomerate of self-indulgent consumers? Angry, soulless, directionless masses? Indifferent, confused citizens? Or a public imbued with confidence, a sense of purpose, a respect for learning and tolerance?"[9]

The classroom can also be a tool to develop values. The education system, and specifically certain disciplines, such as history and civics, can articulate a story about a community with a shared past. If this story tells of the coexistence and mutual respect between different groups (different religious groups, as well as between religious and non-religious citizens), this can help to create a narrative of belonging. If this story excludes the Other or dehumanizes the Other or places the Other in an inferior position in society, this can contribute to abuse, discrimination, unequal treatment in society, and violence. Intolerance can also manifest itself in less obvert ways, such as hostility or benign neglect from teachers toward students from religious minority communities.[10] Developing a common narrative about a shared destiny can contribute to a more peaceful future. As observed in Kenneth Bush and Diana Saltarelli's study, education can usher in positive social change in the development of tolerant individuals or it can perpetuate conflict.[11] Other studies noted that the ideas and values developed as a child can impact attitudes and dispositions

---

[8] I have set aside questions about the rights of parents as it pertains to the education of their children. In this chapter, I have focused on how governments have established an educational system and what impact that can have on religious tolerance or religious intolerance. In a perfect world, there would be a dialogue between school administrators and different-faith communities, as well as humanist societies to discuss various aspects of the curriculum.

[9] N. Postman, *The End of Education: Redefining the Value of School* (New York: Vintage Books, 1996), p. 18.

[10] Bush and Saltarelli note, "Intolerance is also expressed in less tangible ways. Teachers from the majority culture may display negative attitudes towards minority students, expect very little from them and fail to recognize and encourage their individual talents." Kenneth Bush and Diana Saltarelli, *The Two Faces of Education in Ethnic Conflict: Towards a Peacebuilding Education for Children* (Florence: UNICEF, 2000), http://www.unicef-irc.org/publications/269, p. 14.

[11] Bush and Saltarelli, *The Two Faces*.

Table 5.1 Pew Research Center International Religious Freedom and Restrictions scores, Saudi Arabia

Saudi Arabia	2007	2016	2019
Government Regulations Index (GRI)	8.0	7.7	7.2
Social Hostilities Index (SHI)	7.2	5.6	2.5
Average of GRI and SHI	7.6	6.7	4.9

later in life. Thus, the political socialization that occurs early in an individual's life can have lasting consequences.[12]

SAUDI ARABIA

Saudi Arabia is both a place of religious inspiration, as the birthplace of the prophet Muhammad and the holy shrines in Mecca and Medina, as well as a place of hostility and discrimination for the non-Muslims who reside within its borders. Numerous government restrictions, including laws and policies, limit or severely restrict the ability of individuals and faith communities to engage in religious practices or to adhere to deeply held beliefs. The Pew Research Center has consistently reported high scores on both the Social Hostilities Index and the Government Restrictions Index.[13] Saudi Arabia's scores are documented in Table 5.1.

Various non-Sunni religious communities face government obstacles and restrictive policies. Some foreign workers are limited to communal worship in a private house. At times, Christians have been harassed by the Committee for the Promotion of Virtue and Prevention of Vice and arrested.[14] Citizens who follow Shia Islam encounter discrimination and hostility in employment opportunities and in the education system. Many Shiites were arrested after protesting the government's discriminatory policies.[15] During the pandemic,

[12] Robert Hess and Judith Torney, *The Development of Political Attitudes in Childhood* (Chicago: Aldine, 1967).

[13] Pew Research Center, "Global Uptick in Government Restrictions on Religion in 2016. Pew Research Center, "Globally, Social Hostilities Related to Religion Decline in 2019, While Government Restrictions Remain at Highest Levels," September 30, 2021, https://www.pewforum.org/2021/09/30/globally-social-hostilities-related-to-religion-decline-in-2019-while-government-restrictions-remain-at-highest-levels/.

[14] Human Rights Watch, "Saudi Arabia."

[15] State Department, *International Religious Freedom Report for 2014*. Washington, D.C.: US State Department. It is worth noting that in January 2016 a prominent Shia cleric, Sheikh Nimr Baqir al-Nimir, was executed for his criticism of the government.

the government used COVID-19 to further restrict Shia religious rituals, including Ashura.[16] The discrimination against Shiites stems not only from theological differences, but also from the perceived threat from Shia Iran. Riyadh fears an uprising by its Shia minority in its oil-rich provinces in the east.[17]

Atheists are not tolerated by the government. Atheists, such as Raef Badawi, creator of the Free Saudi Liberals website, who challenged the religious policies in the Kingdom have been arrested. Badawi was given a ten-year prison sentence and 1000 lashes, 50 of which were delivered in January 2015, for insulting Islamic figures and apostasy.[18]

Policy makers in Washington criticized the lack of religious tolerance and freedom of religion or belief in Saudi Arabia. Michael Kozak, from the Bureau of Democracy, Human Rights, and Labor, noted in congressional testimony that:

> The government [of Saudi Arabia] does not recognize the right of non-Muslims to practice their religion in public and has applied criminal penalties, including prison sentences, lashings, and fines for apostasy, atheism, blasphemy, and insulting the state's interpretation of Islam. Of particular concern are attacks targeting Shia Muslims, and the continued pattern of social prejudice and discrimination against them. We urge Saudi Arabia to embrace greater protection for religious freedom for all.[19]

The State Department's *International Religious Freedom Report* summed up the widespread denial of religious freedom in the Kingdom:

> The legal system is based largely on sharia as interpreted within the Hanbali School of Sunni Islamic jurisprudence. Freedom of religion is not provided under the law. The government does not allow the public practice of any non-Muslim religion. The law criminalizes "anyone who challenges, either directly or indirectly, the religion or justice of the King or Crown Prince." The law criminalizes "the promotion of atheistic ideologies in any form," "any attempt to cast doubt on the fundamentals of Islam," publications that "contradict the provisions of Islamic law," and other acts deemed contrary to sharia, including non-Islamic public worship, public display

---

[16] Scott Weiner, "Religious Freedom Conditions in Saudi Arabia," USCIRF, September 2021, https://www.uscirf.gov/sites/default/files/2021-09/2021%20Saudi%20Arabia%20Country%20Update.pdf.

[17] Barbara Ann Rieffer-Flanagan, "Rhetoric versus Reality."

[18] Ibid. He spent a decade in prison. He has not had to endure further lashings at the time of writing.

[19] Ambassador Michael Kozak, Testimony before the House Oversight and Government Reform Subcommittee on National Security, October 11, 2017, Washington, D.C.

of non-Islamic religious symbols, conversion by a Muslim to another religion, and proselytizing by a non-Muslim.[20]

Education System

Government policies contribute to the intolerance found in the education system, and this is especially evident in education materials and textbooks used in classrooms. Human rights activists, as well as foreign policy officials, complained about the materials in Saudi textbooks for over a decade. Numerous Islamic studies textbooks in various grades consistently included information that perpetuated a hateful narrative of the religious and non-religious Other. A ninth-grade textbook included intolerant language of Jews and Christians: "The Jews and Christians are enemies of the believers, and they cannot approve of Muslims," and "The Prophet said, The hour [of judgment] will not come until the Muslims fight the Jews and kill them."[21] A high school textbook taught that "Christianity in its current state is an invalid, perverted religion."[22]

Saudi leaders stated that reforms were needed "to prevent our children from being influenced by extremism and intolerance, which has corrupted our Islamic faith."[23] The Tatweer Education Reform Project established by the king in 2007 was a $2.4 billion project to revise the curricula.[24] Saudi political leaders professed that the government has removed information that contributed to extremism and intolerance, but there was little evidence of that for many years.[25] Studies routinely found intolerant language and messages.[26] A study concluded in 2011 found that despite Saudi officials' claims, many

---

[20] State Department, *International Religious Freedom Report for 2020*. Previous reports have also echoed these concerns. State Department, *International Religious Freedom Report for 2013*.

[21] Freedom House, "Saudi Arabia's Curriculum of Intolerance," 2006, https://freedomhouse.org/sites/default/files/CurriculumOfIntolerance.pdf; Elanor Abdella-Doumato, "Saudi Arabia: From 'Wahhabi' Roots to Contemporary Revisionism," in *Teaching Islam: Textbooks and Religion in the Middle East*, edited by Elanor Abdella-Doumato and Gregory Starret (Boulder, CO: Lynne Rienner, 2006).

[22] David Andrew Weinberg, "Prepared Statement for the Subcommittee on Terrorism, Nonproliferation, and Trade, House of Representatives," July 19, 2017, Washington, D.C.

[23] Saudi Royal Embassy, 2005, quoted in Abdella-Doumato, "Saudi Arabia," p. 170.

[24] International Center for Religion and Diplomacy, "The State of Curricular Reform in the Kingdom of Saudi Arabia," June 2012.

[25] In 2005, Prince Turki al-Faisal, then the Saudi Ambassador to the United States, stated, "any material that can be possibly interpreted as advocating intolerance of extremism," has been eliminated. Freedom House, "Saudi Arabia's Curriculum."

[26] Abdella-Doumato, "Saudi Arabia."

textbooks continued to promote hatred and intolerance of various faiths. Anti-Semitism was a particular problem: "Rank anti-Semitism saturates the curriculum. Repeatedly, Jews are demonized, dehumanized, and targeted for violence."[27] There are numerous anti-Semitic themes and references in Saudi textbooks. A seventh-grade textbook taught: "The Jews' nature is treachery, betrayal and breaking covenants."[28] A ninth-grade history textbook depicted Jews as malicious and undeserving of respect:

> From this it is obvious to you the invalidity of any alleged claims by the Jews of their right to inhabit the land of Palestine. The incontrovertible truth is that the Jews lived all their lives without a homeland. Wherever they settle, the peoples hate them and cast them away. They do not relate to any community that they live in except in a relationship of material benefit and interest through extorting money by usury and gambling and bribery in addition to being callers for sedition and people of schemes and conspiracies that they are brought up with. And what the Jews of Medina did to the Prophet (PBUH) in many situations shows their malicious intentions and their evil spirits. In their book, the Talmud, [the text] encourages them to harm anyone who is not a Jew. They also have traditions and lowly maxims, which are rejected by every human being who respects himself.[29]

This content, which is just a small sample of what was in Saudi textbooks, encouraged hatred and animosity. Human Rights Watch's study of the religious studies curriculum in 2017 also indicated that much of the "hateful and incendiary language" toward non-Sunni Muslims was still evident.[30] USCIRF's study of high school textbooks used in the 2017–2018 academic year found the current textbooks more intolerant than those reviewed in 2011–2012 and 2012–2014.[31] Passages that encourage violence included:

---

[27] The study went on to explain "the existence of an Israeli state is de-legitimized and the texts are aimed at mentally preparing the students for eventual war, not peace. As with other history, the accounts are widely distorted and filled with factual errors and tend to blame Jews for all the perceived problems in the world." Hudson Institute, "Ten Years On: Saudi Arabia's Textbooks Still Promote Religious Violence," September 16, 2011, https://www.hudson.org/research/8309-ten-years-on-saudi-arabia-s-textbooks-still-promote-religious-violence.

[28] Hudson Institute, p. 11.

[29] Hudson Institute, p. 25.

[30] "Saudi Arabia's school religious studies curriculum contains hateful and incendiary language toward religions and Islamic traditions that do not adhere to its interpretation of Sunni Islam… The texts disparage Sufi and Shia religious practices and label Jews and Christians 'unbelievers' with whom Muslims should not associate." Human Rights Watch, "Saudi Arabia."

[31] USCIRF, "Special Report: Study Revealed Numerous Passages in Saudi Textbooks Advocating Intolerance and Violence," May 2018, https://www.uscirf.gov/reports-briefs/special-reports/study-revealed-numerous-passages-in-saudi-textbooks-advocating.

"Exposing the people of the Book, explaining the falsity of their doctrines, and encouraging fighting of them until they give the jizya," and "Anyone who makes fun of God, His verses, or His Prophets is an apostate, no excuse is acceptable from him, so either he repents or is killed for infidelity."[32]

Efforts at Reform

For decades there have been calls to reform the Saudi education system and the educational materials used in Saudi classrooms and distributed to madrassas around the world. Unfortunately, the longer the reforms are delayed or limited to merely cosmetic efforts, the longer it will take for the impact to be felt.[33] In addition, teacher training programs and *retraining* programs for educators who have been teaching intolerant material for decades are necessary to change the educational culture in Saudi Arabia. One State Department official expressed her concern that the textbooks used in Saudi classrooms had a significant global reach beyond the Kingdom. She noted that some of these textbooks were used around the world, including in Great Britain.[34] In congressional testimony, David Andrew Weinberg noted that Saudi textbooks were present in 15 countries.[35]

American policy makers often discussed their efforts to revise Saudi textbooks.[36] One person in the Office of Global Programming at the State Department indicated that there had been some progress in textbook revisions in the Kingdom.[37] One US official explained that while there has been "documented progress in reforming textbooks," this is simply because the textbooks "went from terrible to bad."[38] One USCIRF official mentioned that

---

[32] Ibid.

[33] One study noted that educational reform in Saudi Arabia would take over 40 years to have a meaningful impact. Marwan Muasher, *The Second Arab Awakening and the Battle for Pluralism* (New Haven, CT: Yale University Press, 2014), p. 124.

[34] Interview, State Department official, Office of International Religious Freedom, December 14, 2012.

[35] Weinberg explained that "the Kingdom's books have emerged in well over a dozen countries over the years, including Algeria, Austria, Burkina Faso, China, Comoros, Djibouti, France, Indonesia, Nigeria, Pakistan, Somalia, Tanzania, Thailand, the United Kingdom, and previously in the United States." Weinberg, "Testimony." For a further discussion of the global reach of Saudi textbooks, see Hudson Institute, "Ten Years On."

[36] Interview, State Department official, December 14, 2012.

[37] Interview, March 14, 2014.

[38] This official went on to say that, "This is progress but it is still bad. They still include stuff that can lead to violence. They include stories from the Quran that can lead to violence. There are other examples that could promote tolerance [in the Quran] but they are not included in the textbooks." Interview, September 2017.

the Saudis realized the schools created a mindset that could lead to terrorism. He also noted that you have religious leaders cherry-picking verses, and that the worst materials were in the high schools. He concluded by saying that the "revisions are good but incomplete."[39] Another USCIRF official noted that the government agreed to revise their textbooks in 2006 and, while the process is ongoing, it is far from finished: "There are some improvements. But still reserving judgment on others. We can verify some of the textbooks, but who knows what is in the other textbooks?"[40] Despite Washington's efforts, Saudi textbooks contain material that can lead to violence.

Recent efforts to reform textbooks in various grades and subjects have shown some progress, although more is still needed. Some problematic content was removed from textbooks in 2020 and 2021. Descriptions of Jews and Christians as infidels were removed. Chapters praising jihad were removed from various textbooks, including 10th–12th-grade humanities textbooks.[41] Problematic language remained about infidels, polytheism, leaving the Islamic faith, and patriarchal gender roles. One study noted the contradictory aspect of curricular reform:

> In essence, the latest Saudi curriculum seems to be something of a contradiction. On the one hand, there appears to be a real attempt to move away from jihadism. On the other, deep and destructive prejudices remain, including those that are used by extremists to justify religious violence against people demonized as the Other. Progress in the curriculum has been tentative and unsure, with stark limits in some of the most important areas.[42]

The former foreign minister of Jordan, Marwan Muasher, indicated to me that he was not optimistic about the possibility of reform. He noted, "Religious education is still taught in a very rigid way, and almost with no appreciation of other religions. It is still considered taboo to touch this issue, which means it will probably be the last issue tackled in any reforms related to education in the Arab world."[43]

---

39 Interview, March 12, 2014.

40 Interview, July 2017.

41 Eldad J. Pardo, "A Further Step Forward: Review of Changes and Remaining Problematic Content in Saudi Textbooks 2021–22," IMPACT-se, September 2021, https://www.impact-se.org/wp-content/uploads/A-Further-Step-Forward-Review-of-Changes-and-Remaining-Problematic-Content-in-Saudi-Textbooks-2021%E2%80%9322.pdf.

42 Marcus Sheff and David A. Weinberg, "Saudi Textbooks Revised, but Still Incite Hate," March 30, 2020, https://www.longwarjournal.org/archives/2020/03/saudi-textbooks-revised-but-still-incite-hate.php.

43 Electronic communication, May 10, 2018.

It is worth briefly mentioning that despite the bold, perhaps reckless, reforms by Muhammed bin Salman, the Crown Prince, none have specifically addressed religious freedom. The war in Yemen, the crackdown on opposition figures, and Vision 2030 have unsettled many, including conservative clerics, in the Kingdom. There has been some easing of restrictions related to Saudi women and guardianship laws.[44] None of these top-down, autocratic reforms have drastically improved the situation of religious freedom or human rights in Saudi Arabia.

Even as American policy makers discuss the need for greater reform of educational materials, they are also aware of the limitations of these efforts.[45] One State Department official noted, "Yes, we have seen some changes. They have removed some harmful materials. But there is still ongoing intolerant materials, including anti-Shia materials… Even as we have seen a lot of changes, a lot more needs to be done." He went on to say, "Even if we were to see texts that teach inclusion, if you do not see changes in other areas [laws, courts, police], it would still not be enough to change the trajectory."[46]

OMAN

Oman under Sultan Qaboos

If one were looking for a religiously tolerant oasis in the Middle East—a region besieged by sectarian conflict—Oman stands out as an example of a country that paved a unique path. This tolerant path can be attributed to Sultan Qaboos and the educational reforms he initiated. If we compare Oman to Egypt, Israel, or Saudi Arabia, Muscat has a largely favorable record in its approach to religion. While all aspects of Article 18 of the ICCPR were not protected, under Sultan Qaboos religious tolerance existed. There was little evidence of social hostility between religious groups or toward religious minorities over the last decade. The Pew Research Center's Trends in Global Restrictions on Religion bears this out.[47] Pew finds that there are some government restrictions on public preaching, and proselytizing is limited by the government (Table 5.2).

---

[44] Weiner, "Religious Freedom."

[45] Some Saudis in religious institutions resent American interference. Abdella-Doumato, p. 172.

[46] Interview, State Department official, October 13, 2017.

[47] Pew Research Center, "Globally, Social Hostilities Related to Religion Decline in 2019, While Government Restrictions Remain at Highest Levels. The scale used by the Pew Research Center ranges from zero to nine. The lower the score, the less government restrictions and social hostility. High scores (six or better) indicate a denial

Table 5.2 Pew Research Center International Religious Freedom and Restrictions scores, Oman

Oman	2007	2014	2019
Government Regulations Index (GRI)	3.9	4.7	5.4
Social Hostilities Index (SHI)	0.3	0.0	0.4
Average of GRI and SHI	1.96	2.35	2.9

Oman does far better on both government restrictions when compared to Egypt, Israel, or Saudi Arabia.[48] Many have credited the former Sultan Qaboos with the religious environment in the country.[49] One professor noted, "The Sultan has said a lot about Islam and tolerance. He has articulated this very strongly."[50] Sultan Qaboos instituted numerous changes, modernized Oman, and employed a discourse of tolerance.[51] This demonstrates the significant impact and value of a tolerant leader. Sultan Qaboos bin Said promoted religious tolerance in the constitution and in governmental policies. In the mid-1990s, he instituted a new constitution that included a non-discrimination clause.[52] While Islam is the declared state religion, the legal framework allows individuals to practice their "religious rites as long as doing so does not disrupt public order or contradict morals." In addition, there are no laws against leaving one's faith,

of aspects of freedom of religion. See also: https://www.pewforum.org/2019/07/15/a-closer-look-at-how-religious-restrictions-have-risen-around-the-world/.

48 Egypt averaged 6.65 (2007), 7.55 (2014), and 7.45 (2019) on the GRI and SHI scores. Israel's averages were 5.85 (2007), 7.30 (2014), and 6.7 (2019). Pew Research Center, "Trends in Global Restrictions on Religion," June 23, 2016, http://assets.pewresearch.org/wp-content/uploads/sites/11/2016/06/Restrictions2016-Full-Report-FINAL.pdf; Pew Research Center, "A Closer Look at How Religious Restrictions Have Risen Around the World," July 15, 2019, https://www.pewforum.org/2019/07/15/a-closer-look-at-how-religious-restrictions-have-risen-around-the-world/; Pew Research Center, "Globally."

49 A professor of political science in Oman emphasized the role of the Sultan: "I would say the role of his majesty Sultan bin Qaboos is really remarkable, building Oman on strong pillars of tolerance free from any sectarianism." Interview, April 2, 2017.

50 Discussion with Professor of Religious Studies, April 5, 2017.

51 A number of people I spoke to noted that he was a benign dictator who tended to coopt opposition figures. This is far better than other dictators in the Middle East, such as Assad or el-Sisi, who tolerate no dissent.

52 Article 17: "No discrimination amongst [people] on the ground of gender, origin, color, language, religion, sect, domicile, or social status"; see https://www.constituteproject.org/constitution/Oman_2011.pdf. Mirren Gidda, "How Much Longer Can Oman Be an Oasis of Peace in the Middle East?" *Newsweek*, February 10, 2017.

and there is a non-sectarian civil code.[53] While the government does require religious organizations to register, the registration process is not so overly burdensome as to prevent religious groups from carrying out their functions within the country as long as they have a local sponsor within Oman.

Foreigners living in Oman praised Sultan Qaboos's policies. One Christian minister living in Oman said, "[T]here is no proselytizing, they do not want to create divisions and they play down the religious divisions" in the country. He went on to say that the policy of the Ministry for Endowments and Religious Affairs, which directs the content of Friday prayers, was beneficial to keeping the peace and avoiding sectarian conflict.[54] Sermons authorized by the government do not mention confessional difference.[55]

Education System

In addition to the constitution and laws promulgated in Oman, for decades the education system taught students norms of tolerance. Religious studies classes discuss topics in a non-sectarian manner.[56] This avoids the demonization of the religious Other that is so prevalent in Saudi and Egyptian textbooks. Sultan Qaboos bin Said instituted policies to further religious tolerance in the education system.[57] Prior to 1970, Oman's educational system was rather traditional, with students beginning their education with classes in the local mosque.[58] When he came to power in 1970, his administration made significant changes

[53] State Department, *International Religious Freedom Report for 2019* (Washington, D.C.: US State Department).

[54] Discussion with a Christian minister in Oman on April 6, 2017. "However, thanks to its policy of pluralism, coexistence—or what we call al *aish al mushtarak*, or living together—and sound development, Oman has been able to cope with the movements and upheavals that have set several neighboring states ablaze." Sheikh Abdullah bin Mohammed al Salimi, Minister of Endowments and Religious Affairs, Speech in Muscat, Oman, 2014, http://www.mara.om/wp-content/uploads/klmtt-maale-alwzer-balienjleze.pdf.

[55] Marc Valeri, *Oman: Politics and Society in the Qaboos State* (New York: Columbia University Press, 2009), p. 128.

[56] Mandana Limbert, "Oman: Cultivating Good Citizens and Religious Virtue," in *Teaching Islam: Textbooks and Religion in the Middle East*, edited by Eleanor Abdella-Doumato and Gregory Starett (Boulder, CO: Lynne Rienner, 2007), p. 109.

[57] A professor of religious studies indicated to me, "Sultan Qaboos has gone beyond acceptance of other Muslim sects and of the People of the Book by granting land for building Hindu temples and allowing a freedom of worship that is remarkable in the Muslim Middle East." Interview, April 1, 2017.

[58] Abdulrhman al-Salimi, "The Transformation of Religious Learning in Oman: Tradition and Modernity," *Journal of Royal Asiatic Society*, Vol. 21, No. 2 (April 2011), p. 148.

and took "an active role in determining the nature of the religious education to be provided in schools."[59] While Islamic studies are a required part of the curriculum until the 12th grade, non-Muslims can opt out of these classes.

Furthermore, no one denomination or sect is favored in the classroom.[60] An ecumenical or generic form of Islam is taught in schools.[61] A Christian pastor living in Oman told me, "People are taught about Islam, not divisions within Islam. This is good for the social environment in Oman."[62] While Ibadi Islam is the dominant religion in Oman, the government does not emphasize Ibadism to the detriment of other faiths, and it is not taught in an exclusive manner. Al-Salimi explained it this way:

> Although Ibidism is the dominant Islamic tradition in Oman, there are a substantial number of Sunnis and a small yet prominent community of Shi'a. To promote unity and avoid sectarianism, Oman's Islamic Studies curriculum aimed not to favour one tradition over another but rather to focus upon the basic principles of Islam upon which all Muslims agree.[63]

Thus, sectarian differences among Ibadi, Sunni, and Shia Islam are not part of the materials presented to students.[64] The Ministry of Education does not allow textbooks that heighten sectarian identity formation and the hostility toward the Other that is apparent in textbooks in other countries in the region.

Omani students are taught to show kindness and respect toward other faiths.[65] Given the unavoidable impact of globalization and Oman's relationships with diverse states and cultures, the Ministry of Education opted to teach its students how Islamic culture and civilization relate to the broader world.[66] This is in stark contrast to how other societies have demonized other cultures and religious communities.

Oman, when compared to other countries in the Middle East, has developed more tolerant attitudes.[67] The benefits of a non-sectarian approach taught

---

59 Jeremy Jones and Nicholas Ridout, *A History of Modern Oman* (New York: Cambridge University Press, 2015), p. 166.

60 State Department, *International Religious Freedom Report for 2016.*

61 Jeremy Jones and Nicholas Ridout, *Oman, Culture and Diplomacy* (Edinburgh: Edinburgh University Press, 2012), p. 42.

62 Interview, April 6, 2017.

63 Al-Salimi, "The Transformation," p. 149.

64 Jones and Ridout, *A History of Modern Oman*, p. 176. This was also indicated to me by a professor: "schools are not supposed to teach anything sectarian." Interview, April 5, 2017.

65 Limbert, "Oman."

66 Al-Salimi, "The Transformation," p. 155.

67 Jones and Ridout, *Oman, Culture and Diplomacy*, p. 51. While Human Rights Watch's World Report 2017 does note gender discrimination, abuse of migrant

in schools and embedded in everyday social interactions can be seen in the peaceful domestic society that has developed over the last few decades. The benefits are also evident in Oman's relations with other states in the Persian Gulf and beyond.

Oman's tolerance is also related to Ibadi Islam, one of the dominant religions in the country.[68] Ibadism has a long history in Oman, dating to the 7th century. Ibadism developed out of the Kharijite opposition movement. Ibadism incorporates egalitarianism and consultation between the imam and the umma. Therefore, some scholars have referred to Ibadism as a moderate form of Islam.[69] Ibadism has a tradition within Islam that is distinct from Sunni and Shia Islam. One key element of Ibadism is *kufr ni'ma*, which can be understood as being unfaithful or ungrateful for Allah's blessings.[70] Viewing another Muslim from a different tradition as having a mistaken view instead of being an unbeliever allows for tolerance of other Muslims.[71] Ultimately, Sultan Qaboos promoted religious tolerance in Oman to avoid the sectarian conflicts prevalent in the region. These policies were consistent with Ibadism and could draw on centuries of religious teachings.

Since many attribute the religious tolerance found in Oman to Sultan Qaboos, his death in early 2020 raises the possibility of alternative policies or problems. Haitham bin Tariq al Said assumed power within a few days of Qaboos's passing. There has been no indication that he seeks to move Oman to intolerant waters. It is also worth noting that Oman does not have a history of religious intolerance or harassment of religious minorities. Religious tolerance is embedded in Oman's education system and in other institutions in society.

---

workers, and limitations on freedom of expression, it does not mention infringements on freedom of religion; see https://www.hrw.org/world-report/2017/country-chapters/oman.

[68] Ibadis make up approximately 1 percent of Muslims in the world and constitute a majority of the citizens of Oman. Valerie Hoffman, "Ibadism: History, Doctrines, and Recent Scholarship," *Religion Compass*, Vol. 9, No. 9 (2015), pp. 297–307. See also State Department, *International Religious Freedom Report of 2015*. However, there are no official government statistics that break down the different faiths in Oman. It is a government policy not to publish statistics about different faiths in Oman; this is consistent with other policies in which the government attempts to downplay sectarian divisions and deemphasize religious difference. Interview with a Professor of Religious Studies, April 5, 2017.

[69] Thomas Bierschank, "Religion and Political Structure: Remarks on Ibadism in Oman and the Mizah (Algeria)," *Studia Islamica*, Vol. 68 (1988), pp. 107–27.

[70] Hoffman, p. 300. This understanding is different from *kufr shirk* or unbelief or idolatry, which has been used as a justification by some Muslims to kill those with whom they have theological disagreements.

[71] Beyond doctrinal tolerance for non-Ibadi Muslims, in practice this tolerance has been extended to individuals outside of the umma. Hoffman, p. 301.

Therefore, there is no reason to think that the norms of religious tolerance promoted for the last 50 years will change under the new leader.[72]

SWEDEN

Religious minorities and non-theists do not enjoy a religiously tolerant environment in Saudi Arabia or other parts of the Middle East. They fare far better in Sweden according to various indicators, including the Pew Research Center, as noted in Chapter 2. What explains Sweden's more tolerant atmosphere compared to other countries? Sweden is a secular,[73] liberal democracy in Europe. It is in a less violent region than the Middle East and is more committed to universal human rights than some countries in other parts of the world. Another relevant aspect of Swedish society is the educational system. Unlike Saudi Arabia and other societies, Swedish classrooms and textbooks do not teach hate or intolerance of the Other. Understanding how a society teaches its future citizens about religious diversity and religious tolerance is a worthwhile endeavor.

The Lutheran faith became the dominant denomination in Sweden in the 16th century and would remain the official religion until 2000.[74] Religious education classes began in Sweden in the context of an official religion with the goal to create "acceptable members of society"—faithful Lutherans.[75] Over the course of a few hundred years, these classes would change from an emphasis on Lutheranism to Christianity more broadly defined. Parents belonging to Free Churches objected to the heavy emphasis on Lutheranism in the early 20th century, and this eventually resulted in the contemporary non-denominational approach. As Sweden has become less religiously homogenous, its religious

---

[72] The people I spoke to did not believe that religious intolerance was likely to develop after a change in leadership. The Christian minister noted his concerns about the economic stability of the country but added that "the Omani people are not a violent people." Interview, April 6, 2017. A professor told me that Omanis "have never gotten into religious persecution. They never have. I cannot imagine religiously motivated violence" in Oman. Interview, April 5, 2017.

[73] The World Values Survey looks at traditional versus secular-rational values. "Secular-rational values have the opposite preferences to the traditional values. These societies place less emphasis on religion, traditional family values and authority. Divorce, abortion, euthanasia and suicide are seen as relatively acceptable." Sweden has high scores in secular-rational and self-expression values, as do Norway, Japan, Germany, Switzerland, and the Czech Republic, to name a few; see: http://www.worldvaluessurvey.org/WVSContents.jsp?CMSID=Findings.

[74] Karin Kittelmann Flensner, *Discourses of Religion and Secularism in Religious Education Classes* (Cham: Springer, 2017), p. 20.

[75] Kittelmann Flensner, p. 21.

education classes moved to teaching about diverse religious traditions beyond the Lutheran faith.

The goals of the religious education classes according to Skolverket—the National Agency for Education—are to encourage and develop a set of fundamental values in future citizens:

> The national school system is based on democratic foundations. The Education Act (2010: 800) stipulates that education in the school system aims at students acquiring and developing knowledge and values. It should promote the development and learning of students, and a lifelong desire to learn. Education should impart and establish respect for human rights and the fundamental democratic values on which Swedish society is based. The education should be based on scientific grounds and proven experience. Each and every one working in the school should also encourage respect for the intrinsic value of each person and the environment we all share.
>
> The inviolability of human life, individual freedom and integrity, the equal value of all people, equality between women and men, and solidarity between people are the values that the education should represent and impart. In accordance with the ethics borne by Christian tradition and Western humanism, this is to be achieved by nurturing in the individual a sense of justice, generosity, tolerance and responsibility. Teaching should be non-denominational.[76]

Thus, the National Agency for Education aims to instill in its future citizens important values, such as freedom, equality, and tolerance. In the religious education classes, it "aims to present a comprehensive view of different religions without expressing particular views or standpoints about any religious tradition."[77]

To promote tolerance of different religions and non-religious orientations and worldviews, the content of the religious education class introduces students to diverse ideas. The religious education syllabus articulates this as follows: "Through teaching in the subject of religious education, pupils shall be given the opportunity to develop their ability to analyze Christianity, plus other religions and worldviews as well as different interpretations and practices within these."[78] Students learn about Christianity and other religious traditions (Buddhism, Islam, Judaism, Hinduism), as well as ethical traditions. Students are not segregated during these lessons.

---

[76] Skolverket, "Curriculum for the Upper Secondary School," 2013, https://www.skolverket.se/publikationsserier/styrdokument/2013/curriculum-for-the-upper-secondary-school.

[77] Johan Liljestrand, "Education for Citizenship in Swedish RE: Approaches and Dilemmas in Teacher's Talk," *Religion and Education*, Vol. 44, No. 3 (2017), pp. 317–30.

[78] Skolverket, RE Syllabus for Comprehensive Schools, quoted in Kittelmann Flensner, p. 34.

The non-denominational approach has contributed to religious tolerance.[79] Karin Kittelmann Flensner notes in her study of religious education in Sweden that, "in articulations of the Swedish self-image, tolerance was a central value."[80] Swedish students are taught and internalize tolerance in their self-image and identity.[81] Teaching tolerance is not easy, but it is necessary for a democratic political system. One teacher explained it to me this way:

> In a pluralistic society, there has to be a constant negotiation about the borders of freedom of religion, your right to freely practice your religion and my right to avoid religion. And in the classroom, this is sometimes tricky to handle, and I think it must be tricky—it is one of the fundamentals in [a] democracy.[82]

The comparison of diverse countries, such as Saudi Arabia, Oman, and Sweden, has been undertaken to demonstrate the different classroom experiences and educational content to which students are exposed. While this may be expected given that these three societies have different cultural, religious, and historical backgrounds and levels of development, the comparison is worth exploring. The evaluation is not meant to suggest that other countries must become Western liberal democracies in order to achieve religious tolerance in their societies.[83] Diverse societies do not need to mimic Swedish society in all of its facets. But Sweden does offer a window into how to teach about different religious traditions in a respectful manner that encourages tolerance rather than hate. Sweden is a more tolerant society with far fewer violent attacks on religious minorities and their places of worship. The educational system is not the only reason that tolerance developed, but it does contribute to the tolerant environment found there.

---

[79] One Swedish teacher told me that she thought "the construction of RE [Religious Education] contributed to religious tolerance." Interview, May 7, 2018.

[80] Kittelmann Flensner, p.129.

[81] This tolerant self-image did not inhibit students from expressing their bias toward secularism. "One view articulated by students and teachers was… rational and sensible behavior and beliefs in our time do not consist of anything belonging to the religious sphere." Kittelmann Flensner, p. 57. These secular discourses are compatible with the World Values Survey and Sweden's emphasis on secular-rational values.

[82] Interview, May 7, 2018.

[83] It is true that many Western, liberal democracies have proven to be better at protecting a range of human rights, as articulated in the Universal Declaration of Human Rights, ICCPR, and ICESCR. A state does not have to be a liberal democracy to uphold a minimal level of religious tolerance for all its citizens. Oman is a religiously tolerant monarchy.

ENCOURAGING EDUCATIONAL REFORM

Efforts at reforming a country's education system ought to focus on improving the quality of the teachers in classrooms and reforming the lesson plans, curricula, textbooks, and additional materials used by educators. Ultimately, these reforms seek to produce the norms and dispositions in individuals that foster a tolerant environment. Multilateral efforts to address this topic have been undertaken. Policy makers, civil society organizations, and other experts from the international community gathered at a conference in Abu Dhabi in 2019 to discuss educational efforts to combat extremism. The result was the 2019 Abu Dhabi Guidelines for Teaching Interfaith Tolerance to help promote religious tolerance.[84] This document explains the need for educational opportunities to promote religious tolerance. Policy makers involved in this process noted the urgent need for reforms:

> These trends taken together require new approaches for teaching students the importance of interfaith tolerance, peaceful coexistence, and pluralistic societies. However, despite our increasingly interconnected world, the international community has generally steered away from these topics. Billions of dollars are spent annually to help ensure children receive a quality education in reading, writing, and arithmetic. However, donors spend a pittance on equipping students to appreciate pluralistic societies, respect equal citizenship, and prepare them to live in an increasingly religious and ethnically diverse world. There is a need to harness education's power to prepare students for this multi-ethnic, multi-religious future.[85]

Education reform must address the quality of teachers. Lessons on tolerance and respect for the Other in textbooks will have little impact if teachers ignore those chapters or promote intolerance through their words and deeds in the classroom. If instructors use hateful language or engage in proselytization in schools, students may follow their lead. Poorly trained teachers or teachers who promote inaccurate or intolerant messages contribute to a generation of children who are likely to develop into intolerant citizens. One study in Pakistan noted the problems with the individuals who stand in the front of the classroom: "Extensive interviews revealed that public school teachers have a limited or contradictory understanding of religious minorities and their beliefs." It went on to add, "it is important to note that upwards of 80 percent of the public school teachers viewed non-Muslims as 'enemies of Islam' in some

---

[84] See https://www.forb-learning.org/uploads/1/1/3/5/113585003/abu_dhabi_guidelines_on_teaching_interfaith_tolerance.pdf.

[85] Knox Thames, "Teaching Tolerance and Promoting Pluralism: Challenges and Opportunities," Remarks to the Institute of Gulf Affairs, October 22, 2020, https://www.knoxthames.com/post/remarks-to-institute-of-gulf-affairs.

form or another, despite contradictory views expressed in other parts of the interviews."[86] Thus, the individuals who teach about religion must possess not only knowledge of various religious traditions, but also the pedagogical skills and dispositions to teach the materials and interact with students in a respectful manner.

To address some of these issues, governments need to develop and mandate teacher training programs on world religions with particular emphasis on the religious dominations in the country. Teachers should be trained to avoid stigmatizing or accentuating the religious differences in the classroom. Teacher certification programs should include materials on tolerance (of religious communities and non-theists). International actors, including the United States, can help provide funding, information, and educational materials to a country to improve its educational system. It must provide meaningful and continual support.[87] While USAID has funded educational reforms in countries such as Pakistan, some educational efforts have nothing to do with teaching tolerance. A USAID five-year, $155 million basic education project was aimed at merging and consolidating schools in Pakistan.[88] The physical construction of schools or improving efficiency and eliminating redundant schools in some provinces may be needed. However, this will not create tolerant students.

Washington can contribute to better teachers, with the cooperation of the host government, by encouraging teachers and individuals training to be teachers to study in the United States or universities in tolerant countries. Washington can extend scholarships or work with American universities to develop scholarships for students from specific CPC states. Beyond training future teachers, Washington can invite current teachers to the United States to participate in training programs. The US embassy in Saudi Arabia sponsored approximately 30 Saudis to travel to the United States to participate in programs centered on interfaith dialogue and combating extremist ideology.[89] The same could be done with a focus on teacher training and tolerance. The Defense Department developed programs to bring officers from other countries to the United States for training programs. The State Department in

---

[86] USCIRF, "Connecting the Dots," p. 16.

[87] In November 2012, the Bureau of Democracy, Human Rights, and Labor at the State Department offered approximately $1 million to support projects aimed at "promoting mutual respect, tolerance, and interreligious understanding among both teachers and students in the public school system" in Pakistan. Department of State, Bureau of Democracy, Human Rights, and Labor, Public Notice, Request for Proposals for Pakistan. This is too meager an amount to have a long-term impact on Pakistan's education system.

[88] International Crisis Group, Report 257, p. 18.

[89] State Department, *International Religious Freedom Report for 2017*.

conjunction with the Department of Education can develop similar programs. These teacher training programs in the host country or elsewhere must also be sensitive to the concerns and insecurities of the teachers involved. Teachers must be reassured that this will improve their standing and not compromise their own status in the community.

Revising the curricula that guide aspects of an educational system, including lesson plans and textbooks,[90] is potentially more complicated than developing teacher training programs. One State Department official noted that these were sovereign countries, and the US could not force them to make changes.[91] Wherever possible, efforts should be made to remove hateful and derogatory content concerning religious minorities and non-theists. Students should be exposed to positive messages about various religious groups, including materials that discuss the positive contributions that minorities have made to society. Transforming textbooks or educational modules that contain intolerant narratives to tolerant messages of inclusion and respect has the potential to transform a generation and a society. Exposing young children to different religious traditions and cultures through a respectful discussion can help to plant the seeds for tolerant future citizens by addressing and eliminating misperceptions and stereotypes. In these modules on religious diversity and respect for religious difference, the harmful aspects of social media must be discussed. While a comprehensive discussion of social media's impact on children is beyond the scope of this chapter, a few brief points are worth mentioning. Lessons should be developed to raise awareness about the harmful and dehumanizing aspects of some aspects of social media. Teachers can employ case studies to help students identify intolerant content and develop appropriate responses that do not demonize minority communities.

How the topic of religion is taught is also important. To begin, accurate and impartial portrayals of religious communities must be part of the curriculum. An exclusive or separatist approach in which students from different belief communities segregate into separate classes to learn about their community is less likely to encourage tolerance than a more inclusive approach. Teaching a course on comparative religions or world religions where all students engage with the content together in a neutral and objective fashion will provide for a more inclusive and welcoming educational environment. A non-confessional approach to religious education classes that offers neutral, fact-based content on diverse religious and non-religious traditions can be found in numerous

---

[90] Revising textbooks should be a collaborative process between the government, schools, and faith-based communities as well as publishers and authors to ensure accurate information is incorporated in a respectful manner.

[91] Conversation with State Department official, October 13, 2017.

countries, including Norway, Sweden, Botswana, and South Africa.[92] These efforts can plant the seeds for the future development of religious freedom. This is part of the generational struggle that the international community needs to be working on.

One State Department official who has been trying to encourage religious tolerance told me that "education was key. If we could spend millions on education reform, I would do it and it still would not be enough. This would be good to change hearts and minds."[93] Another noted that the State Department saw "educational reform as a really important piece to a more tolerant society."[94] An official at USCIRF echoed these sentiments, explaining that engaging societies in education reform is important as education is a huge part of religious freedom.[95]

US foreign policy should put more emphasis on and funding toward educational reform in countries around the world. One State Department employee explained that "if we had more money we would focus on education."[96] This may be one of the most critical reforms undertaken in CPC countries. Kristina Arriaga, Vice Chairwoman of USCIRF, stated the importance of educational reform:

> USCIRF urges Congress to encourage the State Department, USAID and other entities to prioritize programs that develop and disseminate educational and teacher training materials, especially in countries of concern, on international human rights and religious freedom standards and the centrality of interfaith understanding to achieving development objectives. USCIRF also urges that these programs be implemented especially in countries with public and private education systems that promote religious intolerance and extremism, and that the National Endowment for Democracy and other entities that receive federal funding solicit competitive proposals on specific international religious freedom programming.[97]

---

[92] Kittelmann Flensner, p. 19.

[93] Interview, September 29, 2017.

[94] Interview, October 13, 2017. It is also true that there is deep hostility toward the reforms associated with the West and the US specifically; Madiha Afzal, *Pakistan Under Siege: Extremism, Society and the State* (Washington, D.C.: Brookings Institute Press, 2018), Chapter 4, p. 115. Overcoming the hostility will be difficult.

[95] Interview, March 12, 2014.

[96] Interview, March 14, 2014.

[97] Kristina Arriaga, Testimony before the National Security Subcommittee of the House Committee on Oversight and Government Reform, October 17, 2017, Washington, D.C. Her written testimony can be found at: https://www.uscirf.gov/sites/default/files/October%2011%20testimonyrev3%20--%20as%20of%20October%204%20with%20appendix.pdf

Washington has pursued some limited efforts to assist governments in educational reforms. One Egyptian human rights activist noted that there were numerous problems in Egypt's education system. He mentioned the low quality of teachers, especially in the south. He also commented on the hateful content in textbooks. For example, there is little information about or tolerance for Baha'is or Shiites: "They do not exist for Egyptians."[98] He did note that USAID funded textbook revisions. USAID brought in foreign experts to evaluate the content of textbooks. These efforts were supported by the Egyptian Education Minister. He further explained that in addition to intolerant content, there was also the absence of stories or content about religious minorities, such as Coptic Christians. This resulted in a lack of knowledge of Coptic Christians by Egyptian Muslims: "I [a Coptic] learned about Muslims in school from studying the Quran and Sunna. But there was no real knowledge of Christians."[99] The changes over the last ten years involved including Christian characters in stories.[100] Incorporating positive depictions and stories about Coptic Christians has the potential to introduce the larger Muslim population to understand Copts as equal and non-alienating and hence worthy of dignity and respect.[101]

One essential goal of this educational reform is the development of tolerant dispositions. Changing the content of textbooks or training teachers involves concrete reforms that can be quantified and tracked. Removing intolerant textbooks and literature from classrooms around the world is a worthwhile effort to prevent intolerant and hateful materials from ending up in a child's hands. A further, positive step is also needed to mold tolerant children and ultimately promote tolerant citizens. Embedding tolerant dispositions into young people through a deliberate process of socialization in the education system is also necessary.[102]

---

[98] Interview, October 11, 2013.

[99] Ibid.

[100] Ibid.

[101] One Egyptian educator suggested to me that any education reform would be beneficial: "Anything would be an improvement, even 2 percent would be good," given the environment that students are in. Interview, July 10, 2018.

[102] Education reform alone will not change society by itself. One Palestinian educator told me that a teacher can try to encourage tolerance in children, but if the reality outside the walls of the classroom does not change, we cannot expect the child to change. His point was that we cannot expect lessons on tolerance in classrooms to negate all the hostility and intolerance some children experience outside of the classroom. Interview with Ma'ale Hachamisha, Israel, July 13, 2018.

CONCLUSION

While freedom of religion or belief and the religious tolerance that is necessary for religious freedom is a universal right, it must be constructed and reconstructed generation after generation. Religious freedom must be constructed through a process of thought, language, and social interaction. Therefore, the educational system a child experiences is so important.

When education is mandatory, the government has the ability to influence the values, norms, and dispositions of generations of students for good or ill. Reforming the curriculum and providing teacher training programs will not solve the intolerance problem alone. But it can help to combat some of the intolerant ideas in society. If stakeholders in the community (religious leaders and organizations, civil society activists, etc.) can be persuaded to contribute to a more tolerant education system, this could have a lasting positive impact. This is not to suggest a straight line of causation. In identifying a source of intolerance in Saudi Arabia, I am pointing to an aspect of society which, if reformed, may help to counter some of the demonization of religious (and non-religious) minorities. Encouraging tolerant dispositions in a country is primarily the work of the government and non-state actors within the country. However, the international community has some tools at its disposal to help and encourage the development of tolerant individuals who respect others. Washington and other international actors must approach this as a long-term process that requires the cooperation and input of local actors.

Various aspects of the international community should give greater attention to the development of social norms and dispositions in intolerant countries. Creating tolerant dispositions toward others does not develop overnight. While these changes can be difficult and require the cooperation of the host government, they are essential to establish, at a minimum, religious tolerance and eventually freedom of religion or belief. One former Assistant Secretary of State noted how delicate this was and said policy makers were "nudging not shouting."[103]

This is one part of a long-term strategy. Encouraging governments through programs and diplomatic exchanges to reform the indigenous education system should be combined with a bottom-up strategy with civil society to develop tolerant individuals. One human rights activist noted that it was important for local leaders to encourage these ideas:

> You can begin to develop tolerance. You find people in the culture to promote it within their own culture. The truth of the matter is so much is dependent on indi-

[103] Interview, March 10, 2014, Washington, D.C.

> vidual leaders. Leaders must say that something [stoning] is not part of the culture. How do you elevate their voices?[104]

National governments and civil society actors can work toward reforming the education system, including the materials used in classrooms and the teachers who guide students in those classrooms. The goal is to create and sustain religious freedom or belief for all. Educating young people can encourage the resilience necessary to address periodic intolerance. When citizens hold tolerant dispositions and social norms that respect the religious (or non-religious) Other are embedded in society, there will be less social hostility toward fellow citizens and less need for government action to protect minorities. When members of society believe that the Other deserves a place in the public square, persecution, discrimination, and violence will be less likely.[105] The next chapter builds on some of the lessons of a tolerant leader previously discussed in this chapter (Qaboos) to develop a sustainable environment for religious freedom.

---

[104] Interview, July 18, 2013.

[105] If one looks at those countries with very high scores on the SHI—Iraq, Israel, Syria, Yemen, Pakistan, Sri Lanka, India, Afghanistan, Lebanon, Nigeria—all have experienced violent conflict and discrimination over the last few decades. Pew Forum on Religion and Public Life, "Latest Trends in Religious Restrictions and Hostilities," February 26, 2015, https:// www .pewresearch .org/ religion/ 2015/ 02/ 26/religious -hostilities/.

6. Tolerant leadership in Tashkent: the role of leaders in the promotion of religious tolerance

INTRODUCTION

While many democratic political systems established laws and policies to protect the beliefs and practices of religious (and non-religious) individuals and groups, religious tolerance can develop in a society without a democratically elected leader. History provides evidence of authoritarian rulers who rose to power through skill or brute force, as opposed to the ballot box, and adopted policies that furthered religious tolerance for pragmatic or instrumental reasons. Uzbek President Mirziyoyev ushered in a series of initiatives that *could* transform this country into a religiously tolerant oasis in the heart of central Asia.

One may be forgiven if a land-locked country of approximately 33 million people in central Asia is not the first state one thinks of as a place for hope in a world trending toward global intolerance. Formerly part of the Soviet Union until declaring independence in 1991, Uzbekistan is a country embarking on new political, social, and economic policies.[1] President Mirziyoyev adopted a variety of policies in the last few years. A German professor who has traveled to the country for over a decade commented on the changes occurring there, including more efforts by the government to modernize the economy, improve the country's infrastructure, and promote tourism. This academic added that while it will take time, the "people [of Uzbekistan] were hopeful for the future."

The United Nations High Commissioner for Human Rights explained the extent of the changes: "The volume of constructive human rights-related proposals, plans, and new legislation that has emerged since President

[1] Interview, Tashkent, Uzbekistan, August 8, 2019. It is also worth noting that in August 2019 President Mirziyoyev announced the closure of the notorious Jaslyk prison in which many prisoners were tortured. By the end of 2019 over 300 inmates had been transferred to other prisons throughout the country.

Mirziyoyev took office is remarkable. The successful implementation of those reforms could have a transformational impact on the country's future."[2] One NGO described the reforms as unprecedented.[3] A human rights activist noted, "religious freedom has made strides forward."[4] The Vice President for the European Bank for Reconstruction and Development, Jurgen Rigterink, stated, "Uzbekistan has taken decisive, bold steps towards openness and reform. Since President Mirziyoyev took office in September 2016, he has implemented a far-reaching change process which has taken even long-term observers by surprise in light of its breath and depth."[5] Change is underway. As one journalist from Uzbekistan explained, "I have crisscrossed its regions and… seen a remarkable shift, one that stands in sharp contrast to what often seems like a relentless international trend toward greater repression, increasingly autocracy, and eroding liberties."[6] Whether Uzbekistan will successfully develop into a religiously free society rests largely in the hands of President Mirziyoyev[7] and his commitment and ability to consolidate these extensive social and political reforms.

LEADERSHIP

Religious intolerance, and the dehumanization of the Other that often accompanies this intolerance, has occurred in many societies around the world. The

---

[2] Sean Lees, "Final Evaluation of Joint Project of UNDP [United Nations Development Program], USAID and Supreme Court of Uzbekistan Rule of Law Partnership in Uzbekistan," August 2017. Document is in the possession of the author.

[3] "Beginning in 2006, Uzbekistan was designated a 'Country of Particular Concern' (CPC) for religious freedom by the State Department. However, starting in 2016, Uzbekistan's leaders have ushered in unprecedented political, social, and economic reforms which have attracted worldwide attention"; see https://globalengage.org/programs/uzbekistan. *The Economist* named Uzbekistan its most improved nation in 2019, stating "Uzbekistan still has a long way to go, but no other country traveled as far in 2019."

[4] Steve Swerdlow, "Uzbekistan's Religious and Political Prisoners," webinar, October 13, 2021, https://www.uscirf.gov/events/webinars/uscirf-conversation-new-report-uzbekistans-religious-prisoners.

[5] Jurgen Rigterink, First Vice President of the European Bank for Reconstruction and Development, Speech, Berlin, Germany, January 14, 2019, https://www.ebrd.com/news/speeches/reforming-uzbekistan-challenges-and-opportunities.html.

[6] Navbahov Imamova, "Where Freedoms are Expanding—Slowly," *The Atlantic*, October 5, 2019, https://www.theatlantic.com/international/archive/2019/10/uzbekistan-freedom-slowly-expanding/599446/.

[7] "Reforms—indeed, Uzbekistan's entire decision-making system—remains heavily dependent on Mirziyoyev. Citizens widely view him as the embodiment of the Uzbek government, arguing that unless he says or wants something, nothing changes." Imamova, "Where Freedoms."

coexistence of different-faith communities or believers and non-believers is often more difficult to accomplish. An enlightened or a self-interested leader who allows their citizens to follow their conscience can assist a society in developing religious tolerance. By adopting policies that encourage tolerance, a non-democratic leader *can* place a society on a path to freedom of religion or belief.

An enlightened leader need not be a liberal democrat or a compassionate individual. As noted in Chapter 2, history offers numerous examples of ruthless leaders, with blood on their hands, who not only slaughtered armed opposition, but also tolerated religious communities that could have easily been eliminated. Cyrus the Great, the Persian conqueror, and Napoleon, two centuries later, did not hesitate to use the sword to silence their enemies and enlarge their respective empires. Both emancipated their Jewish populations from repression and instituted policies that offered the Jewish people greater religious tolerance than they had previously enjoyed.

Offering tolerance to a religious minority could contribute to greater security and less conflict in the realm. As noted in Chapter 1, Locke thought people rebel and conspire against the government when they are oppressed. The Lockean insight that repression, not religious freedom, contributes to extremism has been echoed by policy makers and human rights activists.[8]

Some rulers ordered policies to promote religious tolerance because it was deemed essential to enhancing the empire's security or society's economic well-being. Regardless of the motivation (whether social stability, economic prosperity, improved diplomatic ties,.etc.), the perceived social benefits drove the policy, as opposed to a commitment to ethical principles or the fundamental rights and dignity of individuals in society. Can these instrumentally conceived policies for religious tolerance from above by an illiberal leader last? What happens when an authoritarian or unelected leader decides to embrace religious tolerance? Can these policies evolve into a more substantive protection of the right to freedom of religion or belief as articulated in Article 18 of the ICCPR? Current political reforms in Uzbekistan offer a contemporary case study to explore these questions. Will Uzbekistan, under Mirziyoyev, move away from its intolerant past toward more freedom? Can top-down leadership promote a robust religious tolerance that eventually paves the way for religious

---

[8] Nadine Maenza, a commissioner on the United States Commission on International Religious Freedom, noted in an interview: "But, we know freedom of religion does not encourage extremism. What encourages extremism is actually the opposite, is really clamping down, making it difficult for people to practice their faith is much more dangerous than having an open society where people can practice their faith openly." Interview with Navbahov Imamova, Voice of America, October 17, 2019, https://www.amerikaovozi.com/a/5131667.html.

freedom? This chapter charts the policies undertaken by President Mirziyoyev, as well as the additional changes that need to occur before the fundamental human right of freedom of religion or belief is instantiated in Uzbekistan. To demonstrate these changes, this chapter articulates the repressive religious policies under the previous president, Islam Karimov, and then discusses recent policy reforms since Karimov's death in 2016. The chapter also explores what policies need to be adopted to respect the international standards spelled out in the ICCPR. Lastly, this chapter suggests what international actors, especially the United States, can do to help Tashkent on the road to religious freedom.

UZBEKISTAN'S RECENT HISTORY

The area that constitutes contemporary Uzbekistan was ruled by authoritarian leaders, such as Tamerlane/Timur, for centuries. This continued into the 20th century when Moscow created the boundaries for Uzbekistan. Beyond creating the borders for the states of central Asia, Moscow attempted to create identities for the people of central Asia to fully incorporate them as loyal citizens into the Soviet political system. Soviet methods to develop loyal and obedient Uzbeks included harsh anti-religion drives starting in the late 1920s.[9] The Bolsheviks would not tolerate independent religious institutions with a separate base of loyalty and financial support.[10] This hostility toward religion was consistent with Marxist thought.[11] The Soviet policies that promoted atheism included converting madrassahs into museums and disseminating anti-religious propaganda throughout Uzbekistan.[12] Property held by religious institutions was confiscated and nationalized. Many in the ulama were arrested or killed.[13] Individual and communal manifestations of religion were restricted.[14] Throughout the Soviet period, and in the aftermath of independence, the

---

[9] The Soviet Union's anti-religious policies were often articulated by Uzbeks in our discussions in August 2019.

[10] Adeeb Khalid, *Islam After Communism: Religion and Politics in Central Asia* (Berkeley: University of California Press, 2007), pp. 69–70.

[11] In the *Critique of Hegel's Philosophy of Right*, Marx wrote, "The wretchedness of religion is at once an expression of and a protest against real wretchedness. Religion is the sigh of the oppressed creature, the heart of a heartless world, and the soul of soulless conditions. It is the opium of the people." Karl Marx, *Critique of Hegel's Philosophy of Right*, translated by Joseph O'Malley (Cambridge, UK: Cambridge University Press, 1970), p. 131.

[12] Interview, Samarkand, August 12, 2019.

[13] Khalid, *Islam*, p. 72.

[14] Ahmed Shaheed, *Report of the Special Rapporteur on Freedom of Religion or Belief on His Mission to Uzbekistan*, February 22, 2017, A/HRC/37/49/Add.2.

Uzbek people were ruled by repressive leaders who violated many fundamental human rights including freedom of religion.

After gaining independence in 1991, President Karimov's authoritarian rule saw widespread human rights violations, forced labor,[15] corruption, and economic stagnation that resulted in high unemployment for the people of Uzbekistan.[16] He tolerated no dissent. The persistent denial of many basic human rights, including religious freedom,[17] despite being established in the constitution, contributed to a stifling environment in the country and led to numerous criticisms from international organizations, human rights activists, and other states in the international community. Approximately 93 percent of Uzbeks are Sunni Muslims.

A judicial system that upholds the rule of law and protects citizens from discrimination in the name of religion is one of the building blocks of a society that protects freedom of religion or belief. The judicial system, under Karimov, lacked independence and was deferential to political leaders, resulting in widespread problems. One human rights activist explained that the "courts in Uzbekistan had traditionally been subordinated to politics and were overwhelmingly infected by corruption, poor professional ethics, and inefficiency. The absence of a predictable and independent judiciary presented a serious obstacle to economic and social progress."[18]

While many international observers criticized Karimov, some Uzbeks held a more favorable view of him. One person indicated that many people "did not consider Karimov a dictator."[19] Another mentioned that Karimov

---

[15] "For years the Uzbek government has forced Uzbek citizens, including education and health workers, students and people receiving public benefits, to pick cotton for the state-run cotton industry involuntarily and under the threat of penalty, such as dismissal or expulsion from their jobs or loss of benefits." Human Rights Watch, "Uzbekistan: A Year into New Presidency, Cautious Hope for Change," October 25, 2017, https://www.hrw.org/news/2017/10/25/uzbekistan-year-new-presidency-cautious-hope-change.

[16] Forced labor associated with cotton did not begin with Karimov. There were cotton production requirements during the Soviet years.

[17] The constitution adopted in 1992 establishes numerous basic rights. Article 31: "Freedom of Conscience shall be guaranteed to all. Everyone shall have the right to profess or not to profess any religion. A compulsory imposition of religion shall be impermissible." The Constitution can be found at http://constitution.uz/en/clause/index#section2. This right is not always respected in reality.

[18] Mjusa Sever, "Judicial and Governance Reform," in *Uzbekistan's New Face*, edited by S. Frederick Starr and Svante Cornell (Lanham, MD: Rowman and Littlefield, 2018), p. 129.

[19] He included himself among those Uzbeks who did not view Karimov as a dictator. Interview, Tashkent, August 10, 2019.

was a father figure to many Uzbeks and "kept us safe."[20] Karimov guided the country through an economic transition after 1991 with controlled economic policies. These policies, while limiting growth and a free market, prevented an economic implosion similar to the one experienced in Russia after the breakup of the USSR.

Islamic Extremists: Real and Imagined

Karimov's crackdown on Islamic extremists, real and imagined, revolved around threats to his position as the leader of the country. After independence in 1991, Karimov needed to develop his own base of political power after being appointed by Gorbachev. Any individual or group, whether an NGO, opposition political party, or religious organization, who challenged the president could feel the brunt of the government's power. Early in his tenure (November 1991) Karimov was publicly confronted by Adolat, a group that wanted an Islamic state. He did not appreciate being addressed in a disrespectful manner in public.[21] Islamic fundamentalists in neighboring Tajikistan and the creation of the Islamic Movement of Uzbekistan (IMU) by Tahrir Yuldoshov and Juma Nagangani—the latter a soldier in the Tajik Civil War—fueled Karimov's insecurities.[22] The chaos and the violence in Tajikistan reinforced Karimov's view that Islamic extremists were a threat that had to be suffocated.[23] The Karimov regime's aggressive crackdown on Islamic militants ensnared peaceful Muslims in these raids.[24] Human Rights Watch noted that the repressive policies were "a dramatic escalation of a sporadic six-year government campaign against free expression of religion, specifically non-governmental

---

[20] He said, "I cried like a little girl when he first heard that the president died." Interview, Tashkent, August 17, 2019.

[21] "He found the confrontation with Adolat (Justice) personally humiliating, but it also hardened his attitude toward opposition couched in Islamic terms. Ever since, he has been an implacable foe of all expressions of Islam that he has not expressly authorized." Khalid, p. 141. Members of Adolat later formed the Islamic Movement of Uzbekistan.

[22] Chris Seiple, "Revisiting the Geo-Political Thinking of Sir Halford John Mackinder: United States–Uzbekistan Relations 1991–2005," November 2006, https://globalengage.org/_assets/docs/771_seiple_dissertation.pdf, p. 122. IMU collaborated with al Qaeda. Richard Weitz, "Uzbekistan's New Foreign Policy: Change and Continuity Under New Leadership," in *Uzbekistan's New Face*, edited by S. Frederick Starr and Svante Cornell (Lanham, MD: Rowman and Littlefield, 2018), p. 44.

[23] Svante Cornell and Jacob Zenn, "Religion and the Secular State in Uzbekistan," in *Uzbekistan's New Face*, edited by S. Frederick Starr and Svante Cornell (Lanham, MD: Rowman and Littlefield, 2018), p. 203.

[24] One person explained to me that "some KGB guys under Karimov went too far and picked up people who were not extremists." Interview, Tashkent, August 10, 2019.

Islam."[25] The 1999 attack in Tashkent contributed to the president's fear of Islamic extremism and added to the harsh crackdown.[26] Karimov was not the only person who felt threatened. Numerous Uzbeks mentioned, unprompted, the threat of Islamic extremism in the country.[27] One may conclude that the government's efforts, through state-run media, to create support for their policy by spreading fear of Islamic extremists had been internalized by many in the country.

Religious Intolerance under Karimov

Karimov used the threat of Islamic extremism to further develop repressive religious policies, including prohibitions on religious attire, imprisonment of believers, overly complicated registration requirements for religious organizations, and censorship of religious literature.[28] The government also controlled religious life by appointing imams and regulating the sermons delivered at Friday prayers.[29] Many of these restrictions were codified in the draconian 1998 Law on Freedom of Conscience and Religious Organizations. The Special Rapporteur on freedom of religion or belief, Ahmed Shaheed, noted in his report that "the law criminalizes unregistered activity, requires official approval of the content, production and distribution of religious publica-

---

[25] Human Rights Watch, "Republic of Uzbekistan: Crackdown in the Farghona Valley: Arbitrary Arrests and Religious Discrimination," 1998, https://www.hrw.org/legacy/reports98/uzbekistan/. Another crackdown occurred in 2005. In May 2005 there were protests in Andijan, in the Ferghana Valley. People protested the arrest and conviction of over 20 businessmen who were accused of belonging to a banned Islamic group. The government, in its attempt to quell the protests, killed roughly 1000 civilians. Chris Seiple, "Understanding Uzbekistan," Foreign Policy Research Institute, May 6, 2005. See also USCIRF 2016 Annual Report, p. 77. Some have viewed the Andijan unrest as an attempt to limit economic competition rather than an example of religious extremism. See Khalid, p. 195.

[26] Interview, Tashkent, August 10, 2019.

[27] Interviews, Tashkent, Samarkand, Bukhara, August 2019. One Uzbek professor noted "the threat of Hiz-ut-Tahrir and other Islamic groups/individuals, these were pretty real both in the early 1990s and later on. Many of these threats were brought to Uzbekistan from abroad," August 27, 2019. Human Rights Watch, "Republic of Uzbekistan."

[28] USCIRF, Annual Report 2016, pp. 77–81. Institute on Religion and Public Policy, "Religious Freedom in Uzbekistan," October 7, 2008, https://lib.ohchr.org/HRBodies/UPR/Documents/Session3/UZ/IRPP_UZB_UPR_S3_2008_InstituteonReligionandPublicPolicy_uprsubmission.pdf.

[29] In some instances, political authorities have gone so far as to instruct imams to criticize "people conducting illegal religious education" and individuals who organize "small religious gatherings." Institute on Religion and Public Policy, "Religious Freedom."

Table 6.1 Pew Research Center International Religious Freedom and Restrictions scores, Uzbekistan

Uzbekistan	2007	2015	2019
Government Regulations Index (GRI)	7.7	8.0	7.2
Social Hostilities Index (SHI)	1.1	1.1	2.9
Average of GRI and SHI	4.4	4.6	5.0

tions, and prohibits proselytism and other missionary activities." He went on to note that these restrictions "are incompatible with Article 18 of the ICCPR."[30] USCIRF explained that the 1998 law "severely limits the rights of all religious groups and facilitates government control of religious activity, particularly of the majority Muslim community."[31] The law also prohibits anyone other than recognized religious figures from wearing religious attire.[32] One scholar-activist described it as "a terrible law that doesn't allow for anything."[33]

Religious intolerance was demonstrated in the government's crackdown on Islam in 1994–95. The UN Special Rapporteur on freedom of religion or belief noted:

> From 1994 to 1995, the authorities conducted a campaign against "unofficial" Islam: men wearing beards faced harassment and arbitrary detention, while some popular independent Muslim clerics allegedly "disappeared." Following the murder of some police officers in Namangan in December 1997—for which Islamic fundamentalists were blamed—independent mosques were closed and Islamic leaders and other practicing Muslims not affiliated with officially sanctioned Islamic institutions faced broad crackdowns.[34]

Reports from the Pew Research Center also demonstrate that religious freedom was not respected in Uzbekistan, as demonstrated in Table 6.1.[35]

[30] Shaheed, "Report." Article 5 of the law specifically prohibits proselytizing.

[31] USCIRF, Annual Report 2016, p. 77.

[32] Farangis Najibullah, "Uzbek Imam Fired After Deviating from the Script," Radio Free Europe, September 10, 2018.

[33] Chris Seiple, President Emeritus, Institute for Global Engagement, September 25, 2018.

[34] Shaheed, "Report."

[35] The lower the score, the less government restriction and social hostility. High scores (six or better) indicate a denial of aspects of freedom of religion. Pew Research Center, "A Closer Look."

In the ten-year period from 2007 to 2017, government restrictions grew and made publicly practicing one's faith difficult, and at times impossible. One human rights group in Uzbekistan noted that the government had established almost total control over religious people in the country.[36]

The denial of religious freedom and the absence of even a minimal level of religious tolerance was likely a result of residual Soviet hostility toward religion, as well as the Karimov government's authoritarian rejection of the existence of an independent civil society outside of Tashkent's control.[37] The lack of a vibrant and independent civil society continues to be a legacy of the Karimov era in contemporary times.

Given the restrictions on the free practice of religion, Tashkent was often criticized by human rights organizations. In addition, Washington designated Uzbekistan as a CPC in 2006 under the IRFA. This designation remained until December 2018. Despite being designated for a dozen years, Tashkent suffered few consequences, as it received a national security waiver from Washington due to its contributions to the war on terror.

CHANGING LEADERS, CHANGING POLICIES

Top-Down Leadership: Mirziyoyev and Religious Tolerance

Shavkat Mirziyoyev, previously prime minister from 2003 to 2016, assumed the presidency after Karimov's death in 2016. He inherited a brutal regime. Although a product of the previous government, he initiated a wide-ranging reform process after becoming president. Some of the reform projects were developed during his time as prime minister, including a judicial reform initiative. He invited the UN Special Rapporteur on the independence of judges and lawyers to visit the country to help reform the judicial system.[38] Having an

---

[36] Human Rights Society of Uzbekistan, "Report on Civil and Political Rights: Uzbekistan," 2014, https://www.ecoi.net/en/file/local/1321622/1930_1408022470_int-ccpr-ico-uzb-17837-e.pdf

[37] Shaheed noted in his report that "the Government has traditionally been suspicious of the mobilizing power of religion—in particular Islam—and considers symbols of piety as signs of dissent or ambition for political power." Shaheed, "Report."

[38] International Commission of Jurists, "ICJ welcomes the first visit of the UN Special Rapporteur on the independence of judges and lawyers to Uzbekistan," September 20, 2019, https://www.icj.org/icj-welcomes-the-first-visit-of-the-un-special-rapporteur-on-the-independence-of-judges-and-lawyers-to-uzbekistan/. See also International Center for Not-for-Profit Law, "The Presidential Decree on Measures to Further Reform Judicial and Legal System, and Enhance Guarantees for Sound Protection of Rights and Freedoms of Citizens," October 23, 2016, https://www.icnl.org/research/library/uzbekistan_merax/.

independent judiciary is key to ensuring that no one is above the law and that citizens have recourse to deal with corrupt or predatory politicians and security forces.[39]

He also banned the use of forced labor that was prevalent in previous decades. One of the major criticisms involved forced labor connected with cotton. One woman (Delia) explained that her sister and her mother had to work in the cotton fields for a few years. Delia only had to do it for one year: "You had to produce a certain amount of cotton, or they would take money out of your paycheck. Mirziyoyev got rid of that."[40] Since becoming president, Mirziyoyev developed policies to eliminate forced labor and diversify the agricultural sector.[41] Tashkent made strides in abolishing forced labor in the production and collection of cotton by working with the International Labour Organization, promoting awareness throughout the population, and providing outreach and hotlines to call.[42]

The government, under Mirziyoyev, is more responsive to citizens and their concerns.[43] The government passed a law to promote gender equality in September 2019.[44] Some security officials were convicted and sentenced for human rights violations including torture.[45] These actions demonstrate some accountability for wrongdoing that was typically absent under Karimov. The president has repeatedly articulated a commitment to reform and the rule of law and noted the importance of human rights.[46] This commitment was demon-

---

[39] Larry Diamond, *Ill Winds* (New York: Penguin Press, 2019), pp. 19 and 22.

[40] Interview, Samarkand, August 12, 2019.

[41] Human Rights Watch, "Uzbekistan."

[42] The ILO reported progress on forced labor. It has trained hundreds of public prosecutors and human rights activists to better identity forced labor. In addition, it has trained over 12 000 individuals in Uzbekistan who are involved in recruiting labor for the cotton harvest and has strengthened the mechanism by which individuals who are forced to pick cotton can receive assistance. ILO, *Third Party Monitoring on Child and Forced Labour in Uzbekistan*, https://www.ilo.org/moscow/projects/WCMS_704979/lang--en/index.htm. The percentage of forced labor went down 7 points in 2018, from 12 percent the previous year. State Department, *International Religious Freedom Report for 2018*.

[43] Human Rights Watch, "Uzbekistan."

[44] The law, "Guarantees of Equal Rights and Opportunities for Men and Women," seeks to address gender discrimination in the country. USAID helped Tashkent through its Judicial Reform in Uzbekistan Program. USAID, "Uzbekistan Passes Law on Gender Equality," December 19, 2019, https://www.usaid.gov/uzbekistan/program-updates/dec-2019-uzbekistan-passes-law-gender-equality.

[45] State Department, Human Rights Report, 2018.

[46] December 28, 2018, address to the Oliy Majlis. See also a tweet from Imamova on November 22, 2019, reporting on a speech the president gave to Uzbek political leaders: "Uzbekistan President Mirziyoyev: rule of law, media freedom, accountabil-

strated in various speeches to parliament in 2018 and in early 2020. It is worth noting that this reform program was developed in a secure environment. The threat from extremists in neighboring countries had diminished considerably since the 1990s and 2000s. The more secure a country is, and the regional neighborhood is, the more political space there is to promote freedom of religion or belief.

Mirziyoyev's regime made several positive moves, which if followed through, could significantly improve the protection of religious freedom in the country. The government invited the UN's Special Rapporteur on freedom of religion or belief, Ahmed Shaheed, to visit the country. In his report, Shaheed expressed his gratitude for the cooperation from the Uzbek government. He also noted that while religious tolerance existed, additional changes were needed for freedom of religion or belief to be realized since "the exercise of freedom of religion and belief is totally controlled by the state."[47]

The Special Rapporteur noted that the registration process was quite cumbersome and rather restrictive. He also mentioned the state's censorship of religious literature and Tashkent's emphasis on a secular education without inclusion of religious studies. This secular education contrasts with how religious subjects are taught in Sweden and Oman; Chapter 5 noted their more inclusive approach in the classroom. Shaheed concluded:

> What is required is not just the adoption of new laws, but the institutional reform backed by a strong political will and a shift in attitude led and encouraged by the Government. It will also require the support of the international community to both the Government and civil society to sustain the momentum.[48]

Both legislative chambers subsequently adopted a road map on religious freedom based on Shaheed's recommendations in May 2018.

The government also pledged to revise the Law on Freedom of Conscience and Religious Organizations. A draft of the revised law was shared with the international community, including the OSCE, the UN Special Rapporteur

---

ity is key to country's future. Everyone should learn to respect laws and human rights. 'None of us should forget this duty.'"

[47] "The approach taken by the Government tends to promote 'toleration' instead of the positive right to enjoyment of one's freedom. Toleration may be promoted to maintain interreligious harmony, but it fails to guarantee everyone's freedom of religion or belief." Shaheed, "Report."

[48] Shaheed, "Report." It is worth noting that the Uzbek government challenged the Special Rapporteur's findings. In a response on February 16, 2018, Tashkent rejected the idea that it was violating international law. It claimed that the only restrictions on religious individual or groups were "necessary to ensure national security and public order, life, health, morality, rights and freedoms of other citizens."

for religious freedom, and the US Ambassador for International Religious Freedom to solicit feedback for further discussions during the drafting process.[49] The new religion law, signed by the president on July 5, 2021, includes some improvements but does not fully align with international standards. While allowing for more personal freedom on religious attire, it maintains restrictions on unauthorized religious education and religious literature and bans proselytism.[50]

Government officials used the discourse of human rights and expressed their commitment to improving religious freedom in the country.[51] President Mirziyoyev noted, "Uzbekistan always stays committed to its traditions of interethnic harmony and religious tolerance."[52] The Minister of Justice, Ruslan Davletov, stated, "Uzbekistan's new religious policy fully acknowledges international standards and treaties."[53] Uzbekistan's Ambassador to the United States, Javlon Vakhabov, explained that his government is "decisively introducing measures, first, in order to eliminate past practices and, second, to enhance the level of protection of civil rights and particularly religious freedom."[54] He also acknowledged the government's past repressive policies. Saidov, the Director of the National Rights Center of Uzbekistan, stated that all religious communities, large or small, "should enjoy the same range of rights and freedoms."[55] He went on to say, "harmony and religious tolerance are among the priorities of Uzbekistan." In addition, Uzbekistan's Foreign

---

[49] See https://kun.uz/en/news/2019/07/22/uzbekistan-to-revise-law-on-freedom-of-conscience-and-religious-organizations.

[50] USCIRF, Press Release, "USCIRF Concerned by New Uzbekistan Religion Law," July 16, 2021.

[51] Foreign Minister Kamilov: "Ensuring religious freedom is an important component of pol and leg reforms in UZ," "new religious non-Muslim organizations were registered," "education and enlightenment, decriminalization and deradicalization—main approaches in CVE efforts in UZ." Javlon Vakhabov, tweet, July 21, 2019.

[52] December 28, 2018, address to the Oliy Majlis.

[53] National Press Club, July 25, 2018.

[54] "I admit in the past there were restrictive policies in the field of religious affairs." It is a positive sign that the government is acknowledging past repression. Ambassador Jarlon Vakhabov, remarks at the National Press Club, Washington, D.C., December 20, 2018. It is worth mentioning that Uzbek officials periodically refer to the government's five-year Action Plan (2017–2021) and its incorporation of religious tolerance in Area 5. However, religious tolerance is only briefly mentioned, and no concrete steps are outlined on how to make progress on this issue. Presidential Decree of the Republic of Uzbekistan of February 7, 2017, No. UP 4947, "About the Strategy of Actions for Further Development of the Republic of Uzbekistan." *Tashkent Times*, "Uzbekistan's Development Strategy for 2017–2021 has been adopted following public consultation," August 2, 2017, http://tashkenttimes.uz/national/541-uzbekistan-s-development-strategy-for-2017-2021-has-been-adopted-following-.

[55] National Press Club, July 25, 2018.

Minister attended the State Department's Ministerial on Religious Freedom in 2018 and 2019, signaling his attention to this issue.

Further, the government took steps to make the registration process less onerous for religious organizations by eliminating some documents previously required and reducing registration fees.[56] It registered more than a dozen religious organizations between December 2016 and December 2018.[57] In early 2020, the government noted that over 2200 religious organizations were operating legally in the country and that five additional Christian congregations had registered in the second half of 2019.[58] President Mirziyoyev released over a thousand religious prisoners. Some Uzbeks also noticed these changes.[59]

An additional component to establishing freedom of religion or belief in Uzbekistan is the development of a vibrant and independent civil society. Given the many decades of authoritarian rule in the country, a robust domestic civil society does not currently exist. The government allowed more international human rights organizations to travel to the country and report on issues within its borders. These limited steps do not go far enough. A 2015 law regulating the activities of NGOs is still on the books. This law requires civil society organizations to receive government permission to carry out most public activities and therefore significantly limits freedom of association.[60]

The Institute for Global Engagement (IGE), an NGO based in Washington, D.C., engaged in discussions with numerous government officials and religious leaders in Uzbekistan to assist in building religious freedom and strengthening civil society.[61] The IGE signed a memorandum of understanding (MOU) with the government in 2018 and traveled to Uzbekistan in 2019 to begin a series of initiatives, including a religion and rule of law training program to offer religious leaders and government officials a global perspective on the nature of the relationship between the rule of law and religious freedom. While in Uzbekistan, the National Security Council asked the IGE to comment on a draft of the religion law that was being developed.[62] The government's

---

[56] State Department, *International Religious Freedom Report for 2018*.

[57] Knox Thames, Remarks at the National Press Club, December 20, 2018.

[58] Embassy of Uzbekistan, "The Ministry of Justice, the Republic of Uzbekistan Announced the Number of Religious Organizations Registered in the Country," February 21, 2020, https://www.uzbekistan.org/news/view?id=312.

[59] "Now people have more freedom to believe since 2016." Tashkent, UZ, August 10, 2019.

[60] Human Rights Watch, 2020 Annual Report.

[61] IGE, https://globalengage.org/programs/Uzbekistan.

[62] See https://globalengage.org/updates/view/ige-launches-groundbreaking-religious-freedom-initiatives-in-uzbekistan. Individuals from the Ministry of Foreign Affairs, Committee on Religious Affairs, and the National Human Rights Centre were among some of the 40 Uzbek officials to attend the rule of law training program.

cooperation with the IGE is further evidence of its efforts to promote religious tolerance and make progress on religious freedom. Uzbekistan needs indigenous civil society organizations to have the freedom to operate in the country and promote human rights without fear of harassment or incarceration. The role of civil society in the promotion of religious freedom is further explored in Chapter 7.

Motivation for Change

The president initiated a reform process despite being "raised" in an authoritarian system. One American official noted the importance of Mirziyoyev: "From my visits to Tashkent and multiple meetings in Washington, it is clear these reforms are at Mirziyoyev's behest. And they continue. Recent actions now allow children to attend mosques with their parents and the government released some prisoners jailed for 'religious' crimes. These are very welcome actions."[63] Several factors appear to be driving these reforms. Whenever there is a new leader, even one socialized in the previous regime, there is an opportunity for change. In December 2018, Mirziyoyev articulated an ambitious reform agenda that addressed domestic and foreign affairs. He wants Uzbekistan to have a "bright and prosperous future" and promised his citizens that "we will not abandon the path of democratic reforms."[64]

To have a bright and prosperous future, Uzbekistan needs to attract foreign investment, which requires a stable legal environment where contracts are respected. The president mentioned the importance of foreign investment a number of times in his address to parliament.[65] Ambassador Vakhabov noted, "we realize the interconnection between human rights and trade and investment issues."[66] Sam Brownback, the former US Ambassador for International Religious Freedom, suggested "they did it because they saw it as an economic route to move forward."[67] One scholar-activist noted, "They

---

[63] Knox Thames, "A Real Opportunity for Religion Law Reform in Uzbekistan," *The Diplomat,* October 16, 2020, https://thediplomat.com/2020/10/a-real-opportunity-for-religion-law-reform-in-uzbekistan/.

[64] December 28, 2018, address to the Oliy Majlis.

[65] "Since the year 2019 is announced as the year of active investments and social developments, the Ministry of Foreign Affairs and its diplomatic missions abroad should also reconsider their work. From now on, the requirements of our ambassadors will also change. Their activities will be primarily assessed on the basis of efforts they are making to attract the foreign investments and amount of the foreign capital they were able to attract." December 28, 2018, address to the Oliy Majlis.

[66] Remarks at National Press Club, December 12, 2018.

[67] Samuel Brownback, "Faith Angle Podcast with Wajahat Ali," December 31, 2019. The State Department noted an increase in investments by US companies (over

want to be seen as positive global citizens... It is a good thing not to be on the [CPC] list to attract foreign direct investment."[68] An independent analysis of the judicial reforms undertaken to promote the rule of law noted the economic incentives—attracting foreign investment—as part of the motivation for the judicial reforms: "by many accounts the government's judicial reform effort aims to play a big role in its efforts to encourage investor confidence."[69] The government seeks to join the World Trade Organization. In addition to foreign investment, the president also needs to promote private domestic economic activity to contribute to economic growth in the country. A more open and free society is necessary to stimulate that economic activity.[70] Other Uzbek officials noted the impact of US policies: member of parliament Akmal Saidov was quoted as saying, "we don't want to end up on the CPC list again."[71] Others suggested that Uzbek leaders do not want to be in the company of international pariahs, such as North Korea.[72] These economic motivations are unsurprising. As noted in Chapter 2, several political leaders adopted policies for religious tolerance for the potential economic benefits that may result.

AND YET STILL LINGERING PROBLEMS

Despite the positive steps taken by Mirziyoyev, there are lingering problems in Uzbekistan. Change will not occur overnight, especially in a country whose

---

$1 billion) and an increase in trade between the two countries in 2019 (from $315 million to $514 million). Office of the Spokesperson, State Department, "Secretary Pompeo's Visit to Uzbekistan," February 2, 2020.

[68] Conversation with Chris Seiple, President Emeritus, Institute for Global Engagement, September 25, 2018.

[69] Lees, "Final Evaluation."

[70] An Uzbek professor explained it to me this way: Mirziyoyev "knows that without freedoms (religious included), there is no dynamism in economic activity of the population limiting the effects of any possible investments. Investments alone do not produce wealth. It is private economic activity which does. I think this is his logic in pursuing reforms in general and religious reforms in particular." Interview, August 1, 2019.

[71] Imamova, a journalist for Voice of America, tweeted this on May 21, 2019. Thames echoed this, "The Uzbek government welcomed advice from the United States on reform, and we built a productive partnership. The government was especially interested in being removed from the State Department's 'Country of Particular Concern' list for severe religious freedom violators." Thames, "A Real Opportunity."

[72] "Uzbekistan does not want to be on the same list as North Korea." Conversation with Chris Seiple, President Emeritus, Institute for Global Engagement, September 25, 2018. "What is driving this change? ... It could be the promise of greater foreign investment in a country with more dependable legal system. Or the desire to no longer be seen as an international pariah. One thing is clear: Mirziyoyev is driving the shift." Imamova, "Where Freedoms."

elites were dominated by Moscow for decades and later ruled by Karimov: Uzbekistan still has a long way to go. The presidential elections in December 2016 had significant shortcomings, according to the OSCE. The OSCE was invited to observe the presidential elections that Mirziyoyev ultimately won with 88 percent of the vote. They noted a lack of competitiveness, and limitations on freedom of expression and association. This was also true in the 2019 parliamentary elections. The absence of a free, independent media was also an impediment to genuinely free and fair elections.[73] Despite these limitations, "the electoral process of 2016 represented a substantial improvement over prior elections in the country."[74] According to Human Rights Watch, the president "has taken some concrete steps to improve the country's human rights record." However, "the government remains authoritarian. Despite Mirziyoyev's prisoner release, thousands of people, mainly peaceful religious believers, remain in prison on false charges. The security services retain vast powers to detain perceived critics, and there is no genuine political pluralism."[75] The UN Human Rights Committee praised some of the government's reforms, while noting some continuing problems: the lack of an independent judiciary, torture, gender discrimination, and the criminalization of proselytism.[76]

While there have been substantive changes and political and economic reforms in the country since Mirziyoyev became president, freedom of religion

---

[73] The Statement of Preliminary Findings and Conclusions issued on December 5, 2016, concluded that "the 4 December presidential election underscored the need of comprehensive reform to address long-standing systemic shortcomings. The legal framework is not conducive to holding democratic elections… The dominant position of state actors and limits on fundamental freedoms undermine political pluralism and led to a campaign devoid of genuine competition. Media covered the election in a highly restrictive and controlled environment, and the dissemination of a state-defined narrative did not allow voters to receive an alternative viewpoint. Significant irregularities were noted on election day, including indications of ballot box stuffing and widespread proxy voting, despite a concerted campaign to address the latter." See https://www.osce.org/office-for-democratic-institutions-and-human-rights/elections/uzbekistan/306451?download=true.

[74] S. Frederick Starr, "Change and Continuity in Uzbekistan, 1991–2016," in *Uzbekistan's New Face*, edited by S. Frederick Starr and Svante E. Cornell (Lanham, MD: Rowman and Littlefield, 2018), p. 39.

[75] Steve Swerdlow, "Charting Progress in Mirziyoyev's Uzbekistan," Human Rights Watch, October 7, 2019, https://www.hrw.org/news/2019/10/07/charting-progress-mirziyoyevs-uzbekistan#. See also Human Rights Watch, World Report, 2020, https://www.hrw.org/world-report/2020/country-chapters/uzbekistan. "Corruption persists, as do entrenched economic interests, and the security services remain largely unchecked in the eyes of the public, despite Mirziyoyev's pledges that they are indeed being reformed." Imamova, "Where Freedoms."

[76] UN Human Rights Committee, "Concluding Observations on the Fifth Periodic Report of Uzbekistan," May 1, 2020, CCPR/C/UZB/CO/5.

or belief does not yet exist. The government continues to control many aspects related to the practice of religion.[77] The registration process for organizations, while improved, is still complicated. One lawyer who consulted on the draft law indicated continuing concerns about the registration process and the lack of buy-in from local officials.[78] Some groups, such as Jehovah's Witnesses, continue to experience obstacles in their attempts to register with the government. Religious organizations are not truly independent entities in civil society. The government continues to influence or restrict certain religious activities. The government approves sermons that are offered at mosques throughout the country and pays the salaries of religious leaders.[79] The Minister of Justice, Davletov, ruled out revising the religion law to allow for proselytism or missionary activities.[80] The government wants to limit Wahhabi views of Islam within the country. They justified these policies by emphasizing the importance of teaching an appropriate form of Islam. One individual in Tashkent stressed that "the government wants to teach the right religion" and it was important to emphasize "the proper Islam."[81] This sentiment echoes President Mirziyoyev's view. In a speech in June 2017, the president noted the importance of "preserving the true essence and content of [the] sacred Islamic religion."[82] These restrictions are often justified in reference to national security and the threat of extremism.[83]

---

[77] USCIRF, "Country Update: Uzbekistan," January 2020, https://www.uscirf.gov/reports-briefs/policy-briefs-and-focuses/uzbekistan-country-update.

[78] Interview, February 28, 2020.

[79] Some Uzbeks did not seem to be concerned about this and did not view this as intrusive meddling in a religious group's affairs. Interviews, August 2019, Bukhara. State Department, *International Religious Freedom Report for 2018*.

[80] State Department, *International Religious Freedom Report for 2018*.

[81] Interview, Tashkent, August 10, 2019.

[82] A summary of his speech can be found at https://president.uz/en/lists/view/649. The UN Special Rapporteur also noted the government's approach only allowed the correct version of religion: "In the years since independence, the Government has increased its control over religions or beliefs—if not, religious discourse—by determining the parameters of 'proper' belief and worship, the true national tradition and the 'Uzbek way' of practicing Islam, that is, the 'right way' of practicing religion. The Government also distinguishes the 'right' kind of believer from the 'mistaken' or 'dangerous' worshiper."

[83] The UN Special Rapporteur noted in his report: "The fight against extremism came up in almost every conversation that the Special Rapporteur had with his interlocutors in Uzbekistan. Often extremism was described by the authorities as the main challenge facing the country, if not the region, and hence justified the need for strict state control of religion and regulations of religious activities in the interest of 'public security.'"

The national government, as well as local authorities, continue to construct obstacles to freedom of religion. That said, it is also true that there are entrenched interests in authoritarian policies around the country. President Mirziyoyev clearly expressed his preference for Uzbek head scarves over the hijab.[84] By publicly expressing his views, he is tilting the scales toward the mode of religious attire that the government will tolerate, but he is not promoting the basic right of freedom of religion. Under Article 18 of the ICCPR, which Uzbekistan is a party to, individuals can choose what attire accords with their beliefs.[85] Given the president's views, it should come as no surprise that some female students were prevented from attending classes while wearing a hijab.[86] Women are not the only citizens to attract the government's attention. Over a hundred men had their beards forcibly shaved by the police in August 2019.[87] Neither of these policies furthers religious tolerance or religious freedom in Uzbekistan.

Additional problems revolve around local leaders' and security forces' disinclination to follow the national government's guidance on religious freedom. One international consultant noted that some officials in Tashkent mentioned resistance from local officials and that "moving away from the old Soviet mentality isn't easy."[88] Raids continued in 2019 on religious groups in various parts of the country.[89] Local law enforcement continued to harass and detain religious individuals who have not successfully registered with the government. Since an independent judicial system did not exist in the country, often detained individuals required intervention by a national figure to be released.

---

[84] Interview with Maenza, October 17, 2019.

[85] Uzbekistan became a party to the ICCPR in 1995; see https://tbinternet.ohchr.org/_layouts/15/TreatyBodyExternal/Treaty.aspx?CountryID=189&Lang=EN.

[86] Mushfig Bayram, "Supreme Court Challenge to Student Hijab Ban," *Forum 18*, April 29, 2019, http://www.forum18.org/archive.php?article_id=2472.

[87] Umida Hasimova, "Religion, Beards, and Uzbekistan's Secular Government," *The Diplomat*, September 9, 2019, https://thediplomat.com/2019/09/religion-beards-and-uzbekistans-secular-government/. See also Maenza Interview, October 19, 2019.

[88] Interview, February 28, 2020.

[89] Forum 18, "Uzbekistan: Raids, Eviction Threat for Urgench Baptists," October 22, 2019, http://www.forum18.org/archive.php?article_id=2515. Freedom House, "Has Mirziyoyev Really Brought Religious Liberty to Uzbekistan?" January 16, 2019, https://freedomhouse.org/blog/has-mirziyoyev-really-brought-religious-liberty-uzbekistan.

INTERNATIONAL EFFORTS TO PROMOTE FREEDOM OF RELIGION OR BELIEF

This section briefly explores some of the international efforts, in addition to the Special Rapporteur's work as previously discussed, to further freedom of religion or belief in Uzbekistan. These international actors can assist the Uzbek government in developing specific policies that would help plant the seeds that could see this human right flourish in the years to come.

American Foreign Policy

Since Washington continued to emphasize the importance of this right with events such as the State Department's Ministerial on Religious Freedom, it is worth exploring the role of the United States. Uzbek officials specifically noted Washington's impact and CPC status. Has Washington taken concrete steps to address religious freedom in its bilateral relationship with Tashkent?

Washington criticized the Uzbek government for violations of freedom of religion or belief in numerous State Department and USCIRF reports. These reports noted that the 1998 Religion Law restricts various aspects of peaceful religious practice, including "proselytizing, importing and disseminating religious literature, and offering private religious instruction," and could lead to prosecution.[90] These reports repeatedly describe the harassment and imprisonment of peaceful religious adherents. Despite the bleak picture painted by these documents, there were few repercussions.

After 9/11, Washington emphasized Uzbekistan's assistance in the war on terrorism, rather than its record on religious freedom. Uzbekistan is not unique in this respect. Many strategically important countries were largely given a pass on their violations of freedom of religion or belief if they were willing to assist Washington in defeating the Taliban and al Qaeda in Afghanistan and the region. The United States had access to the Karshi-Khanabad base near the border with Afghanistan. Although Uzbekistan was designated a CPC, this did not prevent their government from receiving millions of dollars in assistance from the US. According to the State Department, Uzbekistan received $224.14 million from the US government in FY 2002. From 2003 to 2008, the amount was over $375 million. The budgetary allotments for activities related to human rights and rule of law were a small percentage of the overall assistance

[90] The language found in the 2009 report is similar to previous reports under the George W. Bush administration. State Department, *International Religious Freedom Report for 2009*, https://2009-2017.state.gov/j/drl/rls/irf/2009/127374.htm.

to Tashkent.[91] While these are not large sums from Washington's perspective, providing assistance to a country with a notorious record of religious intolerance, as was the case under Karimov, sends the message that this human right is not a priority and diminishes the criticisms from the State Department and USCIRF. The Obama administration distanced itself from the previous administration's war on terrorism. While it did not make freedom of religion or belief the central component in its relations with Uzbekistan, it did not ignore human rights in its bilateral relations.

US Foreign Policy Going Forward

Washington needs to continue to speak out publicly and privately when public officials in Uzbekistan do not live up to their commitments to protect this fundamental right. Further progress may stall without American and international efforts to continue along the road map. Some have reminded Uzbek officials when the government's policies divert from international standards. USCIRF, for one, has not shied from pressing the government to do more. In their annual report they noted:

> At the same time, local authorities continued to target Christian communities for failing or being unable to register, possessing and distributing religious literature, and engaging in missionary activities, despite government assurances that efforts were underway to decriminalize acts that posed no threat to public safety. This inability to rein in local authorities and police forces throughout the country demonstrates the government's ongoing lack of capacity to fully implement and enforce top-down changes.[92]

---

[91] If we focus on FY 2011–FY 2013, Washington allocated under $7.5 million for programs grouped under Governing Justly and Democratically. Further, $7.5 million out of $36.8 million was allocated for Uzbekistan during this time frame. State Department, "Uzbekistan 2012," http://www.state.gov/documents/organization/193949.pdf; US Department of State, Office of the Coordinator of US Assistance to Europe and Eurasia, Foreign Operations Appropriated Assistance Fact Sheet, December 2009.

[92] USCIRF 2019 Annual Report, April 2019, https://www.uscirf.gov/sites/default/files/2019USCIRFAnnualReport.pdf. Some Uzbek officials have acknowledged the intransigence of some local officials. Ambassador Vakhabov said in reference to the raids on a Baptist Church: "I need to admit there is some difficulties with the implementation of our laws at the local level." He suggests these few incidents were not systematic in nature. Interview, December 20, 2018.

The Vice Chair of USCIRF also noted in an interview:

> I know we worked a lot, spoke out a lot about the hijabs and the right that people should have to practice their faith, and that's a part of their faith. And so, to expect, especially like, you know, a woman that's going into a school to study her faith to take her hijab off, it doesn't make a whole lot of sense. So we're continuing to speak out on that, and the beard shaving.[93]

The United States, as well as other international actors, needs to continue to encourage the president's reform efforts. Many American policy makers reiterated this message in various forums. When Secretary of State Mike Pompeo visited Uzbekistan in 2020, his first meeting was with religious leaders in Tashkent. This was a signal by America's diplomat that furthering religious freedom is a priority.[94] Justin Colbert, the Director for South and Central Asia on the National Security Council, encouraged Uzbek political leaders to make additional progress on the "implementation of social justice reforms and religious freedom." He further suggested that these political and social reforms would help "to promote domestic stability and security" and could "foster a more welcoming business environment."[95] Alice Wells, the former Assistant Secretary for South and Central Asian Affairs, commended the government's efforts to improve the human rights environment in the country: "We applaud the steps Uzbekistan has taken to advance human rights and fundamental freedoms, including freedom of religion, and to end forced labor. The removal of thousands of individuals from 'blacklists' and the release of prisoners of conscience are commendable steps." She then tried to prod Tashkent into taking further steps: "the registration of new churches and adoption of a law that would strengthen protections for religious observance would send a powerful signal of support for tolerance."[96] Some specifically made the instrumental argument linking religious freedom and economic development:

> We would love nothing better than to take Uzbekistan off our Tier 1 list, or our Tier 2 list frankly, and we would if they follow through with the roadmap. And we really feel like if they did get off all of our lists, chances are they'd get more economic

---

[93] Interview, October 19, 2019.

[94] Navbahov Imamova, "Pompeo in Central Asia: State Department Spokesperson says America Brings a New Focus to the Region," February 7, 2020, https://www.amerikaovozi.com/a/5277696.html.

[95] "A New Era for Religious Freedom in Uzbekistan," National Press Club, Washington, D.C., July 25, 2018. Colbert also added "Uzbekistan has a long road ahead of it."

[96] Alice Wells, Assistant Secretary for South and Central Asian Affairs, February 27, 2019, Tashkent, Uzbekistan.

> development, you know. They immediately would be seen as a more stable country for engagement and bilateral agreements.[97]

Programs have been developed at the US State Department to contribute to this human right. The State Department offered a grant for up to $750 000 dollars to organizations undertaking efforts to promote religious freedom in Uzbekistan. This funding opportunity was available to organizations that were engaged in efforts to monitor violations of religious freedom by individuals in society, by law enforcement, and in the judicial system. Programs and workshops to train law enforcement and judicial officials on the important of freedom of religion or belief would also be welcome. Furthermore, the State Department sought programs that would help to reform national laws pertaining to religious freedom that were consistent with international standards and that would reduce harassment of religious activities by peaceful individuals and groups.[98]

Rule of Law

One aspect that the United States, in conjunction with other international partners, should continue to work with Tashkent on is reform of the judicial system and strengthening the rule of law in the country. USAID supported judicial reforms both with technical assistance (an electronic filing system) and with judicial guidance on the rule of law.[99] USAID facilitated American judges' travel to Uzbekistan to discuss the rule of law, human rights, and global norms. US District of Minnesota Judge John R. Tunheim traveled to Uzbekistan nine times "to engage the Uzbeks—government officials, journalists, judges, and advocates—in a dialogue about human rights and international standards." Judge Tunheim said of his numerous visits: "progress may feel slow in a world accustomed to a faster pace, but Uzbekistan is young. It is my hope that we can nurture the rule of law with both patience and persistence. Judges, in particular, need and want human rights training."[100] USAID continued these efforts through its Judicial Reform in Uzbekistan Program. This program, costing $12

---

[97] There is some question as to whether these arguments resonate with political leaders in Uzbekistan. Interview, October 19, 2019.

[98] State Department, Bureau of Democracy, Human Rights and Labor, Notice of Funding Opportunity (NOFO): DRL IRF FY19 Promoting Religious Freedom in Uzbekistan (SFOP0006310), December 12, 2019.

[99] The electronic filing system simplified and sped up the process by which court decisions were published. USAID, Uzbekistan Country Profile. The e-justice system, an electronic case management system is known as ESUD; see https://www.usaid.gov/sites/default/files/documents/1861/072816_UZBEKISTAN_Country%20Profile.pdf.

[100] Judge John Tunheim, "Nurturing Rule of Law in Young Uzbekistan," January 31, 2013, https://blog.usaid.gov/2013/01/nurturing-rule-of-law-in-uzbekistan/.

million, seeks to promote the rule of law by encouraging the development of a professional cadre of lawyers and enhancing the legal space for civil society in Uzbekistan. This 42-month program is a small effort, but one that can have a large impact if NGOs learn to engage the legal system in ways that further independence and accountability.[101]

In addition, USAID worked with the UNDP to advance the rule of law in Uzbekistan. One program, which began in 2014, aimed to "strengthen public access to trust in Uzbekistan's civil court system," promote legal reforms, and to improve the skills, knowledge, and professionalism of judges throughout the country.[102] Azamat Salaev, the Rule of Law Partnership in Uzbekistan project manager, stated that UNDP's efforts were aimed at implementing "best practices in the development of the judicial system" and "increasing the independence of various courts (civil, economic and administrative) throughout the country."[103] Salaev indicated that some progress can be seen in the government's creation of the Supreme Judicial School in 2019. This school was established to educate and train judges and the staff of the various courts to increase judicial independence. UNDP contributed to this capacity-building by developing training materials and manuals that were disseminated across the country.[104] An independent assessment by Sean Lees of the UNDP noted that the program had "led to new levels of justice-sector transparency." His report also suggested that more work needs to be done with civil society organizations.[105]

Since President Mirziyoyev's Development Strategy (2017–2021) specifically discussed the importance of "ensuring the rule of law and further reforming the judicial system," including "improving the system of recruitment, training, retraining, and advanced training, rotation within judiciary, law enforcement and regulatory authorities,"[106] his administration signaled it is receptive to additional help from international actors including Washington.

---

[101] See https://uz.usembassy.gov/marking-16-days-of-activism-against-gender-based-violence/.

[102] See https://www.uz.undp.org/content/uzbekistan/en/home/operations/projects1/democratic_governance/rule-of-law-partnership-in-uzbekistan-.html. The ESUD system has helped Uzbek citizens to access the courts, and has promoted transparency and accountability within the judicial system through the use of this electronic system. UNDP, "E-SUD e-justice System: Making Justice Accessible for Everybody," UNDP document in the possession of the author.

[103] Electronic communication, January 22, 2020.

[104] Ibid.

[105] Lees, "Final Evaluation."

[106] *Tashkent Times*, "Uzbekistan's Development Strategy." The president also stressed the independence of the judiciary in his December 2018 address to the Oliy Majlis.

Independent courts that respect the rule of law are essential to upholding freedom of religion or belief and other fundamental human rights. Efforts by the United States, as well as the UN and NGOs, to facilitate the development of judicial independence in Uzbekistan would go a long way to further freedom of religion or belief.

Other actors in the international realm can offer encouragement and incentives to continue these political reforms related to the rule of law and human rights. The Vice President of the European Bank for Reconstruction and Development noted that, "as a result of the fundamental changes going on in Uzbekistan... we have signed deals for 16 projects worth more than €500 million in total." Rigterink also noted that these economic and political reforms require "transparency, reliability and [the] rule of law [as] firm principles, without which a successful economy cannot be developed on a sustainable basis."[107] Thus, he was articulating a willingness to work with the Uzbek government, so long as these reforms were undertaken with a commitment to improve the rule of law, which is needed for economic growth as well as human rights, such as freedom of religion.

These activities would further the space for religious freedom in the country. The overall goal should be to allow the seeds of freedom of religion or belief to take root. If the roots are deep enough and strong enough, they have the potential to change society, political institutions, and the politicians that come after Mirziyoyev.

CONCLUSION

We should remain cautious with our optimism for a few reasons. Achieving religious tolerance or freedom of religion or belief is not a neat, linear process. Religious freedom does not move forward in a straight line; rather, it ebbs and flows. However, we would be remiss if we did not acknowledge that some policies and personalities can assist the flow in a positive direction. The historical evidence reminds us to be cautious, as religious tolerance does not always outlast the authoritarian leaders who developed these policies. If Mirziyoyev remains in power for a decade or more, religious tolerance may become not only embedded in the dispositions of the Uzbek people, but more importantly in institutions throughout the country, including in local political leaders, security forces, and the judicial system. The latter are key, as the people of Uzbek have historically practiced a tolerant form of Islam and, as the Pew Research

[107] See https://www.ebrd.com/news/speeches/reforming-uzbekistan-challenges-and-opportunities.html.

Center notes, there is little social hostility in the country.[108] By developing strong roots throughout institutions in society, religious freedom may flourish. If Mirziyoyev changes his mind about these nascent policies due to the lack of rewards or perceived security threats, he could reverse the progress that has been made over the last few years. One additional note of caution: if reforms in Uzbekistan are largely dependent on the president, lasting reforms in various political institutions could be set back if a significantly different political leader were to emerge. Ultimately, Uzbekistan moved further away from religious intolerance and repression than most other states, and for that reason we should maintain our hope for the future.

[108] The social hostility that sometimes develops in Uzbekistan tends to involve a Muslim convert to Christianity. State Department, *International Religious Freedom Report for 2017*.

7. The role of civil society: the Institute for Global Engagement and Vietnam

INTRODUCTION

In the village of Plei Lao in the Central Highlands of Vietnam, a church was burned to the ground. One eyewitness explained that after the police ordered the destruction of the church, "the police put fresh earth over the ashes and smoothed it so outsiders could not tell there had ever been a church there."[1] The destruction of religious buildings and the arrest and imprisonment of religious leaders and lay worshipers has been a recurring theme under the communist government in Vietnam. Some of this is due to the country's colonial history and hostility to potential independent political actors. Some limited improvements have occurred in Vietnam since 2006. Evidence for improvement comes from the growth of church affiliation among the Vietnamese population, the renovation of numerous temples, increasing numbers at pilgrimage sites, as well as some government reforms. The UN Special Rapporteur on freedom of religion or belief, Heiner Bielefeldt, also noted "that there was generally more space for the exercise of religious freedom in Viet Nam at present, especially compared with the post-1975 situation."[2] Some of the progress made in Vietnam is due to the persistent effort of some international actors, including the Institute for Global Engagement (IGE), to promote religious freedom through relational diplomacy.

The IGE is one actor in civil society that is attempting to further the fundamental right to freedom of religion or belief. Given Hanoi's approach toward religious groups in its territory, this chapter explains how one NGO—the IGE—tried to influence the Vietnamese government, as well as how the Vietnamese Communist Party responded to international initiatives. This

[1] Marc Galli, "Good Morning, Vietnam!" *Christianity Today*, May 2007, pp. 25–32.

[2] Philip Taylor, "Modernity and Re-enchantment in Post-revolutionary Vietnam," in *Modernity and Re-enchantment*, edited by Philip Taylor (New York: Lexington Books, 2007), p. 1. Heiner Bielefeldt, *Report on Mission to Viet Nam*, January 30, 2015, A/HRC/28/66/Add.2.

chapter uses the IGE to demonstrate the impact an NGO can have when it pursues sustained and thoughtful programs.

Beyond issuing a statement in reaction to discrimination or persecution, can civil society organizations develop sustainable initiatives that further freedom of religion or belief? This chapter begins by explaining the role and activities that actors in civil society play in their efforts to promote human rights. Next, it looks at the history of religion in Vietnam and the policies of the Communist Party in Vietnam to restrict religious organizations and limit religious freedom. The fourth section spells out how various actors in the international community have criticized the Vietnamese government for its repressive policies. Building on previous chapters, we note how the UN and the US have attempted to promote religious freedom in Vietnam. Lastly, this chapter focuses on how one NGO contributed to efforts to advance religious freedom in the country. Given Hanoi's history of Marxism and atheism, more attention will be paid to freedom of religion than to the right not to believe. The IGE's decades-long efforts in Vietnam are assessed to understand what progress has been accomplished, and what work remains to be done.

CIVIL SOCIETY

States play a significant role in the protection of the fundamental right of freedom of religion or belief. States, as demonstrated in earlier chapters, are often responsible for the denial of this basic right, including the persecution of religious groups within their borders. On the other hand, some states, such as the US and Canada, promote this right through various foreign policy proposals and programs. While states are some of the most powerful actors in global affairs, non-state actors also engage in activities that further or limit freedom of religion or belief. As noted in the introduction, the Islamic State and Boko Haram are two non-state actors contributing to religious intolerance in global politics. This chapter focuses on non-state actors in civil society that are working to promote religious tolerance and further the right of freedom of religion or belief.

Civil society refers to private non-profit organizations, including NGOs, human rights activists, and religious associations, to name a few, which seek policy changes at the local, national, or international level by peaceful means.[3] Civil society is constituted by individuals who voluntarily work within

---

[3] I use the term civil society rather than transnational networks. Civil society activists, especially traditional human rights organizations, have played a substantial role in Vietnam. While it may be that we are in the very early stages of a transnational network on freedom of religion or belief, it is still currently an inchoate network. For more on

organizations to advocate for a cause or attempt to advance specific values. These voluntary associations are motivated by principled ideas, morals, and values. They seek to improve society.[4] These private actors engage in various grassroots activities, including lobbying public officials for political change, educating communities about a social concern, and providing services to a population in need. One scholar summarized the role of civil society in the following way:

> As an intermediary between the state and individuals, civil society organizations and institutions perform critical roles, including advocating in support of specific causes or groups or on behalf of aggrieved citizens; educating people about their rights, entitlements, and responsibilities; providing services to areas and people in need; mobilizing public opinion; and serving as watchdogs against violators of human rights.[5]

Often an NGO can act quickly and with more flexibility than a government to respond to a human rights violation, such as religious persecution.

Information

Many civil society organizations collect and disseminate information to the public. NGOs seek to educate policy makers and the larger public in an effort to explain an issue (e.g., what human rights are) or to alert the public to a social problem or crisis. This could lead to policy change in the short term or down the road.[6] For example, efforts to educate citizens about the internment of over a million Uyghurs via social media posts or media interviews can help pressure government officials to confront Beijing. It can potentially lead to the boycott of goods made by forced labor.

---

transnational networks, see Margaret Keck and Katherine Sikkink, *Activists Beyond Borders* (New York: Cornell University Press, 1998).

[4] On the second page of *Activists without Borders,* Keck and Sikkink describe transnational networks in a similar manner: “the centrality of values or principled ideas, the belief that individuals can make a difference, the creative use of information, and the employment by nongovernmental actors of sophisticated political strategies in targeting campaigns.”

[5] Dr. Robert P. George, Testimony before the Africa, Global Health, Global Human Rights and International Organizations Subcommittee of the House Foreign Affairs Committee, July 16, 2016, Washington, D.C.

[6] “Traditional human rights NGOs publish information in the hopes of long-term education. This blends with the objective of influencing policy in the short term through dissemination. Today’s education may become the context for tomorrow’s policymaking.” David Forsythe, *Human Rights in International Relations*, 4th edition (New York: Cambridge University Press, 2017), p. 268.

For many civil society actors, especially human rights organizations, their reputation and their ability to influence the discourse on policy depends on producing credible information and reports. If an NGO is pressured to correct a report due to inaccurate information, this could result in a loss of credibility (crying wolf), and ultimately a loss in diplomatic and financial support from stakeholders.

Lobbying

Civil society activists try to persuade and socialize political leaders to modify their views or to adopt new views. Purposeful activists will develop a narrative framework to encourage social change. Their advocacy work is built on this narrative framework and attempts to convince others (states, IGOs, multinational corporations [MNCs]) of the importance of the ideas embedded in the narrative framework.

When civil society actors lobby governments or IGOs, they attempt to change the policies, behavior, and mindsets of individuals within these institutions. By encouraging a government official to see an individual (in a minority or out-of-favor group) or an activity (blog post, communal gathering, reading a banned book or pamphlet) as non-threatening or harmless, they are attempting to broaden the space in society for greater political acceptance of an individual or a group.

Since NGOs lack the hard power of states (i.e., the military or economic power to threaten or unilaterally sanction), they must rely on the power of persuasion.[7] There are different methods of persuasion. NGOs monitor the protection of a human right in a local context, or for some of the larger Western NGOs, throughout the world. When they write a report, they are trying to influence a state (or IGO, MNC, or financial institution) to change or modify its behavior or policy. Some civil society organizations, such as Greenpeace or Human Rights Watch, attempt to "name and shame" through reports or social media posts. This approach is motivated by the belief that negative publicity will encourage the targeted actor—most often a state—to change its behavior due to the critical public attention it is receiving. Public officials would prefer to avoid the negative attention that human rights violations and social conflict can attract. As one activist noted, "They do not want the light on them. They want the international community out of their hair."[8] Other civil society actors,

---

[7] Ann Marie Clark, "Nongovernmental Organizations," *Encyclopedia of Human Rights* (Vol. 4), David P. Forsythe, editor-in-chief (Oxford: Oxford University Press, 2009), p. 89.

[8] Interview, September 25, 2018.

such as the International Committee of the Red Cross and the IGE, prefer quiet, behind-the-scenes consultation in lieu of public confrontation. In their view, they can accomplish more with private conversations and quiet prodding.[9]

Services

Beyond publishing and disseminating information to public officials and citizens, many civil society organizations provide services to individuals in need and assist those whose rights have been violated. These organizations provide a wide array of services, from legal assistance (representation in court) to training programs to medical procedures (surgery and vaccinations) to development assistance (agricultural support to increase output or constructing a water system so that a village has access to clean water).[10] Given their limited resources, NGOs must develop thoughtful campaigns and policies to avoid wasting resources or causing a backlash and more harm.

In addition to human rights organizations, religious organizations can contribute to the promotion of human rights in their words and deeds. This is especially true in the context of freedom of religion or belief. When religious leaders and religious organizations consistently offer messages of tolerance and acceptance of the religious Other, this can result in a profound and lasting change in attitudes. Many religious leaders enjoy a legitimacy with the members of their community due to the vows they took, the charitable organizations they run to help individuals, or the pious life they have led. Thus, when they speak out against hatred and intolerance and advocate for human rights or social change, this can resonate with a far greater audience than hearing the same message from an American or European diplomat or Western human rights activist.[11]

Declarations such as *Nostra Aetate*, one of the documents produced by the Second Vatican Council or Vatican II, is an example of a message of tolerance by a religious leader (Pope Paul VI) and ultimately a religious institution (the Catholic Church). In *Nostra Aetate*, the church "exhorts her sons, that through

---

[9] David Forsythe and Barbara Ann Rieffer-Flanagan, *The International Committee of the Red Cross: A Neutral Humanitarian Actor* (New York: Routledge, 2016).

[10] "These private actors are crucial especially for grassroots action that directly or indirectly attends to social and economic rights." Forsythe, *Human Rights*, p. 256.

[11] "Other private groups that exist for secular or religious purposes may become international human rights actors at particular times and for particular causes. The Catholic Church in its various manifestations and the World Council of Churches, inter alia, are examples of religious groups that fit this mold… Some faith-based groups, for example, teamed with some secular human rights groups to help achieve greater attention to the right to religious freedom and the right to be free from religious discrimination in the recent past, at least in U.S. foreign policy." Forsythe, *Human Rights*, p. 258.

dialogue and collaboration with the followers of other religions, carried out with prudence and love and in witness to the Christian faith and life, they recognize, preserve and promote the good things, spiritual and moral, as well as the socio-cultural values found among these men."[12] *Nostra Aetate* goes on to encourage mutual respect and understanding for other faiths, including Hindus, Buddhists, and Muslims. It is unequivocal in its rejection of anti-Semitism: "Furthermore, in her rejection of every persecution against any man, the Church mindful of the patrimony she shares with the Jews and moved not by political reasons but by the Gospel's spiritual love, decries hatred, persecution, displays of anti-Semitism, directed against Jews at any time and by anyone."[13] In *Nostra Aetate*, a religious organization articulated a message of religious tolerance to educate its followers and guide their values and actions toward other faiths.

Another example would be the Marrakesh Declaration on the Rights of Religious Minorities in Predominately Muslim Communities in 2016. This declaration encourages individuals, civil society, and states to support freedom of religion for non-Muslims based on the Islamic faith:

> [w]e hereby: Call upon Muslim scholars and intellectuals around the world to develop a jurisprudence of the concept of "citizenship" which is inclusive of diverse groups. Such jurisprudence shall be rooted in Islamic tradition and principles and mindful of global changes.
>
> Urge Muslim educational institutions and authorities to conduct a courageous review of educational curricula that addresses honestly and effectively any material that instigates aggression and extremism, leads to war and chaos, and results in the destruction of our shared societies…
>
> Call upon the educated, artistic, and creative members of our societies, as well as organizations of civil society, to establish a broad movement for the just treatment of religious minorities in Muslim countries and to raise awareness as to their rights, and to work together to ensure the success of these efforts.[14]

This is another statement within a religious tradition about the equal rights for all citizens, regardless of their faith.

Beyond the activities civil society actors engage in is the important question of impact. Can an NGO, religious organization, or other civil society

---

[12] The Vatican, "Declaration on the Relation of the Church to Non-Christian Religions *Nostra Aetate*, Proclaimed by His Holiness Pope Paul VI," October 28, 1965, https://www.vatican.va/archive/hist_councils/ii_vatican_council/documents/vat-ii_decl_19651028_nostra-aetate_en.html.

[13] Ibid.

[14] Marrakesh Declaration, "Executive Summary," Marrakesh Declaration on the Rights of Religious Minorities in Predominantly Muslim Majority Communities, January 27, 2016, https://www.marrakeshdeclaration.org/declaration/index.html.

actor contribute to the development and promotion of a basic human right or social change, and how should we understand the impact of a civil society organization's activities? How can we measure the influence or success of a non-state actor that is seeking social and policy change? One scholar offered this approach:

> In dealing with the sometimes elusive notion of success or achievement, sometimes it helped to distinguish among the following: success in getting an item or subject on the agenda for discussion, success in achieving serious discussion, success in getting procedural or institutional change and finally success in achieving substantive policy change that clearly ameliorated or eliminated the problem.[15]

Can an NGO bring more attention to an issue and influence public discourse on this topic? Is a civil society organization able to create rules or standards in conjunction with states? Thus, standard-setting is another activity that human rights organizations engage in.[16] If, after much effort, they are able to establish human rights standards in international treaties, domestic laws or policies adopted by MNCs, financial organizations, or IGOs, then NGOs can measure compliance with these standards. The rest of this chapter explores the situation of religious freedom in Vietnam and efforts to advance the acceptance of this right in society.

VIETNAM

The religious makeup of contemporary Vietnam was influenced by foreigners and the ideas and ideologies they brought to the country. Out of a population of roughly 100 million people, less than 15 percent identified with a religious tradition in the 2019 census. Six million are Catholics, with another million belonging to a Protestant community. The second largest group in Vietnam is the roughly 5 million adherents of Mahayana Buddhism. Other smaller religious minorities include Hoa Hao Buddhists and Cao Dai, which account for less than 5 percent of those individuals with a religious affiliation. Millions of Vietnamese are not affiliated with any recognized religious community or choose not to report any religious affiliation due to a fear of the social or legal consequences of doing so.[17]

---

[15] Forsythe, p. 273.

[16] Clark, p. 91.

[17] State Department, *International Religious Freedom Report for 2020*, May 12, 2021, https://www.state.gov/reports/2020-report-on-international-religious-freedom/vietnam/.

The Denial of Religious Freedom under Foreign Rule

Foreigners ruled the territory that is contemporary Vietnam for centuries. Foreigners controlled or influenced life in the territories of present-day Vietnam from roughly the 10th century to the middle of the 20th century. The Chinese were defeated in 939, and a series of dynasties ruled the area until French colonial rule was cemented in the mid-1800s. After a series of French military victories, the French established control over all of Vietnam by 1883. A Vietnamese resistance movement of communists and nationalists eventually forced the French to withdraw in 1954. The Chinese, Portuguese, and French brought aspects of their culture, including religion, with them. Confucian, Buddhist, and Christian beliefs left a mark on Vietnamese society whether the land was under foreign control or during periods of independence.

In the 16th century, Portuguese and French missionaries traveled to Vietnam to spread the faith. Religious organizations and individuals associated with these communities often had tense relationships with the political powers in charge of the territory, whether domestic or foreign.[18] Some local leaders targeted Christians, particularly Catholics. As Charles Keith noted: "The 19th century was, of course, a time of widespread and severe repression of Catholicism in Vietnam, both official and popular, which not only strongly discouraged conversions but also led to as many as 100 000 Catholic deaths across the Nguyen kingdom."[19] This violence was often motivated by the European, especially French, association with the religious tradition or the perception of the interconnectedness of the French with Catholicism. Some nationalists portrayed Catholic missionaries as the tools of French imperialism.[20] According to a Catholic bishop in Vinh in the late 19th century, "among the pagans, Catholic is synonymous with friend of the French, and whoever embraces the religion is regarded as an enemy."[21]

Despite the perception of a close relationship, the Catholic hierarchy and French colonial administrators did not always see eye to eye. As one scholar noted, "Indeed, powerful ideological differences and competition for influence over the Vietnamese population meant that Catholic missions and the colonial state could often be each other's most bitter rivals."[22] Many officials within the Catholic Church in Vietnam did not believe that the colonial officials were

---

18 John Gillespie, "Human Rights as a Larger Loyalty: The Evolution of Religious Freedom in Vietnam," *Harvard Human Rights Journal*, Vol. 27, pp. 107–49.

19 Charles Keith, *Catholic Vietnam: A Church from Empire to Nation* (Berkeley: University of California Press, 2012), p. 20.

20 Taylor, "Modernity," p. 43.

21 Keith, p. 56.

22 Keith, p. 65.

adequately addressing their concerns about security or poverty. Many in the Vatican held more humane views of the people of Indochina and rejected the label of barbarians that some French colonizers held. This is not to suggest that Buddhists always enjoyed religious tolerance at the hands of the French administrators. Colonial administrators were often brutal to the Vietnamese, regardless of their religious commitments. This colonial legacy would impact religious policy under Communist Party rule.

Communist Vietnam

After Vietnam was unified in 1975 following the defeat of the Americans, the communists under Ho Chi Minh did not embrace freedom of religion or belief—quite the contrary. The revolutionaries were influenced by Marxism. Marxist ideology was imbued with atheism, as Marx had expressed his disdain for religion as the opiate of the masses, among other reasons. In *Critique of Hegel's Philosophy of Right*, Marx wrote: "The wretchedness of religion is at once an expression of and a protest against real wretchedness. Religion is the sigh of the oppressed creature, the heart of a heartless world, and the soul of soulless conditions. It is the opium of the people."[23] Thus, this new independent state would be forcefully secular. The Communist Party in Vietnam also had concerns about the Catholic Church in Vietnam due to their perceived ties to the French colonial regime. Given their opposition to foreign domination, they "feared that faith groups would become a threat to the government" because they would be manipulated by a Western power.[24] In addition, the Communist Party has been suspicious of any independent civil society actors who were outside of the government's control and who could exploit the proletariat.[25] Independent organizations in civil society can mobilize and become a threat to the regime's stability and grip on power. Vietnam is an authoritarian political system where the Communist Party holds all political power (executive, legislative, and judicial).[26] The approach of the government is one of strict control. The government often banned and imprisoned individuals advocating for human rights or criticizing Hanoi's policies. Government policies regularly

---

[23] Marx, p. 131.

[24] Hien Vu, conference call, September 11, 2014.

[25] Hien Vu, Stephen Bailey, and James Chen, "Engaging Vietnam and Laos on Religious Freedom," *The Review of Faith and International Affairs*, Vol. 14, No. 2 (2016), pp. 86–92.

[26] Reg Reimer and Hien Vu, "Towards the Rule of Law for Freedom of Religion and Belief in Vietnam," *The Review of Faith and International Affairs*, Vol. 14, No. 4 (October 2016), p. 81. Freedom House, "Freedom in the World Report 2020: Vietnam," https://freedomhouse.org/country/vietnam/freedom-world/2020.

persecute Buddhists and Christians because some in the government still embrace a strain of Marxism that is hostile to any group that could be a threat to the government's power.[27]

While freedom of religion or belief was included in the 1980 constitution, this provision was not upheld in practice by state agencies or the judicial system.[28] Although Vietnam became a party to the ICCPR in 1982,[29] this did not result in a change to the government's approach to religion.

Government Policies

Since 1986, the Communist Party has developed an economic reform package known as Doi Moi, or Renovation, in an attempt to reinvigorate the economy. These efforts to move from a command economy toward a market economy significantly impacted Vietnamese society. Besides encouraging private markets, the government slowly began strengthening the legal system to provide the stability required for contracts and foreign investments.[30] The rule of law is useful to reassure businesses that their investments will not be confiscated by an arbitrary decision by an agent of the state. Doi Moi also created more openness in the area of religion, and initially allowed for more freedom for religious activities.[31] This was demonstrated in the increased private financial assistance given to religious institutions to support religious festivals, religious education, and the construction of churches, temples, and pagodas.[32] This raised red flags, as some of these independent activities alarmed government officials. This led to increased efforts to regulate religious organizations. One example was Ordinance 2004.

The 2004 Ordinance on Beliefs and Religions was an effort by the Vietnamese government to exert control over religious organizations. The ordinance established requirements for religious organizations in the areas of education, fundraising, ritual observation, and personnel matters. Religious organizations needed approval for the curricula used in religious schools, for fundraising drives, for conducting religious services and rituals, as well as for

---

[27] James Chen, Executive Director at IGE, radio interview, Ave Maria Radio, May 30, 2018.

[28] Gillespie, p. 121.

[29] Ratification of Human Rights Treaties, Vietnam University of Minnesota Human Rights Library, http://www.1umn.edu/humanrights/research/ratification-Vietnam.html.

[30] Gillespie, p. 123.

[31] Chung van Hoang, *New Religions and State's Response to Religious Diversification in Contemporary Vietnam* (Cham: Springer, 2017), p. 6.

[32] van Hoang, p. 8.

the individuals in leadership positions in the faith community.[33] Bielefeldt and Michael Wiener describe the regulations in Vietnam and their consequences: "special licenses are needed for performing worship, conducting youth activities, performing missionary work, importing and selling religious literature, and other activities… Hence people always move in a grey zone of legal insecurity, which has a chilling effect on their activities."[34]

Ordinance 2004 is an example of a government regulation that inhibits freedom of religion or belief. For freedom of religion or belief to be a right that is protected and not a meaningless article in a constitution, individuals must have the ability to develop the religious infrastructure that they deem necessary. This infrastructure includes the building and maintenance of property where individuals can congregate, the creation and maintenance of legally recognized charitable organizations and schools, as well as the ability to produce literature related to essential ideas and beliefs. Vietnam's regulations hinder the development and maintenance of religious infrastructure. Since it does not involve violence, regulations typically receive less international attention. This form of regulation, which can involve harassment by local officials, is nevertheless an obstacle for individuals who want to pursue a faith or live in accordance with deeply held beliefs. Thus, the Vietnamese government sought to manage these independent organizations to ensure they would not be used as the foundation of a protest movement that would challenge the centrality of the Communist Party, influence public opinion in undesirable ways, or threaten the stability of the government.[35]

New Religion Law

Given Vietnam's economic and strategic motivations, the government undertook reforms to the laws related to religion. Hanoi drafted and adopted the Law on Belief and Religion, which went into effect in January 2018. The IGE engaged in a dialogue with Hanoi about revisions to the new draft law. They

---

[33] Gillespie, p. 125. Decree No. 92/2012/ND-CP on Detailed Regulations and Enforcement Measures to Implement Ordinance on Belief and Religion, November 8, 2012. It provides for the regulation of various activities, including religious festivals and religious schools. These activities require religious groups to submit documents and register with local officials. The UN Special Rapporteur on freedom of religion or belief was critical of the "excessive requirements of Decree 92." The English translation is available at: http://reachingvietnam.com/wp-content/uploads/2013/03/ND92_EnglishTranslation.pdf.

[34] Bielefeldt and Wiener, p. 132.

[35] Gillespie, p. 125. I heard a similar sentiment from a Buddhist nun in Hue, Vietnam. She noted that the government does not interfere in their activities so long as they are not involved in politics. Interview, August 20, 2018.

were able to convince the government to make some changes to the law.[36] This law is an improvement over the previous law on religion since it refined the process for registration and reduced the waiting period for recognition to five years, but it is still flawed in many ways. The new law gave the government a greater ability to monitor and control religious individuals, practices, and especially religious organizations. Hien Vu, a program manager at the IGE, noted in a coauthored article that "early critiques by both domestic and international organizations agreed that the law did not provide legal protection of religious freedom but seemed more a means for the Vietnamese government to better monitor religious practices and to limit evangelism."[37]

Various American officials noted their concerns about the draft law. David Saperstein, the Ambassador-at-Large for International Religious Freedom in testimony before the House of Representatives explained:

> We have also engaged extensively with Vietnamese authorities to bring about needed changes in their proposed draft law on religion and belief. As currently written, it appears that the draft legislation will continue to require religious groups to undergo an onerous and arbitrary registration and recognition process to operate legally. Even with such registration, I understand that groups must still obtain specific approval for almost all activities, including religious events, building renovations (beyond normal construction requirements), and the establishment of seminaries or religious classes. Currently, persons undertaking these activities without certain approvals have been subject to harassment, arrest, or detention.[38]

USCIRF concluded, "the law—both as written and as implemented—contravenes international human rights standards, particularly Article 18 of the International Covenant on Civil and Political Rights."[39]

Despite the flaws in the revised religion law, it is worth noting that Hanoi did engage with international actors (NGOs, Washington) in the process of drafting and revising this law.[40] While the law still has significant limitations, including the government's ability to limit and regulate religious organiza-

---

[36] James Chen told me, "there were certain clauses in the first draft that changed." Interview, August 9, 2018.

[37] Reimer and Vu, p. 79. See also State Department, *International Religious Freedom Report for 2016.*

[38] David Saperstein, Ambassador-at-Large for International Religious Freedom, Statement for the House Foreign Affairs Committee Subcommittee on Africa, Global Health, Global Human Rights, and International Organizations, June 16, 2016, Washington, D.C.

[39] Dominic Nardi, Policy Analyst USCIRF, "Country Update: An Assessment of Vietnam's Law on Belief and Religion," November 2019.

[40] "The Vietnamese government reached out to IGE for written feedback on the draft law." James Chen, Interview, August 9, 2018.

tions, the willingness to listen to international actors is an important aspect of a continuing dialogue. One scholar who has worked with the Vietnamese government said that "it is positive that the government had been willing to engage on this issue, but that there was still resistance within the government." She went on to say that "the control mentality frames the whole thing."[41]

INTERNATIONAL CONCERNS

Various sources have documented the denial of religious freedom in Vietnam. The Pew Research Center reports significant government regulation of religion for over a decade.[42] Human rights organizations criticized the government for numerous violations of freedom of religion or belief. According to Freedom House:

> Religious freedom remains restricted. All religious groups and most individual clergy members are required to join a party-controlled supervisory body and obtain permission for most activities... [A] 2016 Law on Belief and Religion... reinforced registration requirements [and] will allow extensive state interference in religious groups' internal affairs, and give authorities broad authority to penalize unsanctioned religious activity. Members of unregistered Christian, Hoa Hao, Cao Dai, and other groups also face regular arrests and harassment from local and provincial authorities, and dozens of people are believed to be behind bars in connection with their religious beliefs.[43]

Human rights organizations consistently note that religious organizations have not registered with the government either because of government obstacles and obstruction or fear of being monitored and harassed. Individuals affiliated with unregistered religious groups have been detained, imprisoned for years, and tortured.[44]

Often, Western criticism about the situation of human rights in Vietnam was met with charges of cultural relativism. Government officials argued that "no country has the right to impose any political, economic, or cultural model on others."[45] Furthermore, the government articulated a communitarian approach in which the national interests of the country will take precedence over

---

[41] Interview, February 28, 2020.

[42] GRI 6.6/SHI 1.2 (2007); GRI 6.6/SHI 2.3 (2015); GHI-7.6/SHI-1.5 (2017). Pew Research Center, "A Closer Look."

[43] Freedom House, "Freedom in the World 2018 Vietnam."

[44] Human Rights Watch, "Human Rights Watch Submission to the European Union for the EU–Vietnam Human Rights Dialogue," February 18, 2002, https://www.hrw.org/news/2020/02/18/human-rights-watch-submission-european-union-eu-vietnam-human-rights-dialogue.

[45] Quoted in Gillespie, p. 109. See his footnote 10.

individual rights, including freedom of religion. The 2013 constitution states in Article 15 that "the practice of human rights and citizens' rights cannot infringe upon national interests, and the legal and legitimate rights of others."[46] Hanoi was unmoved by arguments by Western states and civil society actors of the inherent right of all individuals to believe what they want. National interests concerning economic development would prove to be more persuasive.

The United Nations

In addition to criticism from NGOs, IGOs such as the UN have highlighted numerous problems pertaining to this human right. Bielefeldt, the UN Special Rapporteur on freedom of religion or belief, also noted his concerns. He issued an unfavorable report on the situation of religious freedom in Vietnam after his visit in 2014:

> Whereas religious life and religious diversity are a reality in Viet Nam today, autonomy and activities of independent religious or belief communities, that is, unrecognized communities, remain restricted and unsafe, with the rights to freedom of religion or belief of such communities grossly violated in the face of constant surveillance, intimidation, harassment and persecution.[47]

He was critical of various government policies, the overly broad language in the constitution, and Ordinance 21, and expressed his concerns about the intimidation and harassment of members of faith communities in Vietnam. He noted, "independent Buddhist communities currently could not exercise their freedom of religion or belief." Bielefeldt complained that some individuals were warned against meeting him,[48] presumably by agents affiliated with the government: "He experienced firsthand and received credible information that some individuals with whom he wanted to meet had been heavily surveilled, warned, intimidated, harassed or prevented from traveling by the police. Even those who successfully met with him were not free from different degrees of police surveillance or questioning."[49]

---

[46] Quoted in Reimer and Vu, p. 79.

[47] Bielefeldt, *Report*.

[48] Marty Petty, "U.N. Religion Expert Concerned Over 'Interrupted' Vietnam Visit," *Reuters*, July 31, 2014.

[49] Bielefeldt, p. 3.

The government of Vietnam challenged Bielefeldt's conclusions at the UN Human Rights Council meeting in March 2015. The Vietnamese representative defended the government's record, stating that Vietnam:

> deeply regretted that the report failed to correctly present the real situation in Vietnam. Today around 95 percent of the population practiced a religion or belief and the religious life was vibrant. Freedom of religion or belief was enshrined in the Constitution and protected by the laws; the Government was doing its best to facilitate religious practices while promoting unity, harmony, equality and non-discrimination. There were no cases of threat, harassment or reprisal against persons who had engaged with the Special Rapporteur during his visit. While there was room for further improvement, Vietnam believed that efforts and achievements in the promotion of freedom of religion should have been reflected in the report in an objective and comprehensive manner. Viet Nam was disappointed by the imbalanced and partial approach by the Special Rapporteur and was unable to support his recommendations.[50]

It is worth contrasting Vietnam's defensive reaction and denial of the essence of Bielefeldt's findings with Uzbekistan's openness to Shaheed's visit in 2017 and the report that resulted from his visit.

Foreign Policy: US–Vietnamese Relations

We have also seen states raise the subject of freedom of religion or belief with Vietnam in their bilateral relations. As we saw in Chapter 4, the United States gave greater attention to this right starting in the 1990s, and this affected its relationship with Vietnam. It took decades for Washington and Hanoi to move beyond their troubled and violent past and restore bilateral relations. When the IRFA was passed in 1998, diplomatic tensions again came to the surface. Hanoi's repressive treatment of religious individuals and organizations eventually led Washington to designate Vietnam as a CPC. In September 2004, the Ambassador for International Religious Freedom noted the George W. Bush administration's concerns, including Vietnam's imprisonment, beating, and killing of religious individuals, especially Protestants and Buddhists. He also noted that the government had closed or prohibited access to houses of worship.[51]

---

[50] UN OHCHR, "Human Rights Council Starts Interactive Dialogue with the Special Rapporteur on Freedom of Religion or Belief," March 10, 2015, https://www.ohchr.org/EN/NewsEvents/Pages/DisplayNews.aspx?NewsID=15678.

[51] USCIRF, "Religious Freedom in Vietnam: Assessing the Country of Particular Concern Designation 10 Years After Its Removal," February 2017, https://www.uscirf.gov/sites/default/files/Vietnam.%20Assessing%20the%20Country%20of

CPC status created a problem for Hanoi. The Vietnamese government wanted to normalize trade relations with Washington and to join the World Trade Organization. To make progress on either goal, Vietnam needed to improve its record on freedom of religion or belief, since the threat of sanctions loomed. Economic obstacles, via sanctions, could contribute to economic isolation and hurt foreign investment, which was needed to create jobs in the country. Economic self-interest motivated these changes. According to Vu, Vietnam did not want to miss out on any economic opportunities due to the CPC designation. CPC status would likely result in less foreign investment.[52]

Hanoi decided to work with Washington and change some policies related to religion. Washington developed a road map with Hanoi to see progress on this human right. The State Department noted in its 2005 annual report that Vietnam committed to improving its approach to religion by agreeing to:

> fully implement the new laws on religious activities and to render previous contradictory regulations obsolete; to instruct local authorities to strictly and completely adhere to the new legislation and ensure their compliance; to facilitate the process by which religious congregations are able to open houses of worship; and to give special consideration to prisoners and cases of concern raised by the United States during the granting of prisoner amnesties.[53]

If Hanoi followed through on these policies, the Bush administration agreed to reappraise Vietnam's CPC designation.[54] Vietnam was removed from the CPC list in 2006. Washington reassessed Vietnam due in part to the policy changes made by the government. The IGE supported Washington's decision to remove Vietnam from the CPC list. One program manager at the IGE indicated that "the State Department made a timely decision to remove Vietnam off the CPC list. Vietnam desperately needed to learn more about rule of law, international trade treaties, [and] human rights."[55] Many were not convinced that Hanoi had turned a corner or made enough progress to warrant being removed from the CPC list. Some at the State Department privately expressed their concerns that removal from the list had not resulted in significant progress.[56] An official at

---

%20Particular%20Concern%20Designation%2010%20Years%20after%20its%20Removal.pdf, pp. 2–3.

[52] Hien Vu, conference call, September 11, 2014. Vietnam eventually joined the World Trade Organization in 2007.

[53] State Department, *International Religious Freedom Report for 2005*, https://www.state.gov/j/drl/rls/irf/2005/51535.htm.

[54] State Department, *International Religious Freedom Report for 2005*, https://www.state.gov/j/drl/rls/irf/2005/51535.htm.

[55] Hien Vu, August 9, 2018, electronic communication.

[56] One individual in the Office of International Religious Freedom noted that, since the CPC designation, there had been some improvements, but this had stagnated. Interview, Washington, D.C., December 14, 2012.

USCIRF also expressed similar reservations: "We [USCIRF] have advocated for CPC designation. We think State [Department] let them off too easily."[57] USCIRF continued to voice their concerns about the situation in Vietnam:

> Law enforcement officials continue to detain, arrest, and/or imprison individuals due to their religious beliefs or religious freedom advocacy. The scope and scale of these violations make clear that Vietnam still is a long way from respecting the universal right to freedom of religion or belief as defined by international law and covenants.[58]

USCIRF urged the Obama administration to use a visit by the President of Vietnam to press for greater protections of religious freedoms. Further, USCIRF noted the continuing harassment and discrimination of independent religious groups and the intimidation and detention of lawyers representing individuals and religious organizations.[59]

Although USCIRF called for the reinstatement of CPC status, many policy makers resisted this.[60] The US Ambassador to Vietnam Michael Michalak argued against reinstatement of CPC, noting there had been some improvements:

> Vietnam's poor handling of the situations at the Plum Village Community at the Bat Nha Pagoda and the Dong Chiem Catholic parish last week—particularly the excessive use of violence—is troublesome and indicative of a larger GVN [Government of Viet Nam] crackdown on human rights in the run-up to the January 2011 Party Congress.
>
> However, these situations are primarily "land disputes," do not meet the statutory requirement in the 1998 International Religious Freedom Act, and should not divert our attention from the significant gains in expanding religious freedoms that Vietnam has made since the lifting of CPC designation in November 2006. These gains include increased recognition and registration of scores of new religions, implementation of a new legal framework on religion, and training programs at the local and national level. Catholic and Protestant communities, including those in the

[57] Interview, Washington, D.C., March 12, 2014. USCIRF's 2020 Annual Report reiterated its view that the State Department lifted the CPC designation too early and that Vietnam should be redesignated in light of systematic and continuing violations of religious freedom.

[58] USCIRF, "Religious Freedom."

[59] Press Release, July 22, 2013. It is worth noting that the State Department held a meeting with Vietnamese government officials, US civil society groups concerned with freedom of religion and belief, and USCIRF to address some of these continuing concerns. Media Note from the Office of the Spokesperson, "Meeting on Religious Freedom in Vietnam," July 25, 2013, Washington, D.C.

[60] USCIRF, Press Release, "USCIRF Urges President Obama to Raise Religious Freedom with Vietnamese President," July 22, 2013. See also USCIRF's Annual Report, 2020.

> North and Northwest Highlands, continue to report improvements, as do members of the Muslim, Baha'i, and Cao Dai faiths throughout Vietnam. The widespread, systematic religious persecution that existed prior to Vietnam's designation in 2004 does not exist anymore. Post therefore recommends that the Department not re designate Vietnam and instead use high-level engagement opportunities to press the GVN to continue to expand religious freedom in Vietnam.[61]

The Obama administration publicly acknowledged that Vietnam needed to do more to protect this fundamental human right in congressional testimony:

> A frequent refrain I hear whenever I visit Vietnam is the need for better implementation of laws that are on the books. Constitutionally, citizens have the right to free speech, freedom of religious belief, and other human rights. But we all know, for example, that many members of Christian, Buddhist, and other groups face harassment and are required to, but then not allowed to register. The New Decree 92, which came into effect in January, could be implemented in a manner that further restricts, rather than promotes, religious freedom guaranteed in the constitution.[62]

Furthermore, the administration stated that this was an important part of US–Vietnam bilateral relations. This was echoed in the Joint Statement Between the United States of America and the Socialist Republic of Vietnam, which affirmed both countries' commitment to further support for human rights and fundamental freedoms. The statement noted: "Both sides recognize the contributions that social and religious organizations continue to make in the fields of education, health care, and social services in both countries."[63] It is worth noting that the Obama administration did not use the language of universal human rights as codified in the ICCPR—to which Vietnam is a party. Rather, the statement incorporates a discourse about religious organizations that highlights their contributions to society. The narrative of non-threatening religious organizations who further the progress of society was employed. This is unsurprising since the Vietnamese government had to agree to the language in the statement. But it also demonstrates a narrative that the Vietnamese government finds acceptable and can be used to further the protection of freedom of religion or belief in the country. Hanoi recognizes that religious organiza-

---

[61] Michael Michalak, "Vietnam Religious Freedom Update – The Case Against CPC," E.O. 12958, https://www.theguardian.com/world/us-embassy-cables-documents/244345.

[62] Daniel Baer, "U.S.–Vietnam Bilateral Relations," Deputy Assistant Secretary, Bureau of Democracy, Human Rights, and Labor, Prepared Statement to the House Committee on Foreign Affairs Subcommittee on Asia and the Pacific, June 5, 2013, Washington, D.C.

[63] White House, Office of the Press Secretary, "Joint Statement: Between the United States and the Socialist Republic of Vietnam," May 23, 2016.

tions and individuals can make a positive contribution to society through its charitable activities.[64]

Removing the CPC designation led to some improvements, but problems continued to revolve around the government's attempt to manage religious organizations and to perceive organized communities of faith as potential threats to the stability of the regime. Additionally, local officials have been unwilling to comply with the central government's policies and reforms. USCIRF noted, "nearly all the religious groups USCIRF met during its trip blamed implementation problems on local and provincial authorities rather than on the central government."[65] Despite continuing problems, it is worth acknowledging that some progress was made and that Washington used the leverage it had in its foreign policy tool kit to encourage Hanoi to change some of its policies. This demonstrates and reiterates the role that a state's foreign policy can play in addressing religious persecution, as well as the impact of instrumental motivations for reform.

THE IGE IN VIETNAM

This section explores the goals, activities, targets, and resources used by one NGO to encourage Hanoi to stop its persecution of religious minorities and non-atheists and to make additional improvements in the protection of this fundamental right. The IGE has been active in Vietnam for approximately 20 years in a long-term effort to see freedom of religion or belief take hold.

The IGE is a human rights organization created in 2000 by Robert Seiple, the former US Ambassador-at-Large for International Religious Freedom. The IGE's philosophy is centered on relational diplomacy.[66] Relational diplomacy revolves around building relationships of trust with local communities and government officials. They believe that local buy-in throughout a society is necessary to see progress on freedom of religion or belief. They recognize the need to work with local organizations (when possible) and individuals throughout society. The IGE adopted a long-term approach of tirelessly cultivating partnerships with local political and religious leaders in an effort to encourage religious freedom and the rule of law.[67] The IGE works in various countries around the world, including Laos, Uzbekistan, and Myanmar. They try to encourage change by informing political leaders of the empirical

[64] Vu, Bailey, and Chen, p. 86.

[65] Nardi, "Country Update."

[66] James Chen, Executive Director at IGE, radio interview, Ave Maria Radio, May 30, 2018.

[67] One person mentioned, "IGE is in the business of relational diplomacy over the long haul." Interview, September 25, 2018.

evidence that demonstrates that countries that protect religious freedom have more social stability and economic growth. One individual who worked at IGE noted, "the argument we always made is religious freedom is better for security and stability… It is against your interests to deny religious freedom."[68] Their arguments often revolve around the instrumental benefits of protecting freedom of religion or belief. Beginning in 2004, the IGE assisted "national leaders and the people of Vietnam to build religious freedom."[69] One of the IGE's goals is to raise awareness about the importance of religious freedom. They do this through an open dialogue which they hope will contribute to a relationship built on trust.

The IGE engaged in various activities to promote freedom of religion or belief in Vietnam. They traveled to Vietnam multiple times to meet with and lobby government officials, including the president and members of parliament, as well as religious leaders and citizens. They met with registered and unregistered churches. This is part of an effort to establish a respectful dialogue. It is also an effort to collect information about the situation of religious freedom in the country, which allows them to disseminate information to various stakeholders and to lobby government officials in Hanoi and Washington. For example, the IGE's former president gave testimony on Capitol Hill and lobbied Congress to lift CPC status. Seiple suggested that CPC status should be withdrawn with the caveat that Congress should hold Hanoi to their commitments on freedom of religion or belief.[70] His testimony was an effort to lobby US policy makers to revise their approach to Vietnam.

In addition, the IGE developed and convened conferences on religious freedom and the rule of law. They undertook numerous steps to begin this process, including signing a letter of intent and an MOU with the Vietnam–USA Society (an organization affiliated with the Vietnamese government). The letter of intent includes an agreement to hold a dialogue on human rights and religion in Washington, D.C., and for the IGE to organize a conference on the rule of law and religion in Hanoi and conduct "field visits for further understanding of the implementation of the Ordinance on faith and religion at

[68] Interview, September 25, 2018.

[69] See https://globalengage.org/programs/vietnam. My focus on an American NGO in this chapter stems from the fact that there is not a mature or vibrant civil society in Vietnam.

[70] Chris Seiple, Testimony before the Senate Finance Committee, July 12, 2006, on "S.3495—A bill to authorize the extension of nondiscriminatory treatment (normal trade relations treatment) to the products of Vietnam," https://www.finance.senate.gov/hearings/to-hear-testimony-on-s3495a-bill-to-authorize-the-extension-of-nondiscriminatory-treatment-normal-trade-relations-treatment-to-the-products-of-vietnam.

the local level." The MOU clearly articulates that the IGE's work in Vietnam will involve mutual respect for "one another's national and cultural context, and the rule of law, and each country's legal system."[71]

The IGE's efforts to educate and strengthen the rule of law in Vietnam are necessary to protect human rights, including freedom of religion or belief. While freedom of religion is established in laws and in the constitution, an independent judiciary is needed to uphold these rights. Promoting the rule of law has an added benefit from the government's perspective. The rule of law is necessary for economic investment because foreign investors want to know that their business disputes will be adjudicated fairly and investments will not be lost. Thus, promoting the rule of law for economic reasons can also be used to protect individual human rights, including the rights of individuals who want to live according to their deeply held beliefs.

In these conferences, the IGE teaches individuals, and especially government officials in places such as Vietnam, what the principles of the rule of law are and how they relate to the principles of freedom of religion or belief. The IGE has held "Religion and Rule of Law" training programs in various locations throughout Vietnam, including Hanoi, Ho Chi Minh City, Da Nang, Northwest Highlands, and the Mekong Delta region. Since the IGE developed these training programs in 2012, more than 4000 Vietnamese government officials, policy makers, advisors, and faith leaders have attended these seminars.[72] The IGE's speakers explain how these principles are implemented in other countries. By comparing how different societies, including non-Western societies, implemented these principles, the IGE offers examples of what could help a country such as Vietnam. In addition, it creates a space for government officials and religious leaders to discuss this issue and hopefully provides a means to continue the dialogue.[73]

These training programs are an effort to teach and influence future leaders in order to plant the seeds of religious freedom in the future. The Vice President of IGE noted that they "try to shape or influence the mindset of these officials because this would lead to changes at policy levels."[74] Additional long-term educational efforts include the development of a Vietnamese language text-

---

[71] Letter of Intent between the Vietnam–USA Society and the IGE, Hanoi, Vietnam, July 1, 2005. MOU between IGE and Vietnam–USA Society, November 27, 2012. These documents are in the possession of the author.

[72] Hien Vu, August 9, 2018, electronic communication. See also https://globalengage.org/updates/view/ige-to-hold-groundbreaking-religious-freedom-programs-in-vietnam-and-laos.

[73] See https://globalengage.org/updates/view/ige-to-hold-groundbreaking-religious-freedom-programs-in-vietnam-and-laos.

[74] Interview, August 9, 2018.

book titled *Law on the Right to Freedom of Religion or Belief*. The IGE worked with scholars at Vietnam National University to draft and publish this work. This book is important because it is in the local language and because it will be used in classes at Vietnam National University's law school, further planting the seeds for the development of future generations.[75] The IGE wants to change the mindset of people to show that religious individuals and organizations are not a threat to the government. The organization is specifically trying to work with government officials to show the benefits of freedom of religion and to facilitate a dialogue between the government and religious leaders in Vietnamese society.

The IGE also met with individuals who have been persecuted in the past, including pastors and Protestant leaders in the Central Highlands. By meeting with these individuals, local officials are aware that the IGE is concerned about their well-being. This could protect them from further persecution.

In sum, the IGE's campaign in Vietnam seeks to educate government officials, religious leaders, and citizens about the importance of the rule of law and religious freedom in the country. They seek to teach current and future policy makers that religious individuals are not a threat and can offer positive contributions to society. Their training programs and quiet diplomacy seek to establish respectful relations with various elements within the country to help Vietnam open up a greater space for religious freedom in society. The IGE's work is not reactive. They have developed a long-term strategy to build a sustainable religious freedom policy in Vietnam and elsewhere. Their efforts involve planting a seed and cultivating it for decades, as Kennan advocated for in foreign policy.

CONCLUSION

While the full protection of freedom of religion or belief as articulated in Article 18 does not yet exist in Vietnam, there has been progress. Even though the government continues its attempt to manage religious organizations, there have been improvements for individuals engaging in private (non-threatening) worship. In the more than a dozen years since the CPC designation was removed, the government strengthened the rule of law, revised a law on religion, and trained local officials on religion. Hanoi has adopted a less hostile approach to religion and religious groups in the last few years. In August 2019, Prime Minister Nguyen Xuan Phuc praised the social and charitable activities

---

[75] See https://globalengage.org/updates/view/ige-facilitates-publication-of-first-ever-vietnamese-textbook-on-religious-freedom.

that some religious groups have undertaken.[76] According to James Chen, "they have a long way to go, but the general trend has been encouraging."[77]

This progress can be attributed to a number of factors. Hanoi's desire for economic growth and pressure from international actors, including the CPC designation by the United States, added pressure on the government. In addition, the IGE's continual efforts at relational diplomacy also played a role. While measuring the exact impact of an NGO (or other actor) is often difficult, it would be hard to argue that the IGE has not made a positive contribution to freedom of religion or belief and the rule of law in Vietnam. The IGE engaged with various stakeholders in Vietnam to advance this fundamental right. They raised awareness with government officials and religious leaders. While the IGE did not independently eliminate the problem of religious repression, there have been improvements in Vietnamese society, including procedural and legal changes.

Civil society organizations, such as the IGE, can play a positive role in the promotion of the right to freedom of religion or belief if they develop a thoughtful long-term approach. Not every NGO has the resources and human capacity to develop long-term goals and work on freedom of religion or belief in a country for decades, as the IGE has done. But this is a method that has a greater chance of having an impact compared to alternative approaches. They can train government officials on the legal and policy protections for religious freedom. They can try to persuade a government to stop the harassment and intimidation of individuals in society by noting the positive contributions of faith-based groups. Civil society should encourage religious leaders to work across religious lines. If they develop a long-term strategy in conjunction with individuals on the ground, they have the ability to slowly strengthen this basic human right.

---

[76] USCIRF, 2020 Annual Report.

[77] James Chen, Executive Director at IGE, radio interview, Ave Maria Radio, May 30, 2018. It is worth noting that some in Washington are more pessimistic. One State Department official suggested that "Vietnam was not doing so well overall. I think they [IGE] are too optimistic." Interview, March 14, 2014, Washington, D.C.

8. Promoting religious freedom in Egypt

INTRODUCTION

In many countries around the world, the situations of citizens who are members of a belief community are deplorable. Egypt is one such country. All Egyptians are not free to practice their religion or live according to their deeply held beliefs. Religious freedom does not exist. In Egypt, Coptic Christians are treated as second-class citizens, while Shiites and other non-Sunni Muslims face legal discrimination from the government and social hostility from other members of society. This chapter explores why various religious minorities (Copts, Shiites) cannot safely engage in religious practices. Further, what can be done in this society where individuals have been killed for who they are and what they believe? What is needed for Egypt to move from its current state, where some Egyptians are harassed for their beliefs, to one where freedom of religion or belief is a basic right for all and protected throughout society? This chapter applies the conceptual architecture and building blocks developed in previous chapters concerning educational reform, political leadership initiatives, multilateral efforts, and civil society activities to understand what could assist in promoting this fundamental right in Egypt.

For Egyptians to experience, first, a more tolerant atmosphere, and then eventually one where religious freedom is a right protected by the government, several changes are needed. A multidimensional approach is required to improve the situation. First, political leaders, especially President Abdel Fattah el-Sisi, must—at a minimum—embrace a genuine religious tolerance for all and consistently speak out against the dehumanization of the religious Other in society. El-Sisi must also initiate some domestic reforms specifically targeting educational and judicial institutions. He needs to understand that this is in his political interests. Other states, especially the United States, can help to encourage these changes either by making instrumental arguments about the economic and security benefits of freedom of religion or through their foreign policies and assistance programs. International organizations, such as the UN and its Special Rapporteur for freedom of religion or belief, can amplify this message. Civil society organizations, if they are allowed to operate within the country's borders, can help implement these policies and programs on the ground. All these efforts are necessary to see progress on this fundamental human right. The process of building the architecture of religious freedom in Egypt will take decades to take hold. Thus, sustained engagement with political and social leaders must be nurtured on a continual basis.

RELIGIOUS INTOLERANCE IN EGYPT

The freedom to follow and adhere to an established set of religious beliefs, particularly beliefs that diverge from Sunni Islam, is not a protected right for millions of Egyptians. Unfortunately, this has been true for decades. Although Egypt has been a party to the ICCPR since 1982, the government has not made protecting Article 18 for all its citizens a priority. The denial of freedom of religion or belief has been documented by the Pew Research Center. In 2007, the GRI for Egypt was 7.2 and the SHI was 6.1. Over a decade later, the environment in Egypt had deteriorated further. By December 2018, Egypt's GRI was 7.7 and its SHI was 7.5.[1] Egypt consistently recorded high levels of both government restrictions and social hostilities within its borders.[2] Various organizations also noted concerns about Egypt's disregard for international standards.[3] According to one NGO activist, "Egypt has been going in the wrong direction for a long time."[4]

To understand the troubling results from the Pew Research Center's reports, we need to understand how Egypt's laws and policies inhibit some citizens from adhering to their beliefs. Various administrations, from Nasser to el-Sisi, used the tools and power of the government to limit religious institutions and religious citizens for more than 50 years. The Egyptian government also failed to consistently address violence against religious minorities.

Since the 1960s, various presidents have attempted to regulate aspects of religion. Some scholars have explained these efforts to regulate and control religion in Egypt in terms of statism. The government, by limiting autonomy increasing the powers of the state, tries to control various aspects of society.[5] When applied to the religious environment in Egypt, we see that various administrations attempted to regulate, limit, and control religious activities and

---

[1] Pew Research Center, "In 2018, Government Restrictions."

[2] Pew Forum on Religion and Public Life, "Latest Trends."

[3] European Parliament Intergroup on FoRB and RT, *2014 Annual Report: The State of Freedom of Religion or Belief in the World*, Brussels, Belgium, https://www.oursplatform.org/wp-content/uploads/European-Parliament-Intergroup-on-Freedom-of-Religion-2014-Report-State-of-Freedom-of-Religion-or-Belief-in-the-World.pdf; USCIRF, "2019 Annual Report"; USCIRF, "2020 Annual Report."

[4] Interview, July 18, 2013.

[5] Paul Hirst, "Statism, Pluralism, and Social Control," *British Journal of Criminology*, Vol. 40, No. 2 (2000), 279–295. Paul Hirst, *From Statism to Pluralism* (London: UCL Press, 1997).

institutions. President Nasser's restrictive religious policies were one aspect of his attempt to control Egyptian society. Nasser asserted the right to appoint the Grand Sheikh of Al-Azhar, a respected religious institution founded in 972. The result was a loss of some of Al-Azhar's religious and institutional independence.[6] For decades, the government of Hosni Mubarak regulated and controlled many aspects of religious life, from the construction of religious places of worship to religious institutions. The government argued that regulation of aspects of religious life was necessary to prevent sectarian violence and extremism. The regime controlled Sunni mosques throughout the country by selecting the imams, monitoring their sermons, and paying their salaries.

The more that authoritarian rulers, such as Nasser, Mubarak, and el-Sisi, implement statist policies, the less room there is for freedom of religion or belief to exist in society.[7] President el-Sisi has not hidden his authoritarian tendencies or his desire to control Egyptian society. As noted by the Deputy Director for Research at the Project on Middle East Democracy:

> This is not run-of-the-mill Middle East authoritarianism. More and more, it appears that al-Sisi's state seeks to dominate all aspects of life, including the non-political and the private. Security agencies aim to control what Egyptians can watch, read and say online, and listen to, as well as where they can worship, travel, and live.[8]

El-Sisi maintained this inheritance and used it to further his legitimacy. One scholar explained, "the current instrumentalization of religion is employed as a buttress to state authority and legitimacy and in furtherance of the Egyptian regime's statist vision."[9]

---

[6] Bruce Rutherford, *Egypt After Mubarak* (Princeton, NJ: Princeton University Press, 2008). Nathan Brown and Michele Dunne, "Who Will Speak for Islam in Egypt—and Who Will Listen?" Carnegie Endowment for International Peace, June 7, 2021, https://carnegieendowment.org/2021/06/07/who-will-speak-for-islam-in-egypt-and-who-will-listen-pub-84654.

[7] Michael Wahid Hanna, "Public Order and Egypt's Statist Tradition," *The Review of Faith and International Affairs*, Vol. 13, No. 1 (2015), pp. 23–30. This is not to suggest that the Morsi administration promoted freedom of religion or belief for all Egyptians. Scott noted that Morsi and the Justice and Development Party continued many of these statist policies they inherited. Rachel Scott, "Managing Religion and Renegotiating the Secular: The Muslim Brotherhood and Defining the Religious Sphere," *Politics and Religion*, Vol. 7 (2014), pp. 51–78.

[8] Amy Hawthorne, Deputy Director for Research, Project on Middle East Democracy, "Hearing on Egypt: Trends in Politics, Economics, and Human Rights," Testimony before the Subcommittee on Middle East, North Africa, and International Terrorism, House of Representatives, September 9, 2020, Washington, D.C., https://docs.house.gov/Committee/Calendar/ByEvent.aspx?EventID=110989.

[9] Wahid Hanna, "Public Order," p. 25.

The results of these statist policies are discrimination in legislation and policies, as well as bureaucratic harassment. For Coptic Christians, who are estimated to make up approximately 10 percent of the population, the unwillingness of security forces to protect them from physical harm or protect their property is a form of discrimination and a denial of equality based on their faith. If a person's right to life is violated, other basic human rights become irrelevant. One Coptic Christian described the situation of his community: "In vain, the victimized Copts have sought the protection of the state, the laws, and the security forces and guarantees of their rights. But in every case, they found the state weak-kneed, the law frozen, and officials closing churches while they turn a blind eye to the crimes of other victimizers."[10]

Beyond specific policies and the lack of protection from government officials, discrimination is built into the legal system. Religious minorities, especially those who share some aspects of the Islamic faith (Shiites and Quranists, for example) but do not identify as Sunni, faced numerous legal and bureaucratic barriers due to their perceived heretical beliefs. The Baha'i faced problems in society because they have struggled to have their religious community recorded on government-issued identity cards. National identity cards record an individual's religious affiliation as either Muslim, Christian, or Jew. This leaves the Baha'is without any options that recognize their faith. Baha'is view Baha Allah (also spelled Bahā'ullāh) as a prophet, and this is inconsistent with the views of most Muslims who regard Muhammad as the last prophet. The inability to obtain an identity card creates problems when attempting to obtain other legal documents, including birth certificates and marriage licenses. Although the government indicated it would allow Baha'is to use a dash instead of one of the three recognized religions, many continued to report problems in obtaining these important documents.[11] Beyond obtaining identification cards, the government also discriminates against the Baha'i in the judicial system. Judicial rulings have denied the Baha'i equal legal status in Egypt.[12] Without official government recognition, the Baha'i have difficulty owning property and engaging in public forms of worship.

---

[10] Quoted in Mahmoud Farouk, Amy Hawthorne, and Ahmed Rizk, *Prayers Unanswered: Assessing the Impact of Egypt's 2016 Church Construction Law*, December 2018, Project on Middle East Democracy, https://pomed.org/wp-content/uploads/2018/12/CCL_Report_181212_FINAL.pdf.

[11] Cable from the American Embassy in Cairo to Secretary of State, "Egypt's Baha'i Frustrated with Lack of Progress on Identity Cards," August 3, 2009, Ref ID: 09CAIRO1495. Efforts by the US government to address this issue have not resulted in significant changes to date.

[12] Saba Mahmood and Peter Danchin, "Immunity or Regulation? Antinomies of Religious Freedom," *South Atlantic Quarterly*, Vol. 113, No. 1 (2014), pp. 129–159; Ishak Ibrahim, "Egypt's Officials Don't See Unrecognized Religious Minorities," The

We can also see discrimination and the denial of freedom of religion or belief for all Egyptians in the constitution that was created after a coup overthrew the government of President Morsi. The constitution approved in 2014 allows for some protections for freedom of religion but falls short of the protections articulated in Article 18 of the ICCPR. Egypt reserves the right to reject sections of the covenant if those sections conflict with sharia. Beyond reservations concerning religion, the Egyptian government has not felt bound by its legal obligations under the ICCPR. The constitution states that Islam is the religion of the state, and the principles of sharia are the main source for legislation in the country.[13] Article 2 of the constitution protects some citizens' right to practice their religion. Article 64 guarantees that freedom of belief is absolute in Egypt, while Article 65 codifies freedom of thought. On paper, Egyptians are free to believe according to their conscience. However, all citizens are not free to practice or engage in public activities related to their religious beliefs. That is reserved for Sunni Muslims, Christians, and Jews. The constitution is explicit in its discrimination and inequality.

One improvement in the 2014 constitution that *could* enhance aspects of religious freedom for some citizens is Article 235. This article required the government to develop legislation related to the building and renovation of places of worship. This could have positive consequences for Coptic Christians who have been waiting decades to renovate some churches if fully implemented.[14]

The much-anticipated Church Construction and Renovation Law (Law 80/2016) finalized in September 2016 has not lived up to its potential or fulfilled the needs of many Christian denominations in Egypt. Many Christian communities hoped the law would improve the process by which they could secure official permits to build new churches, obtain legal recognition for unlicensed churches, and repair property after years of obstruction by government officials. The law did establish a clear process by which a church could obtain official recognition and permission to renovate an existing building. This bureaucratic clarity is a step in the right direction.[15] However, these efforts

---

Tahrir Institute for Middle East Policy, June 2, 2021, https://timep.org/commentary/analysis/egypts-officials-dont-see-unrecognized-religious-minorities/.

[13] Egypt Constitution. The English translation of the 2014 constitution can be found at: https://www.constituteproject.org/constitution/Egypt_2014.pdf; State Department, *International Religious Freedom Report for 2020*.

[14] This has been a continuing problem over the last few decades. Over a hundred applications were submitted requesting approval to build new churches for the Coptic community in 2006. Often these applications were simply ignored by local officials. USCIRF, *International Religious Freedom Report for 2013*.

[15] Farouk, Hawthorne, and Rizk, *Prayers Unanswered*.

encountered further delays, with only 1638 permits receiving government approval out of the over 3700 applications submitted by 2020.[16] However, final approval has been limited to 200 church properties.[17] Some Protestant denominations also received permits. Copts continue to encounter bureaucratic delays and obstacles.

It is unlikely that this law will create new opportunities for Shiites in the country. Shiites experience difficulties due to their perceived heretical beliefs. For example, in 2015 the Religious Endowment Ministry prevented Shia followers from commemorating Ashura, the holiday that honors Hussain's death in Karbala during the 7th century, by closing the Imam Hussain Mosque. This was justified by the government as necessary to stop the dissemination of "Shia untruths" on this holiday.[18]

While the 2014 constitution does allow the Grand Sheikh of Al-Azhar to be selected by senior religious scholars (Article 7), the government continues to influence the finances of the organization. The Ministry of Religious Endowments provides content and guidelines for what can be disseminated at Friday prayers.[19]

In addition to inequality in the legal system and constitution, there is also discrimination in employment. Only a few religious minorities served in high-level political positions or in the foreign service. Samuel Tadros, an expert on Coptic issues in Egypt, explained that "there are sections of the Egyptian state that are closed to Copts."[20]

---

[16] Samuel Tadros, "Hearing on Egypt: Trends in Politics, Economics, and Human Rights," Testimony before the Subcommittee on Middle East, North Africa, and International Terrorism, House of Representatives, September 9, 2020, Washington, D.C., https://foreignaffairs.house.gov/hearings?ID=56A33A4A-8ACB-4D21-B321-A4AFC0118F98.

[17] USCIRF, *International Religious Freedom Report for 2020*.

[18] Mina Ibrahim, "Ashura: A Day in History of Discrimination against Egyptian Shi'as," *Daily News Egypt*, October 24, 2015, http://www.dailynewsegypt.com/2015/10/24/ashura-a-day-in-history-of-discrimination-against-egyptian-shias/.

[19] Efforts by the ministry to have government-written sermons read at Friday prayers were ineffective because of objections by Al-Azhar. Brown and Dunne, "Who Will Speak"; Georges Fahmi, "The Egyptian State and the Religious Sphere," Carnegie Middle East Center, September 18, 2014, https://carnegie-mec.org/2014/09/18/egyptian-state-and-religious-sphere-pub-56619.

[20] Samuel Tadros, IDC webinar, "Briefing on Egypt: Egypt Must Confront Christian Persecution," January 15, 2021, https://religionunplugged.com/news/2021/1/15/are-egypts-christians-persecuted-why-copts-say-no

Social Hostility

The absence of freedom of religion or belief is also seen in the interactions among citizens within a society. When individuals in society harass, insult, or attack others because of their membership in a community, the result is social intolerance and an inability to engage in deeply held religious beliefs or activities. Without a consistent message from the government, civil society, the media, and other elements of society that all Egyptians, regardless of their beliefs, ought to be tolerated and respected, the more expansive right to freedom of religion or belief will not develop in the long run.

Numerous religious minorities have experienced hostility from someone of a different faith. Violence directed at Coptic Christians and Shiites occurred repeatedly in the last 40 years. There were attacks against Coptic homes and churches in the early 1990s in various towns and cities (Imbala in 1991 and Asyut in 1994). Twenty-one Copts were killed in El Kosheh, a town to the south of Cairo, in 2000.[21] The perpetrators were cleared of any wrongdoing.[22] The attacks have continued in the years since the Egyptian revolution. Social hostility is evident in the destruction of unlicensed churches. Many Muslims do not want a church in their towns and villages.[23] Unfortunately, the security services failed to hold anyone accountable for these attacks. One scholar was highly critical of the lack of convictions of individuals who perpetrate violence against Christians.[24] Instead of punishing the perpetrators, local officials hold reconciliation meetings with limited results. Reconciliation sessions are not led by a neutral official. Pressure is often applied to Copts to forgo a criminal process in the judicial system. One human rights activist noted the failure of these reconciliation meetings and the spiral of impunity that resulted: "If after communal violence you use reconciliation meetings, you will not have accountability. And if there is no accountability you will have reoccurrence. Nothing happens if you are a Muslim who attacks someone else. They just have reconciliation meetings in Egypt."[25]

After the 2011 Egyptian revolution removed President Mubarak from power, the situation deteriorated. The number of attacks on Coptic Christians

---

[21] Samuel Tadros, *Motherland Lost: The Egyptian and Coptic Quest for Modernity* (Stanford, CA: Hoover Institution Press, 2013). Some sectarian violence between Coptic Christians and Muslims is motivated by an economic grievance or perceived insulting behavior. Attacks on Coptic Churches are related to religious difference and intolerance of a religious minority.

[22] Farouk, Hawthorne, and Rizk, *Prayers Unanswered.*

[23] Ibid.

[24] Tadros, IDC webinar.

[25] Interview, July 18, 2013.

increased from 45 in 2010 to 112 in 2012. The attack in October 2011 on Copts at the Mary Girgis Church concluded with a reconciliation meeting and no accountability for the attackers.[26] Security forces did not intervene when the Cathedral of Saint Mark in Cairo was attacked in 2013. These repeated attacks without any accountability or an appropriate response from the government leaves Coptic Christians in fear, with little hope of long-term security. One Coptic from Fanous expressed his impotence and anxiety when a Coptic building was destroyed:

> Although we recognized the village youths who participated in the demolition work, we could not name any of them as we are a minority living in the village and we do not want to have problems because we fear for the safety of our children. We go away to work in Cairo, leaving our families behind in the village. I believe that as Copts we are destined to be always persecuted.[27]

In the months following the coup that imprisoned President Morsi, some Egyptians took revenge on Copts. Pope Tawadros II was one of a coalition of leaders that defended the military coup that removed President Morsi and the Muslim Brotherhood from office.[28] For some supporters of the Muslim Brotherhood, Coptic Patriarch Tawadros II's decision to support General el-Sisi was intolerable.[29] Hundreds of Coptic homes and schools were burned in August 2013.[30]

The Shia minority also experienced violence in Egypt. Shia Islam is portrayed in the media and by Al-Azhar as ideas that should not be allowed to spread in the country. Four Shiites, including Sheikh Hassan Shehata, were killed in June 2013 when a mob descended on them in the village of Zawyat

---

[26] Cairo Institute for Human Rights Studies, "Islamist Groups Must Stop Inciting to Sectarian Violence; Protection of Christians Responsibility of the State," August 7, 2013.

[27] Mary Abdelmassih, "Muslims Demolish Church Building in Egypt," *Assyrian International News Agency*, January 16, 2013.

[28] Farouk, Hawthorne, and Rizk, *Prayers Unanswered*; Al Arabiya, "Egypt's Coptic Church Announces Support for Army, Police," August 17, 2013, http://english.alarabiya.net/en/News/middle-east/2013/08/17/Egypt-s-Coptic-Church-announces-support-for-army-police.html.

[29] Mariz Tadros, "Vicissitudes in the Entente between the Coptic Orthodox Church and the State of Egypt," *International Journal of Middle East Studies*, Vol. 41, No. 2 (2009), pp. 269–87; Sanaa Hassan, *Christians versus Muslims in Egypt: The Century-Long Struggle for Coptic Equality* (Oxford: Oxford University Press, 2003).

[30] Dr. M. Jasser, Testimony before the Committee on Foreign Affairs, Subcommittee on Africa, Global Health, Global Human Rights and International Organizations, House of Representatives, December 10, 2013, Washington, D.C.

Abu Musalam. The victims were referred to as infidels.[31] The security forces in the area again refused to intervene and help the Shiites during the attack.

Egyptians' Views

That many Egyptians would attack members of a different belief community should not surprise us given some public opinion polls over the years. Polls conducted over the last decade indicate that a proportion of the Egyptian population does not believe in freedom of religion or belief for everyone, and the public is aware that not all Egyptians are free to follow their faith. Further, 46 percent of Egyptians articulated the view that they are free to practice their religion, while only 31 percent believe that non-Muslims are free to practice their faith. Approximately one-fifth of those polled (18 percent) stated that non-Muslims were not too free or not free at all to practice their religion.[32] More troubling is the fact that two-thirds of those who indicated that non-Muslims were not free to practice their faith do not view this denial of freedom of religion as a problem.[33] In the same survey, the vast majority of those polled (88 percent) believed that someone who left the Muslim faith deserved the death penalty. In another poll conducted by Gallup in 2012, 25 percent of Egyptians did not agree that all individuals should be able to freely observe and practice a religion of their choice.[34] These polls suggest an awareness that freedom of religion or belief is not a protected right for all Egyptians. Thus, we should not be surprised by the violent attacks or the fear experienced by minorities in Egypt. That some Egyptians do not feel safe is also troubling. In one poll, 90 percent of Christians indicated that they were not satisfied that the government would keep them safe.[35] This demonstrates a religious minority that is aware

---

[31] Egyptian Initiative for Personal Rights, Press Release, "A Report on the 'Shiite Massacre' in the Abu Muslim Corner in Giza," June 26, 2013, http://eipr.org/pressrelease/2013/06/26/1750; Amnesty International, "Egypt: President Morsi Must Send a Clear Message Against Attacks on Shia Muslims," June 24, 2013, https://www.amnesty.org/en/latest/news/2013/06/egypt-president-morsi-must-send-clear-message-against-attacks-on-shia-muslims/; Human Rights Watch, "Egypt: Lynching of Shia Follows Months of Hate Speech," June 27, 2013.

[32] Neha Sahgal and Brian Grim, "Egypt's Restrictions on Religion Coincide with Lack of Religious Tolerance," Pew Research Center, July 2, 2013, http://www.pewresearch.org/fact-tank/2013/07/02/egypts-restrictions-on-religion-coincide-with-lack-of-religious-tolerance/.

[33] Ibid.

[34] Muasher, p. 67.

[35] Zogby Research Service, "After Tahrir: Egyptians Assess their Government, their Institutions, and their Future," June 2013, http://static.squarespace.com/static/52750dd3e4b08c252c723404/t/52928b8de4b070ad8eec181e/1385335693242/Egypt%20June%202013%20FINAL.pdf.

of the violence that occurs in their towns and villages. At a minimum, Egypt needs to develop citizens with tolerant dispositions toward other members of society if progress is to be made on freedom of religion or belief.

THE BENEFITS OF A TOLERANT LEADER: CAN EL-SISI RISE TO THE OCCASION?

Abdel Fattah el-Sisi, who assumed power after initiating a coup against a democratically elected president, is far from a liberal democrat with a history of protecting human rights. As we discussed in Chapter 2, authoritarian political leaders, with no commitment to democracy, have initiated policies to promote religious tolerance in their societies. As previously noted, the goals of economic prosperity or stability motivated these authoritarian leaders. These instrumental motivations worked in the past and could be deployed to encourage el-Sisi to adopt new policies to put Egypt on the road, first, to greater tolerance, and then to religious freedom. Instrumental arguments ought to be offered. One US official indicated that "Egypt is a country that very, very deeply cares about its image. I have seen the Egyptian government make incremental shifts because they see it as playing a part in its improved international image."[36] Even minimal efforts, such as promoting respectful attitudes toward all religious minorities and confronting hatred and religiously inspired violence, would benefit Egyptian society.

The Egyptian government can play a positive role in encouraging religious tolerance and laying the foundation for freedom of religion or belief. A society that protects all aspects of Article 18 of the ICCPR will ensure that a community can meet in public and peacefully assemble to carry out various rituals and activities. The government must not only allow individuals to rent or own buildings for these activities, it must also provide security for them if there are hostile or violent individuals and organizations in society that seek to do them harm. El-Sisi has provided more security to Coptic Churches over the last few years in response to attacks on Coptic houses of worship in Cairo (2016) and Alexandria (2017).[37] Other religious minorities must protect themselves.

---

[36] Interview, July 15, 2021.

[37] Walsh and Youseff, "Gunmen Attack." The effectiveness of these additional security measures remains to be seen. According to the Tahrir Institute for Middle East Policy, "Religious freedom remains severely restricted throughout Egypt, where citizens are not free to believe or not believe, nor are they are able to practice their beliefs as they see fit. Although the Constitution of 2014 provides an absolute right to belief, it limits the practice to Abrahamic religions, and legal and social structures further restrict the free exercise of religion." These concerns have been echoed by others including

President el-Sisi initiated some positive, albeit limited, steps toward religious tolerance for Coptic Christians.[38] More needs to be done for other religious minorities and those Egyptians without religious commitments. The president made symbolic gestures toward Coptic Christians. He visited a Coptic Church for Christmas mass in January 2015 and again in 2021. At the services in 2015, el-Sisi decried the religious tensions between Christians and Muslims and added, "it is not right to call each other anything but Egyptians. We must only be Egyptians."[39] This inclusive discourse, noticed by American officials, is a welcome change from his predecessors. One USCIRF official noted, "Sisi has always spoken positively about Copts," and "his rhetoric has been very positive."[40] Another official explained that these symbolic actions were "especially important coming from the president himself."[41] The president also appointed two Coptic Christians to be governor of the Damietta Governorate (Dr. Manal Awad Mikhael) and Dagahleya Governorate (Dr. Gamal Gad Saad).[42] These modest changes are welcome, but far more needs to be done, as noted by USCIRF Commissioner Maenza: "Egypt still has a way to go to truly establish religious freedom in the country," as "systematic and ongoing discrimination of Coptic Christians" and smaller Muslim communities continues.[43]

Beyond small gestures, the president must ensure that laws and government policies do not discriminate against people of certain faiths or those with no religious affiliation. Given the authoritarian nature of the regime and the expansive powers of the president, el-Sisi could implement policy changes that would lead to greater protection of freedom of religion or belief. Regardless of

---

NGOs and Western governments. For more information, see Tahrir Institute for Middle East Policy, "A Fragile Egypt."

[38] One US official who has been focused on Egypt for decades told me that he believed el-Sisi has "a little bit more of a personal tolerance for the Coptic community, certainly more than Mubarak." Interview, July 15, 2021.

[39] David Kirkpatrick and Merna Thomas, "Egyptian Leader Visits Coptic Christmas Eve Service," *New York Times*, January 6, 2015, https://www.nytimes.com/2015/01/07/world/middleeast/egyptian-leader-visits-coptic-christmas-eve-service.html.

[40] Kurt Werthmuller, Webinar, "Are Egypt's Christians Persecuted? Why Some Copts Say No," January 15, 2021, https://religionunplugged.com/news/2021/1/15/are-egypts-christians-persecuted-why-copts-say-no. In a June 2020 cabinet meeting, the president urged "giving the highest priority to spreading awareness among students of the principles of all religions, including freedom of belief, tolerance and acceptance of difference." State Department, *International Religious Freedom Report for 2020*.

[41] Nadia Maenza, USCIRF commissioner; see Werthmuller, "Are Egypt's Christians Persecuted?"

[42] See House Resolution 49, "Supporting Coptic Christians in Egypt," January 16, 2019.

[43] Werthmuller, January 15, 2021.

one's faith or beliefs, the legal system should not create barriers, bureaucratic nuisance, or hardships for individuals.[44] Unfortunately, this is the case for atheists, Shiites, Baha'i, and others who do not belong to the Sunni majority. The president should institute a policy removing religious identification from identity cards. He should also prevent the use of reconciliation sessions that do not result in just outcomes and further the cycle of impunity. El-Sisi should instruct the judiciary to hold perpetrators accountable. This has been suggested by numerous American policy makers and human rights advocates.[45]

To see genuine respect for all aspects of freedom of religion or belief, significant judicial reforms that strengthen the rule of law are necessary. The reform and retraining of the security forces with an emphasis on respect for all citizens is also needed. Beyond passing laws, the government must also develop mechanisms for individuals to report a denial of religious freedom and have that complaint addressed. A complaint can be addressed by the judiciary in a courtroom. A legal process allows an individual or community of believers the ability to sue the government if laws or government institutions discriminate based on religious beliefs. It also allows businesses or organizations in society to be sued for discrimination. Thus, the courts, by respecting the rule of law, can help protect this fundamental right.

These long-term institutional reforms would ensure that this human right and other fundamental freedoms are protected throughout society. Since el-Sisi assumed power over the political system, there has been little evidence that he intends to move in a more democratic and rights-protective direction. This does not preclude progress on promoting religious tolerance for all Egyptians or laying the foundation for greater protection of freedom of religion and belief over time. Minimizing violence and prosecuting the perpetrators of violence while using inclusive and tolerant language for all individuals will not threaten el-Sisi's hold on power. These steps could also enhance his international reputation. As one US official noted, "Egypt loves that, they like being acknowledged for those positive things."[46] Over time, as the security and economic situations improve in the country, el-Sisi may take further steps along the road to religious freedom. This would not result in a democratic political system. Nor would it address other human rights violations, such as politically motivated detentions or executions. But it would still be progress in this authoritarian political environment and improve the lives of millions of Egyptians.

---

[44] Bielefeldt and Wiener (p. 54) refer to this as religious infrastructure.

[45] See House Resolution 49.

[46] Interview, July 15, 2021.

EDUCATION REFORM

Egypt's education system is both part of the problem that contributes to intolerance in society and a potential means to improve the environment if reforms are undertaken and consistently supported. As noted in Chapter 5, when schools teach children to hate and denigrate those with different beliefs, the consequences are detrimental to various communities. Conversely, we also noted that teaching children the values of tolerance and respect for religious pluralism can have a positive impact on a society. The lessons that students are taught in the classroom can contribute to the level of tolerance in a country.[47] Classrooms, and the messages promoted in classrooms, can have a lasting effect on students, contributing to their social and political views.

Unfortunately, children in Egypt received an intolerant message about non-Sunni Muslims for decades. Anti-Semitism was part of the curriculum, and Coptic Christians were often absent from lesson plans despite their being a significant portion of the population. Various textbooks contained anti-Semitic messages.[48] Some textbooks taught that Judaism and Christianity were deficient, or that non-Muslims are going to hell.[49] An eighth-grade textbook taught children that, "Whoever desires other than Islam as religion—never will it be accepted from him, and he in the hereafter will be among the losers."[50]

Simply removing the negative depictions of minority religious traditions in Egypt is not enough for a religiously tolerant society to develop there. Incorporating positive descriptions and accurate information about religious minorities also needs to be a part of the Egyptian education system. Egyptian students, regardless of their faith, will learn about Islam and the Qur'an from their Arabic classes. A human rights activist who is a Coptic Christian described his educational experiences and the absence of information on Christianity or other faiths: "I had to learn about Muslims and Islam, but Muslims had no real knowledge of Christians."[51] Without discussing other

---

[47] Fatima Al Sadi and Tehmina Basit, "Religious Tolerance in Oman: Addressing Religious Prejudice through Educational Intervention," *British Educational Research Journal*, Vol. 39, No. 3 (2013), pp. 447–72.

[48] Jasser, "Testimony."

[49] Arnon Groiss, "Jews, Christians, War and Peace in Egyptian School Textbooks," 2004, http://www.impact-se.org/docs/reports/Egypt/EgyptMarch2004.pdf; Yohanan Manor, "Inculcating Islamist Ideals in Egypt," *Middle East Quarterly* (Fall 2015), https://www.meforum.org/5480/inculcating-islamist-ideals-in-egypt.

[50] Muasher, p. 135.

[51] Interview, October 11, 2013.

religious communities beyond stating that they are losers and mistaken in their views, it is difficult to see how tolerant attitudes can take hold.[52]

Egypt's public education system is underfunded and often denies its young people a quality education or the knowledge and skills needed in the 21st century. This does not excuse the intolerant messages that students are taught that could contribute to social hostility or violence in the future. In addition to a greater emphasis on critical thinking and contemporary skills to contribute to the growth of the economy, the government also needs to encourage "education policies that promote pluralism, tolerance, [and] respect for different points of view."[53] This requires curriculum reform and retraining educators. The Minister of Education, Tarek Shawky, has taken steps to revise textbooks and "remove sectarian language and encourage respect."[54] Some changes have been implemented. A ninth-grade geography textbook incorporates more tolerant language concerning Israel and is part of some additional, albeit limited, reforms in religious texts to encourage tolerance and remove passages that could be used to promote violence and extremism.[55] A 12th-grade textbook on Islam discusses acceptance of the Other, as well as fair treatment of the People of the Book.[56] More reforms are needed, and sustaining these efforts is key to a more tolerant future.

Reforming the curriculum would involve removing intolerant context and incorporating materials that promote respect for religious diversity and religious pluralism. Teaching young Egyptians about the different belief systems within the country and throughout the world in history classes and incorporating positive depictions of religious minorities in various courses would demonstrate the value and dignity of others.[57] In addition, many educators will need to be provided with additional training and materials to prevent hateful messages from being disseminated by teachers with personal bias toward reli-

---

[52] One human rights activist indicated that, for Egyptians, the Baha'is and Shiites simply "do not exist at all." He went on to explain that there was only one Christian character in his textbooks. Interview, October 11, 2013.

[53] Muasher, p. 179.

[54] Werthmuller, January 15, 2021.

[55] Ofir Winter, "Egypt Enhances its Peace Education, One Step at a Time," An Impact Brief, March 2016, https://www.impact-se.org/wp-content/uploads/Egypt-Report-Ofir-Winter.pdf.

[56] David Andrew Weinberg, "Egyptian Textbooks Send Mixed Messages about Jews," ADL, June 22, 2021, https://www.adl.org/blog/egyptian-textbooks-send-mixed-messages-about-jews.

[57] There are various ways that positive depictions of religious minorities can be incorporated throughout the curriculum. Lesson plans to develop reading comprehension can incorporate positive stories about an individual of a religious minority. These discussions do not have to be limited to history classes.

gious minorities. If these educational reforms are consistently implemented, this would start the process of educating Egyptians to better comprehend other citizens (Coptic Christians, Shiites, Baha'i) in their society and would help to combat the intolerance and social hostility within the society. This step is necessary to eventually see religious freedom develop in the country.

Reforming the education system and the development of tolerant attitudes will take time, but it could have generational benefits. If norms of tolerance and the value of religious pluralism are cultivated in various classrooms across Egypt, this would result in a decrease in social hostility. If young people are taught to tolerate and respect the religious (and non-religious) Other in schools, members of these minority groups can become citizens who have a place in the public sphere. This would lessen the need for security forces to patrol religious spaces or deal with religiously motivated violence against minorities. However, this is not the only domestic social institution that could help promote tolerant views and values. Civil society actors can also contribute to these changes.

US FOREIGN POLICY

Washington, and other states, should use various elements in their foreign policy tool kit (diplomacy, economic incentives, military relationships) to encourage the government to advance religious freedom throughout Egyptian society. Given the difficult environment in Egypt, instrumental arguments should be deployed to start nudging el-Sisi to start the process of reforming political institutions, but the United States must also stress the inherent value of this fundamental human right. At a minimum, Washington cannot ignore or downplay flagrant human rights violations.[58] Presidential statements and Congressional resolutions on the importance of human rights and freedom of religion or belief not only affirm American support for these values, but also demonstrate solidarity with those individuals who are on the front lines fighting for their fundamental rights.

Washington used public and private diplomacy to prod Egypt to improve its protection of this right. The President, State Department, the USCIRF, as well as some members of Congress publicly criticized Egypt's government for its unwillingness to ensure freedom of religion or belief for all Egyptians. During Barack Obama's time in office, various members of the executive branch noted their concerns about violence directed at religious minorities and the denial of

---

[58] One activist with the Cairo Institute for Human Rights told me, "Only one demand to stop false public statements by senior officials on Egypt's human rights record." Interview, April 2, 2010.

human rights. President Obama condemned the attacks on Coptic Christians in the aftermath of the coup that removed President Morsi from office:

> We call on the Egyptian authorities to respect the universal rights of the people. We call on those who are protesting to do so peacefully and condemn the attacks that we've seen by protesters, including on churches. We believe that the state of emergency should be lifted, that a process of national reconciliation should begin, that all parties need to have a voice in Egypt's future, that the rights of women and religious minorities should be respected, and that commitments must be kept to pursue transparent reforms of the constitution and democratic elections of a parliament and a President.[59]

The State Department's annual report on religious freedom did not gloss over or ignore the discrimination and intolerance in the country. One report noted: "Senior U.S. officials, including President Barack Obama, raised deep U.S. concerns about increased religious violence and discrimination against Copts with senior Egyptian officials, including concerns about the government's failure to prosecute perpetrators of sectarian violence."[60] Comments such as these can be found in each report over the last 15 years. Further, various officials criticized the unjust detention of individuals, including religious minorities such as Ramy Kamel.[61] The Assistant Secretary for the Bureau of Democracy, Human Rights, and Labor visited Cairo and stated:

> I did meet with a range of religious leaders both Christians and Muslims, and will continue to do that. I think it's important that we do whatever we can to encourage harmony and tolerance and the ability of every person to have the freedom to practice their faith. Our job is not to prefer one religion over another; our role is to promote religious freedom, which means that every individual should pursue their faith.[62]

---

[59] Office of the Press Secretary, "Remarks by the President on the Situation in Egypt," August 15, 2013, https://obamawhitehouse.archives.gov/the-press-office/2013/08/15/remarks-president-situation-egypt.

[60] State Department, *International Religious Freedom Report for 2011*.

[61] USCIRF Commissioner Nadine Maenza said, "USCIRF implores the Egyptian government to immediately release Mr. Kamel and dismiss all charges against him, after more than a year of unjust pre-trial detention. His lifelong commitment to highlighting the Coptic Church community's struggle to attain full religious freedom and other rights as equal citizens of Egypt makes the situation even more troubling." Press Release, "USCIRF Calls for Release of Ramy Kamel," December 30, 2020.

[62] Michael Posner, Press Roundtable at the US Embassy in Cairo, October 9, 2010.

One State Department official told me that "in every conversation we have with Egyptian leaders we bring up the need for freedom of religion for all Egyptians."[63]

Unfortunately, despite the various public and private messages, there have been few improvements in Egypt. There is little indication that Egyptian policy makers are addressing all of Washington's concerns about religious freedom. Moreover, some government officials have complained about Washington's interference in domestic affairs. The foreign ministry rebuked the criticisms of one International Religious Freedom Report, saying that "interference by foreign parties in matters that only concern the domestic sphere is unacceptable."[64]

American pressure has not had a discernable impact on el-Sisi. President Trump was not critical of the Egyptian President and did not put much emphasis on human rights. His rhetorical comments about the importance of religious liberty, often for domestic electoral purposes, did not extend to el-Sisi. Furthermore, the Egyptian government often played a mediating role between Israel and Hamas, as it did in the military confrontation in May 2021. The Egyptian president may believe some limited improvements for the Coptic Christian community and his rhetoric encouraging a moderate Islam will buy him enough goodwill with American policy makers to stem calls for more significant reforms.

Despite the limited results thus far, Washington should leverage its bilateral assistance to the promotion of human rights and freedom of religion or belief in Egypt. Washington could reduce some military assistance to Cairo to encourage more attention to this right. Even a 15 percent or 20 percent reduction could force the Egyptian government to reform some of its policies. Various international human rights organizations, including Amnesty International, the Cairo Institute for Human Rights Studies, and POMED, called for a decrease in foreign military financing and expressed their dismay that President Biden maintained the same level of financial assistance to the Egyptian government in the budget request for FY 2022.[65] Some religious minorities also sug-

[63] Interview, December 2012, Washington, D.C.

[64] US Embassy Cable, "Egypt Reacts to 2008 Religious Freedom Report," 08CAIRO2135_a, September 30, 2008, https://search.wikileaks.org/plusd/cables/08CAIRO2135_a.html.

[65] Statement by Amnesty International, Cairo Institute for Human Rights Studies, The Freedom Initiative, Human Rights Watch, and the Project on Middle East Democracy, May 28, 2021. This statement can be found at: https://pomed.org/wp-content/uploads/2021/05/Statement-on-FY22-Egypt-Request.pdf.

gested "thinking about sanctions" and aid conditionality.[66] Limiting access to International Monetary Fund loans is also possible. Individual judges or policy makers who discriminate against religious minorities or atheists can be targeted under the Magnitsky Act, limiting their ability to travel or engage in financial transactions. At a minimum, it would signal to Cairo that the status quo of discrimination, violence, and impunity by reconciliation sessions and unjust judicial decisions will have consequences.

This will not guarantee results overnight. The Obama administration cut some assistance to Egypt in the aftermath of the coup in 2013. The spokesperson for the State Department explained that the Obama administration would "hold the delivery of certain large-scale military systems and cash assistance to the government pending credible progress towards an inclusive, democratically elected civilian government through free and fair elections."[67] This did not alter el-Sisi's authoritarian impulses or policies since his goal was to maintain power. Attempts to encourage change on issues that do not threaten President el-Sisi's hold on power could see greater results. However, consistently decreasing foreign assistance will have an impact over time, especially for an economy as weak as the one in Egypt.

The United States can also reward el-Sisi if he makes significant changes, including reforming some laws and policies, which result in greater protection of freedom of religion or belief. Additional access to bilateral financial assistance or loans from the World Bank could provide a positive incentive to continue to address this issue. Washington can also develop programs to help encourage religious tolerance throughout society. The American embassy in Cairo can host roundtable discussions, lectures, and community-building activities where religious leaders and NGO activists can interact and communicate community needs. Washington can also provide grants to organizations throughout Egypt who are developing activities aimed at furthering tolerance.[68] When a more tolerant environment is established in the country, more attention should be directed toward the protection of freedom of religion or belief as articulated in Article 18 of the ICCPR.

Washington can encourage education reform by developing materials, in conjunction with Egyptian educators, that promote tolerance and respect for

---

[66] Sherif Mansour, a Quranist, articulated this in a discussion with USCIRF. "Quranists in Egypt," July 23, 2021. This USCIRF podcast can be found at https://www.uscirf.gov/news-room/uscirf-spotlight/quranists-egypt.

[67] Jen Psaki, State Department Press Release, October 9, 2013.

[68] Government Affairs Office (GAO), "International Religious Freedom Act: State Department and Commission Are Implementing Responsibilities but Need to Improve Interaction," GAO Report 13-196, March 26, 2013, https://www.gao.gov/products/gao-13-196.

all citizens, regardless of their beliefs. This should include revising textbooks and lesson plans to ensure that negative stereotypes about religious minorities are removed. USAID has provided aid for a variety of educational programs. For example, between 2017 and 2024, USAID estimates it will provide over $75 million to fund STEM programs, early-grade learning, and teacher training programs in Egypt.[69] Some of this funding could be used to incorporate religious tolerance in lessons and to train Egyptian teachers about freedom of religion or belief.

Outside of the classroom, Washington can help children to develop religious tolerance through educational programs and activities. USAID provided funding for the television program Alam SimSim. This is an indigenous version of Sesame Street. One goal was to "increase female participation in quality basic education" to promote gender equality in Egypt. To accomplish this goal, a group of educational experts, Egyptian television producers, and advisors from Sesame Street came together to develop programming where girls were depicted in a positive manner and boys and girls engaged in activities on an equal footing.[70] More than 85 percent of the population reported that their children watched the program.[71] Washington can also fund television programs that depict Coptic Christians, Shiites, Jews, Baha'is, and other religious minorities in a positive and respectful manner. This would be an additional step toward combating the negative stereotyping of religious minorities in society.

American bilateral programmatic diplomacy need not be limited to the field of education. Washington can and should provide technical and financial assistance to reform the judicial system and police forces. When the police or security forces refuse to respond to instances of religiously motivated violence, or when a judge does not uphold the rights established in laws and the constitution for all religious individuals, this results in religious discrimination and a denial of freedom of religion or belief. The United States frequently brings military officers from other countries to train with American soldiers. These programs should be expanded to include other institutions. The Egyptian police and security forces are poorly trained and have committed numerous human rights violations over the years. Efforts to reform the security forces by offering training modules on international norms, protection of minorities, and appropriate crowd dispersal techniques could go a long way toward restoring faith in law and order for minorities in society. Washington can train Egyptian

---

[69] USAID, "Basic Education Fact Sheet," July 2020, https://www.usaid.gov/sites/default/files/documents/USAIDEgypt_Education-Basic_Fact_Sheet_2020_EN.pdf.

[70] Final Report, Alam SimSim, http://pdf.usaid.gov/pdf_docs/PDACA924.pdf.

[71] Ibid.

judges in Article 18, the rule of law, and equal protection. This will not happen overnight, but it could contribute to stability in the long term.

Washington should strengthen aspects of civil society by offering grants to NGOs and religious organizations that develop activities related to religious freedom. It can also help media organizations to learn about religious pluralism and ensure that programs from various media outlets are sending a tolerant message throughout their shows and articles. The United States should help with training programs to ensure that television anchors are not only using tolerant language, but that negative depictions of religious minorities are removed from broadcasts. This is also true of religious institutions at the grassroots level.

INTERNATIONAL EFFORTS

The international community must apply more pressure and push the Egyptian government to uphold this basic right. Egypt ratified the ICCPR and is therefore legally required to uphold Article 18. The UN, EU, and other international actors can remind the government of its international obligations. There is no pressure from other countries in the Middle East to promote freedom of religion or belief. This is not surprising, as countries such as Saudi Arabia violate this basic right. Therefore, a consistent message from IGOs, such as the UN, EU, and other states who are part of the International Religious Freedom Alliance, is critical to convincing Egypt to protect this fundamental right.

At a minimum, when religiously motivated violence occurs, the international community should speak forcefully against it. Catherine Ashton, the former EU Foreign Policy Minister, stated that the Egyptian government should address the sectarian violence:

> I strongly condemn the attack which led to several deaths and injuries during a Coptic wedding on Sunday… I call on the Egyptian authorities to ensure that the perpetrators of this unacceptable act are promptly brought to justice. States have an obligation to do everything in their power to prevent acts of violence against persons based on their religion or belief.[72]

States have used the UN Human Rights Council to urge Cairo to do more to address freedom of religion or belief in the country. During Egypt's Universal Periodic Review in 2010, several states noted their concerns about Coptic

---

[72] Ahram Online, "EU condemns Egypt church violence, urges end to religion-based attacks." October 22, 2013. https://english.ahram.org.eg/News/84468.aspx

Christians, religious intolerance, and the difficulties associated with having one's religion on identity cards.[73]

Furthermore, there should be consequences if the government fails to address these violations. The EU and other IGOs, such as the International Monetary Fund, can limit financial assistance to Egypt if it is unwilling to address religious intolerance and discrimination against religious minorities. The EU can advise Cairo that it will discourage the citizens in member states from traveling to Egypt as tourists or investing in Egypt, which would decrease the foreign currency coming into the country. This is needed to help finance government services and national projects. President el-Sisi does not need further economic problems that could provoke protests or instability. Economic conditions deteriorated in the first few years of his administration. Youth unemployment and poverty increased.[74] COVID-19 contributed to these economic problems as well as the collapse of tourism in 2020.

The EU, UN, and those states that are part of the International Religious Freedom Alliance discussed in Chapter 3 need to present a consistent message to the Egyptian government that religious intolerance, if ignored, will have consequences. One Egyptian NGO activist forced into exile explained that, without an international response, more human rights violations will occur.[75]

Various actors in the international community can encourage el-Sisi and the Egyptian government to promote this fundamental human right in terms of their self-interest. Violence and discrimination are detrimental to economic growth. Violence and instability can limit foreign investment from multinational corporations. Violence and instability also have a detrimental impact on tourism and the revenue that tourists bring to the country. Egyptian citizens, if they are the target of attacks and property destruction, may decide to emigrate from the country. If religious minorities do not feel safe, they can take their skills and wealth out of the county. Over 90 000 Copts left Egypt in the four

---

[73] UN Human Rights Council, 2010, A/HRC/14/17. The states expressing these concerns were Austria, Canada, Chile, Finland, Germany, and the United States.

[74] Brown and Dunne, "Who Will Speak."

[75] "However, if there is no sustained push back from the international community against this unjust sentence, then many other Egyptian human rights defenders and pro-democracy critics of the government will be subjected to similar treatment." Bahey eldin Hassan, Director of the Cairo Institute for Human Rights Studies, "Hearing on Egypt: Trends in Politics, Economics, and Human Rights," Testimony before the Subcommittee on Middle East, North Africa, and International Terrorism, House of Representatives, September 9, 2020, Washington, D.C., https://docs.house.gov/Committee/Calendar/ByEvent.aspx?EventID=110989.

years after the revolution (2011–2015).[76] This is not in the self-interest of the president or the government.

CIVIL SOCIETY

Civil society, if allowed to operate freely in Egypt, can contribute to an inclusive, tolerant, and religiously free society. A broad range of actors within civil society, if they promote a narrative of the value of religious pluralism and respect for the religious (or non-religious) Other, can help to move Egyptian society on the path to freedom of religion or belief within local communities. Grassroots efforts from NGOs,[77] human rights activists, religious institutions, and media organizations can have a positive impact, especially when combined with state and international efforts. Local actors within civil society often have legitimacy due to their previous work in the community and their knowledge of the local environment. This is especially true of religious organizations. Given their long history in the community, resources, and support from their followers, they have a legitimacy that outsiders or foreign NGOs lack. They can monitor the situation of this human right, lobby policy makers to protect this right, convene interfaith dialogues, educate citizens, and dispel inaccurate information. They can denounce violence and visit the victims of violence. And perhaps most importantly, they can voice a simple message of the fundamental dignity and rights of all individuals. When these themes are repeated over and over, they will take hold in a society.

Various organizations and individuals in Egypt engaged in efforts to promote religious tolerance. Two NGOs, Beit el-Aela el-Misruyah and the Coptic Evangelical Organization for Social Services, developed interfaith dialogue programs. They repaired damage done to places of worship from violence or normal wear and tear.[78]

---

[76] Yohanan Manor, "Inculcating Islamist Ideals in Egypt," *Middle East Quarterly*, (Fall 2015), https://www.meforum.org/5480/inculcating-islamist-ideals-in-egypt.

[77] El-Sisi has engaged in a harsh crackdown on independent NGOs, arresting individuals associated with human rights organizations. The NGO law passed in 2019 did not dramatically improve the situation. Some have argued that it is worse than the previous restrictive NGO law. POMED, "Fact Sheet – Egypt's 'New' NGO Law: As Draconian as the Old One," September 23, 2019, https://pomed.org/fact-sheet-egypts-new-ngo-law-as-draconian-as-the-old-one/.

[78] In Chapter 6, Makari discusses efforts by NGOs to promote reconciliation between Christians and Muslims as well as new efforts at conflict resolution and conflict prevention. Peter Makari, *Conflict and Cooperation: Christian–Muslim Relations in Contemporary Egypt* (Syracuse, NY: Syracuse University Press, 2007). See also Eurasia Review, "Egyptians Unite to Repair Houses of Worship," 2013, https://www.eurasiareview.com/24112013-egyptians-unite-to-repair-houses-of-worship/.

A religious institution with a long history and legitimacy in Egypt and in the Muslim world is Al-Azhar. Al-Azhar developed initiatives and activities to promote religious tolerance for some in Egypt. They have engaged with Muslims and Coptic Christians in different towns in Egypt in an effort to reduce tensions and violence.[79] One initiative is the Family Home. This initiative promotes a narrative that focuses on the multi-denominational nature of Egyptian society. By arguing that different-faith communities are part of a shared public space in Egypt, it is offering an inclusive message to citizens throughout society.

The Grand Sheik of Al-Azhar, Dr. Ahmed El-Tayyeb, repeatedly offered a message of tolerance and the need for freedom of belief, which he explained is guaranteed in Islam. He signed the Document on Human Fraternity for World Peace and Living Together with Pope Francis and other religious leaders in 2019.[80] The ideas contained in this interfaith dialogue are disseminated in textbooks used in Al-Azhar schools throughout the country.[81] Further, he stated:

> Accordingly, any aspect of compulsion, persecution, or discrimination on the basis of religion is prohibited. Everybody in society has the right to embrace any ideas he chooses, without encroaching upon the right of society to the maintenance of divine faiths, in light of sanctity accorded to all the three Abrahamic faiths; so, everyone is free to perform his rituals, and none should hurt the other's feelings or violate the sanctity of his rites whether by words or deeds, and without breaching the public order.[82]

This is not limited to religious institutions. He noted the role that the media can play in promoting tolerance:

> We appeal to those working in the field of religious, cultural, and political rhetoric over the media to pay attention to this important dimension in their practices and to seek a wise approach that helps form a public opinion marked by tolerance, broad-mindedness, resort to dialogue, and rejection of fanaticism.[83]

---

[79] US State Department, *International Religious Freedom Report for 2011*.

[80] See https://www.vatican.va/content/francesco/en/travels/2019/outside/documents/papa-francesco_20190204_documento-fratellanza-umana.html.

[81] State Department, *International Religious Freedom Report for 2020*. Further, a ninth-grade Azhari textbook on Islamic culture discusses the fundamental value of interfaith tolerance in Islam. See Weinberg, "Egyptian Textbooks."

[82] Ahmed Tayyeb, "Al-Azhar Document," 2012, http://danutm.files.wordpress.com/2012/04/al-azhar-document-for-basic-freedoms.pdf.

[83] Ibid.

There are aspects of the Al-Azhar document that are valuable. It clearly rejects violence and hostility toward members of Abrahamic faiths. This is a step toward greater tolerance in Egyptian society. However, this tolerant message does not extend to Shiites, Baha'is, and other religious minorities. Al-Azhar attempted to "counter atheism" and developed programs "to prevent youth from falling into disbelief."[84] Al-Azhar's fatwas failed to incorporate a tolerant message concerning the Baha'i; instead, members of this group were deemed apostates.[85] Offering a welcoming public space to Baha'is, Shiites, and other religious minorities has been difficult for a Sunni institution like Al-Azhar. However, this is a needed step to see religious tolerance take root in Egyptian society. Still, we should not dismiss Al-Azhar's efforts simply because they are incomplete. Their efforts to improve Muslim–Christian relations are important. Some in Washington noticed. One American official explained, "Al-Azhar can play a positive role. They have a lot of credibility. They have spoken out against intolerance."[86] This is a foundation that can be further developed.

The media can also contribute a tolerant message within society. When newspapers and other media outlets develop segments and programs that discuss religious minorities in a positive manner and their contributions to society, this can reinforce the basic message that all Egyptians deserve a place in society and ought to be treated in a respectful and tolerant manner. If programs and stories describe religious minorities as untrustworthy, deceitful, or worse, violence could result. Many Egyptians received negative depictions of religious minorities; this is especially true of anti-Semitism. Articles and talk-show guests in public (state-run) and private media outlets often depict members of the Jewish faith in a degrading manner.[87] The Egyptian government could prevent these hostile messages, given the controlling nature of the administration.

Many human rights organizations that seek to promote this right are constrained by government policies. Some have been shut down in el-Sisi's attempt to limit any independent organizations that criticize him. Religious institutions, such as Al-Azhar, do not face the same level of government hostility.

---

[84] State Department, *International Religious Freedom Report for 2020*.

[85] Ishak Ibrahim, June 2, 2021.

[86] Interview with USCIRF Commissioner Katrina Lantos Swett, July 10, 2013.

[87] State Department, *International Religious Freedom Report for 2011*; Michele Dunne and Katie Bentivoglio, "Is Sisi Islam's Martin Luther?" January 16, 2015, https://carnegie-mec.org/diwan/57738.

CONCLUSION

There is not much to be optimistic about in the decade since Egyptians filled Tahrir Square during the Egyptian revolution. Some have argued that the current situation in Egypt is worse under President el-Sisi than President Mubarak.[88] Although there has been little progress since Egyptians took to the streets in 2011 and much bloodshed, a combination of efforts on the part of the Egyptian government, international assistance via state foreign policy and international organizations, and grassroots efforts in civil society could promote a more religiously tolerant society. All these aspects are necessary because they play different roles in society and offer a multifaceted approach to tackling the lack of religious freedom in the country.

The Egyptian government under President el-Sisi must reform some institutions and develop additional policies to begin this process. Encouragement and international pressure from other states and international organizations can help el-Sisi to see the benefits of adopting new policies. The Egyptian president and other government officials must adopt inclusive and respectful language when discussing all religious minorities and Egyptians who do not adhere to religious beliefs. The government must articulate a clear message denouncing violence against religious minorities. This message must be repeated so that all Egyptians understand there will be consequences for violent and intolerant behavior. Perpetrators of violence must understand that the judicial system will punish them if they harm other individuals. If individuals who attack religious minorities or places of worship understand that there will be consequences, this could help deter some violence in the short term. In the long term, the government must develop programs in the legal and educational systems to encourage the development of tolerant attitudes so that Egyptians see religious (and non-religious) minorities as equal members in society.

Egypt must also stop its harassment and legal persecution of civil society organizations and the individuals who are attempting to promote human rights. Various NGOs and religious institutions could help to promote religious tolerance, as Al-Azhar has done in its interfaith efforts with the Coptic Church. These interfaith dialogues must also be expanded to other religious minorities within Egypt. Tolerant messages, as opposed to the demonization of some religious minorities, from the media will improve the climate in Egypt.

President el-Sisi has not demonstrated a commitment to the fundamental human rights of all Egyptians or a willingness to make legal and policy changes that would ensure the judicial system protects freedom of religion or

---

[88] Hawthorne, "Testimony." Mike Posner, Policy Statement on Human Rights in Egypt, April 10, 2014. Interview with NGO activist, April 11, 2014.

belief for all. Despite his apparent hostility to democracy and the rule of law, there are tools that can persuade him of the benefits of religious tolerance and freedom of religion or belief. States, such as the United States, can limit foreign assistance if he continues to allow violence and intolerance to go unpunished in society. International organizations can also demonstrate that there will be economic and reputational consequences for the lack of accountability in Egypt. Despite the persistent intolerance in Egypt over the last few decades, progress is possible. Furthermore, since Egypt is the most populous country in the Arab world and is home to the Al-Azhar, progress in this country could have ripple effects throughout the region.

9. Tending to human dignity in the garden

INTRODUCTION

When the Islamic State came to Sinjar, Iraq, in 2014, they destroyed and defiled a people and their ancestral homeland. The Islamic State viewed the Yazidis as pagans. Yazidis suffered brutally as a result. In Kocho, Islamic State fighters shot men in the back of the head. Yazidi women disappeared into a web of sexual slavery across the border in Syria.[1] These reprehensible facts are part of a complicated story of fear, tragedy, and American assistance. It is also a story of what is possible when individuals and organizations sound the alarm and work together to address religious persecution.

News of the Islamic State's arrival in Sinjar came to the United States via phone calls from desperate family members who sought refuge on Mt. Sinjar. Over 200 000 Yazidis fled in one week in August.[2] Recent immigrants in Nebraska, Texas, and Virginia listened as distraught relatives fled their villages in advance of Islamic State fighters. Yazidi immigrants in the United States formed a group, the Sinjar Crisis Management Team, to lobby Washington to respond to the impending massacre. They contacted individuals at the State Department's Office of International Religious Freedom. They also spoke to USAID and White House officials. The Obama administration responded with air strikes on ISIS positions. Additional assistance involved food and water supplies dropped on Mt. Sinjar to provide temporary relief until those Yazidis who fled could be evacuated to safety. While the initial American response

---

[1] Jenna Krajeski, "The Daring Plan to Save a Religious Minority from ISIS," *The New Yorker*, February 19, 2018, https://www.newyorker.com/magazine/2018/02/26/the-daring-plan-to-save-a-religious-minority-from-isis.

[2] Assistant Secretary Anne Richard, "U.S. Humanitarian Assistance in Response to the Iraq Crisis," Testimony before the House Foreign Affairs Subcommittees on Africa, Global Health, Global Human Rights and International Organizations and the Middle East and North Africa, September 10, 2014, Washington, D.C., https://docs.house.gov/meetings/FA/FA16/20140910/102642/HHRG-113-FA16-Wstate-RichardA-20140910.pdf.

was far from perfect, it demonstrates the importance of an immediate response to religious persecution.

In the aftermath of the Islamic State's brutality, diverse elements of the international community developed initiatives to respond to this massacre. Besides the immediate humanitarian aid, the United States assisted in efforts to rebuild areas in Ninewa. These efforts addressed the extensive needs of Yazidis and other religious minorities targeted by the Islamic State. Washington provided medical assistance, food, tents, and psychological assistance to those violated by ISIS.[3] The UN established UNITAD. The UN Investigative Team to Promote Accountability for Crimes Committed by Daesh/ISIL collected evidence and helped to identify mass graves and exhume the bodies of victims of the Islamic State. Civil society organizations embarked on various activities to assist and rebuild communities targeted by ISIS. Nadia Murad, a Yazidi survivor, established Nadia's Initiative. This organization, started with assistance from Germany and the United Arab Emirates, advocated for justice for the Yazidis with human rights lawyer Amal Clooney.[4] Other organizations, such as the Free Yezidi Foundation, formed to provide educational opportunities to address the marginalization of the Yazidi community. The Iraq Heritage Stabilization Program sought to preserve Iraqi heritage by restoring buildings of religious minorities in northern Iraq. This program helps religious minorities return to their communities.[5] This coalition of diverse actors and organizations demonstrates the need for a multilayered approach to help a threatened religious minority. The Yazidis have a long way to go, and thousands of women and girls remain missing. More than 100 000 were able to return to their homeland.[6] While justice remains elusive, many Yazidis were saved by these collective efforts. Progress is possible when the appropriate actors are motivated to do so.

---

[3] State Department, "Iraq," *International Religious Freedom Report for 2019*, June 10, 2020, https://www.state.gov/reports/2019-report-on-international-religious-freedom/iraq/.

[4] UN News, "Six Years after Genocide, International Community Must Prioritize Justice for Yazidi Community," August 3, 2020, https://news.un.org/en/story/2020/08/1069432.

[5] Darren Ashby, a professor at the University of Pittsburg, specifically noted that restoring religious buildings and shrines was necessary to help individuals return to their communities. Without these important places, many might not return. Webinar, "Strategies to Build Peace from the Ground Up: Protecting Religious Diversity, Coexistence, and Cultural Heritage in Iraq," July 19, 2021. This webinar was organized by the Religious Freedom Institute.

[6] UN News, "Six Years."

A PATH TO PROGRESS

Unfortunately, persecution is prevalent around the globe. We find it in every region. We find various political figures and social groups discriminating against and, in many cases, persecuting the Other because they differ in beliefs or practices. Some politicians target a religious minority to score political points with a domestic audience. Indian Prime Minister Narendra Modi and Hungarian Prime Minister Viktor Orban both targeted and disparaged Muslims in an effort to boost their popularity with a portion of the electorate. These facts, while disturbing, are not the end of the story. The international community can engage in policies and practices to not only combat persecution, but also promote the fundamental right of freedom of religion or belief that is found in numerous international documents, including the ICCPR.

An important step to promote this human right and protect people in diverse regions with different-faith commitments is to understand and identify religious intolerance. Which actors are preventing individuals from gathering to discuss a religious text? Do state authorities arrest individuals at religious services? Do police officers shave a man's beard or remove a woman's hijab? Or does the denial of religious freedom or the harassment of those who hold no religious beliefs stem from groups in society? Are religious minorities or atheists set upon in society as heretics? Is there social pressure to convert? Who engages in religious repression? Who enables religious intolerance? Identifying the source of the violation is the first step. After identifying the source of the intolerance or repression, a clear and forceful response is necessary. Otherwise, a culture of impunity will develop when discrimination or violence goes unpunished or unaddressed.

While there is no simple path to religious freedom, we can learn lessons from history to address religious intolerance. First, we must understand that the minimal aspects of religious tolerance are not equal to the fundamental human right established in Article 18 of the ICCPR. Examples from history and in contemporary times demonstrate that religious tolerance moves a society closer to freedom of religion or belief. Pursuing religious tolerance for pragmatic or instrumental reasons can start a society on the road to greater religious freedom. Although instrumental motivations for religious tolerance failed in some instances to develop a rights-protective society, they should be pursued in the short term. Religious tolerance provides a framework and a foundation on which to build in the future.

We must be mindful in each society of the history, religious diversity, and social conditions that impact the development of religious freedom. Religious tolerance developed in various territories (Dutch Republic, Ottoman Empire) regardless of the dominant faith. Understanding the history of societies that encouraged religious tolerance and the arguments put forth by philosophers (Spinoza, Locke, Hobbes) and political and religious leaders (William Penn, Roger Williams, William of Orange) for religious tolerance indicates the long quest for this basic right. The yearning for religious freedom is not a recent development. It is a basic desire and an aspect of human dignity. The past does not offer a teleological approach, but it suggests that certain policies and initiatives are worth pursuing. Therefore, acknowledging the historical and political context is essential to identifying successful strategies.

Given the extensive religious persecution throughout the globe, moving from religious intolerance to a rights-protective society where all individuals are free to believe and act in accordance with those beliefs is important for individual dignity and social stability. Ultimately, I argued that a long-term strategy that combines international efforts, national reforms, and active civil society engagement has the greatest chance of creating a religiously free society where all are protected and accepted. States are key actors in the global environment. They can ratify a treaty, work cooperatively in an international organization, and develop targeted sanctions. Targeted sanctions are an easy tool that can be deployed to promote religious freedom. The United States passed the Global Magnitsky Human Rights Accountability Act in 2016, which empowers the government to issue visa bans and freeze the assets of individuals who violate human rights, including those who persecute others based on their religious commitments. But states are not the only actors that can engage in policies and activities that slowly help to make headway on this issue.

Multilateral efforts by IGOs, such as the EU or the UN, can articulate norms, set standards, engage in quiet diplomacy, and develop policies to further religious freedom around the world. Different actors bring different strengths and different tools to the table. These diverse actors with their different perspectives are important because they employ different advantages in pursuit of this right.

Institutions and policies at the national level are important. Thoughtful policies and basic laws are necessary for a robust form of religious freedom to take hold in a society. To establish this right, clear language is needed in the constitution or in the legal system. Transparent language must prohibit the government and individuals in society from restricting the religious freedom of citizens. States can accomplish this by adopting the language of Article 18 of the ICCPR or by drafting national laws guided by the ICCPR and Declaration on the Elimination of All Forms of Intolerance and Discrimination Based on Religion or Belief. Beyond the codification of legal standards, a government needs to develop mechanisms and offices to uphold this right. The government must enforce the laws that were created. All citizens must be held accountable under the law. To uphold the rule of law, officials in law enforcement must understand and enforce these legal obligations. Equally important is the judiciary's commitment to applying the law equally and without discrimination based on an individual's faith. In concrete terms, the police cannot arbitrarily arrest a member of a minority religious tradition out of personal disgust or due to contrary beliefs. The courts must not allow acts of discrimination or violence by the majority faith to go unpunished, as is often the case in Egypt.

To uphold all aspects of freedom of religion or belief, the government should also offer some individuals limited accommodations for their religious beliefs. This may involve granting conscientious objector status or allowing specific religious attire to be worn (head scarf, burkini, kippah), or providing alternative meals to respect dietary restrictions (halal meals). These accommodations demonstrate respect for religious individuals and promote religious freedom in society.

Beyond legal and judicial institutions, societal attitudes concerning acceptance of the religious Other are also essential for a religiously free society. Societies need to manifest tolerant beliefs about those with different religious commitments. The lack of acceptance in society for minority religious traditions leads to abuse, discrimination, and violence. The development of a society that embraces religious freedom often takes decades. This is why the education system is so important. Children grow over the years and develop in response to what they learn in school (and in society). The education system must teach students to be tolerant and to value those in society, regardless of their religious commitments. When teachers encourage tolerant dispositions and create an environment in the classroom of respect for all, norms of acceptance and tolerance can take hold in children. These dispositions, if taught throughout a child's early years, can have long-lasting effects. Developing tolerant beliefs in children can result in behavioral changes in a society. Citizens can learn, from an early age, that religious freedom is a fundamental right of every member of society.

I also argued for the importance of a tolerant leader. The value of a tolerant leader who adopts policies or pushes their society to embrace religious tolerance for all cannot be stressed enough. Political leaders do not have to have a deep commitment to religious freedom. If they see religious tolerance as being in their self-interest and if they are willing to compromise, progress is possible. Self-interest is an acceptable motivation to begin this process. The development of values, which is necessary for religious freedom, will take time. We should not expect that these values will develop overnight in political leaders or in the population more broadly. Despite the long-term nature of this process, a national leader can push a society toward religious freedom.

Political leaders, especially the head of government, must employ a discourse that demonstrates respect for religious diversity. If an individual uses disparaging language or endorses violence targeting religious minorities, or those with no faith, political leaders must challenge those destructive views directly and forcefully in public. A leader who promotes public discourse that is tolerant and encourages religious freedom for all through public policies can move the needle in society. Uzbekistan demonstrates just how quickly a tolerant leader can institute reforms that change society.

Civil society can amplify these norms and attitudes. Human rights organizations, religious communities and their leaders, and other actors in civil society can play a positive role in the development and protection of the right to freedom of religion or belief. As one imam noted, "civil society has a big role to play" in helping to advance religious freedom on the ground.[7] Collaborative efforts by prominent religious leaders, such as Pope Francis's efforts with the Grand Sheik of Al-Azhar and declarations (2016 Marrakesh Declaration, 2012 Rabat Plan of Action, and 1965 *Nostra Aetate* by Pope John Paul VI), affirming the rights of different religious minorities are essential because they come from within the religious community and cannot be dismissed as foreign "interventions."[8] In the last few decades, prominent religious actors from different faiths worked diligently to promote this basic right.

ADDITIONAL WORK REMAINS

In addition to the multifaceted framework I established in this work to promote religious freedom, it is worth noting some roadblocks that can impede these efforts. Threats, both traditional and virological; corruption; and the lack of trust obstruct efforts to further the right to freedom of religion or belief.

Fear motivates some religious intolerance. Fear and anxiety of the religious Other can develop when people wear distinctive religious attire or engage in practices perceived as weird, deviant, disruptive, or immoral. This fear and anxiety can cause feelings of distaste or disgust, sometimes resulting in efforts to isolate the Other or cleanse the society of this dangerous Other. The violence and discrimination that follow from this fear is then justified as defensive in nature. The religious Other, often a minority, is described and perceived as a threat that must be dealt with for the good of society. Fear is a powerful unifier and needs to be addressed via education and leadership.

---

[7] Imam Magid, IRF Summit, July 27, 2021, Washington, D.C., https://www.youtube.com/watch?v=bO-Q957UgDY.

[8] *Nostra Aetate* reaffirms the fundamental dignity of all: "No foundation therefore remains for any theory or practice that leads to discrimination between man and man or people and people, so far as their human dignity and the rights flowing from it are concerned. The Church reproves, as foreign to the mind of Christ, any discrimination against men or harassment of them because of their race, color, condition of life, or religion." Pope Paul VI, Vatican, "Declaration."

China shows how brutal a government can be when it perceives a community as a threat. The Chinese Communist Party (CCP) demonstrates how perceived threats can trigger a vicious reaction. The CCP surveilled, detained, and tortured millions of Uyghur Muslims in Xinjiang. After a few isolated incidents of violence by Uyghurs, the Chinese government established a brutal and technologically sophisticated program to control and reengineer the more than 12 million Uyghurs in the northwest province. Facial recognition technology and apps allow the CCP to control the Uyghur population through constant monitoring. Beyond watching Uyghurs as they move from street to street, the CCP indefinitely detained more than a million Uyghurs in reeducation camps. These camps monitor every move an individual makes. Further, the camps employ teachers to "educate" detainees in Mandarin and in "correct" ideological thinking. Correct ideological thinking demands love of China and a secular framework devoid of Islam.[9] The CCP's efforts to rid this population of its culture, religion, and ideas stems in part from the government's view of Islam and the Uyghur community as a threat to its long-term stability.[10] These repressive Orwellian policies, as well as hostility toward Christians and Tibetan Buddhists, made China the most restrictive country, according to the Pew Research Center.[11] The use of technology, including artificial intelligence in China, is a worrying sign for the future, especially if other states employ these technological tools to persecute religious minorities.

Countering narratives concerning threatening groups will assist in the process of addressing religious intolerance. Numerous examples demonstrate that religious tolerance is more likely when a society and political leaders feel secure. The less secure a society and political leaders feel, the less likely they will be to tolerate religious diversity and minorities within their midst.[12] Napoleon could open the political and social space to the Jewish community in various territories around Europe due to his position and, for several years, the inability of others to threaten his power.

This was also true of the Ottoman Empire. As noted in Chapter 2, when the sultans of the Ottoman Empire enjoyed prosperity and security, they were

---

[9] The Uyghur language is a Turkic language more similar to Uzbek than to Mandarin.

[10] Yuting Wang, "Prospects for Covenantal Pluralism in the People's Republic of China: A Reflection on State Policy and Muslim Minorities," *The Review of Faith and International Affairs*, Vol. 19, No. 2 (2021), pp. 14–28.

[11] On the GRI, China's score of 9.3 is higher than any other country. Pew Research Center, "Globally."

[12] E. Gregory Wallace, "Justifying Religious Freedom: The Western Tradition," *Penn State Law Review*, Vol. 114, No. 2 (2009), p. 514. Wallace makes this point in reference to Christianity in the 4th century, but his point has applicability beyond the 4th century.

willing to tolerate various religious minorities, knowing that these communities were not a threat and contributed to the stability of the realm. Uzbekistan demonstrates this as well. As documented in Chapter 6, a decrease in threats from extremists in the name of Islam opened a space for some of the political and social changes currently taking place in that country.

Threats assume various, even invisible, forms. COVID-19 is a social and economic threat that has been difficult for most countries to contain. The instability and fear that arose in connection with COVID-19 disrupted life. Unfortunately, the virus also contributed to religious intolerance and discrimination for some religious minorities. The UN Special Rapporteur on freedom of religion or belief noted, "the pandemic has further eroded protection of freedom of thought, conscience and religion or belief."[13] Some governments limited religious services and activities to stop the spread of the virus. The ban on social gatherings, especially in the early months of the pandemic, was not a denial of religious freedom. When policies are developed in a neutral and non-discriminatory manner, this temporary restriction on religious gatherings is not a denial of a basic human right. When applied to all faiths and communities, it is an understandable response motivated by health guidelines.

Unfortunately, many states imposed social restrictions on some religious minorities. Saudi Arabia limited Shia gatherings in the eastern provinces in a discriminatory manner. Beyond government policies, religious minorities experienced social hostilities. In some countries, religious minorities were accused of spreading the virus. This should not surprise us. In the 1340s, Jews in various regions of Europe were blamed and ostracized for the plague that killed millions of people. In one extreme example in 1349, the people in Trier condemned the Jewish residents living there for the Black Plague and murdered them.[14] In contemporary times, a proactive campaign by a government, including a clear, tolerant message from the head of state, can avert many of these issues.

Systemic Corruption

An additional barrier to the successful promotion of freedom of religion or belief is systemic corruption. Corruption shreds the fabric of society because it damages social trust. The less trust there is between religious communities, the less likely these groups will be to interact and cooperate. Individuals will

---

[13] Shaheed, "Conversation with USCIRF Spotlight Podcast."

[14] James Carroll, *Constantine's Sword: The Church and the Jews* (New York: Houghton Mifflin Company, 2001), p. 226. See also Fordham University, *Jewish History Sourcebook: The Black Death and the Jews 1348–1349 CE*, https://sourcebooks.fordham.edu/jewish/1348-jewsblackdeath.asp.

come to rely on members of their own faith instead of the government or others in society. This results in separation and can lead to discrimination and hostility. The lack of social trust hurts the development of religious tolerance and freedom of religion or belief.

If corrupt officials accept bribes or prey on the population, reforms in education related to religious tolerance or the passage of legislation criminalizing religious discrimination will have little impact. Efforts by national leaders to use tolerant language and encourage respect for religious minorities are meaningless if national leaders turn a blind eye to shakedowns and other venal forms of corruption in society. When a leader allows corruption to go unimpeded, he is tainted by his inaction. As the 14th-century theologian, William of Pagula, noted, "one who permits anything to take place that he is able to impede, even though he has not done it himself, had virtually done the act if he allows it."[15] Foreign policy approaches that simply ignore corruption impede progress on religious freedom. If international actors, including human rights organizations and foreign governments, ignore corruption, the local population may view this as tacit consent.[16] Indifference to corruption can taint international efforts on a range of issues including the promotion of religious freedom. It can also further religious conflict in a society. It is worth recalling that one of Martin Luther's concerns in the 16th century was the corruption in the Church and, specifically, the selling of indulgences.

Social Media

There is widespread recognition that social media platforms contribute to hatred and violence of the Other when demonizing content is not removed and algorithms encourage toxic content to attract more users and engagement on the platform. This was evident in the vile content shared on Facebook about the Rohingya Muslims of Myanmar, as well as the demonization of Christians in Sri Lanka and Jews in Europe. The UN Special Rapporteur for freedom of religion or belief noted, "social media is a huge problem."[17] Beyond sowing the seeds of violence, social media can undercut formal education and the tolerant lessons taught in schools, especially if children spend more time on Facebook and Instagram than in a world religions class.

Social media platforms need to do more to manage and remove harmful content, regardless of the financial implications. If they will not make changes

---

[15] Quoted in Sarah Chayes, *Thieves of the State: Why Corruption Threatens Global Security*, (New York: W. W. Norton and Company, 2015), p. 41.

[16] Chayes, p. 41.

[17] Ahmed Shaheed, Discussion of Report on Anti-Semitism, September 19, 2019, New York.

for altruistic reasons, then governments and MNCs need to encourage these changes. Governments can establish regulations to control some of this content. While there are legitimate concerns about freedom of expression, advocating and inciting violence should not be protected content. Article 20 of the ICCPR allows the prohibition of speech that incites hostility or violence. Businesses should refrain from advertising on certain platforms if the social media companies continue to allow their sites to promote hatred and violence. If enough businesses boycott a platform for a month, a financial message will be sent. Economic sanctions of this kind can encourage policy changes on these platforms.

PROGRESS

I documented progress in some countries. Uzbekistan shows that progress, albeit slow, is possible. Additional signs of hope are also apparent. One aspect of progress is encouraging various faith communities to fight for freedom of religion or belief for all, and not just their own faith community. We have seen more interfaith initiatives. There are more efforts by diverse-faith communities to speak out when others are persecuted or discriminated against because of their faith. This is a positive development over the last few decades.

Another positive development in the cause of religious freedom is a growing imperative to protect this right. There is more attention to the promotion and protection of Article 18 by governments and civil society. More resources have been deployed to address this human right since 2000. More interfaith and intergovernmental alliances respond to violations of religious freedom. Governments created positions to focus on and monitor freedom of religion or belief, including special envoys and ambassadors dedicated to this right (Germany, Denmark, Lithuania).

As Knox Thames, the former Special Advisor for Religious Minorities in the Near East and South and Central Asia at the State Department noted:

> It's been very positive to see more countries get in the game to set aside resources, either by identifying particular offices or naming diplomats to play an envoy role. It used to be just the United States by ourselves with our ambassador-at-large, and now there's probably twelve or thirteen special envoys of different natures from around the world, both, of course in North America and Europe, as you'd expect. We've seen them in Taiwan and Mongolia, demonstrating this isn't a Western issue, but really a global issue that touches on every community around the world.[18]

---

[18] Knox Thames, "The Council on Foreign Relations Religion and Foreign Policy Webinar Series," September 22, 2020.

The Pew Research Center found that social hostilities declined in 2019 compared to 2018; 27 percent of countries (53 countries) had high or very high levels of social hostility in 2018. In 2019, the number dropped to 22 percent (43 countries). While a 5-percent decrease in one year is far from overwhelming, and can be reversed, it is still progress. Some of the countries discussed in this work saw a decline in social hostility, including Sweden and Egypt.[19]

CONCLUSION

The basic human right of freedom of religion or belief requires constant attention. Far too many political and religious figures have opportunistically exploited hatred and spread misinformation about religious minorities. Hatred can be confronted with responsible leadership from political figures and supportive messages from civil society actors. Patient policies developed by national leaders and encouraged by international actors are needed since many societies will take decades to move from religious intolerance to religious tolerance and ultimately freedom of religion or belief. Progress can be achieved, but it will not develop overnight. Slow progress is still progress. This work will take generations to take hold. Despite the sometimes-exhausting efforts needed to uphold this right, there is nothing more fundamental to human dignity than the ability of any individual to believe and act in accordance with those deeply held convictions.

---

[19] Sweden: SHI in 2018 was 3.3, and in 2019 SHI was 1.5. Egypt: SHI in 2018 was 7.5, and in 2019 it was 6.5. Pew Research Center, "Globally."

References

Abdelmassih, Mary, "Muslims Demolish Church Building in Egypt," *Assyrian International News Agency*, January 16, 2013.
Afzal, Madiha, "Education and Attitudes in Pakistan," US Institute of Peace, Special Report 367, April 2015.
Afzal, Madiha, *Pakistan Under Siege: Extremism, Society and the State*, Washington, D.C.: Brookings Institute Press, 2018.
Al Arabiya, "Egypt's Coptic Church Announces Support for Army, Police," August 17, 2013. http://english.alarabiya.net/en/News/middle-east/2013/08/17/Egypt-s-Coptic-Church-announces-support-for-army-police.html
Al Sadi, Fatima, and Tehmina Basit, "Religious Tolerance in Oman: Addressing Religious Prejudice through Educational Intervention," *British Educational Research Journal,* Vol. 39, No. 3 (2013), pp. 447–472.
Al Salimi, Abdullah bin Mohammed, Minister of Endowments and Religious Affairs, Speech in Muscat, Oman, 2014. http://www.mara.om/wp-content/uploads/klmtt-maale-alwzer-balienjleze.pdf
Al-Salimi, Abdulrhman, "The Transformation of Religious Learning in Oman: Tradition and Modernity," *Journal of Royal Asiatic Society,* Vol. 21, No. 2 (April 2011), pp. 147–57.
Albert, Eleanor, and Lindsay Maizland, "The Rohingya Crisis," *Council on Foreign Affairs*, January 23, 2020. https://www.cfr.org/backgrounder/rohingya-crisis
Ambrosewicz-Jacobs, Jolanta, "Religious Tolerance, Freedom of Religion or Belief, and Education: Results of the 2001 UN Conference," in *Facilitating Freedom of Religion or Belief: A Deskbook,* edited by Tore Lindholm, W. Cole Durham, and Bahia G. Tahzib-Lie, Leiden: Martinus Nijhoff Publishers, 2004, Chapter 37.
American Embassy, Tunis, "Tunisia Religious Engagement Report," June 16, 2010, EO 12958.
Amnesty International, "Egypt: President Morsi Must Send a Clear Message Against Attacks on Shia Muslims." June 24, 2013. https://www.amnesty.org/en/latest/news/2013/06/egypt-president-morsi-must-send-clear-message-against-attacks-on-shia-muslims/
Anti-Defamation League (ADL). "Global Anti-Semitism: Selected Incidents Around the World in 2016," December 31, 2016. https://www.adl.org/news/article/global-anti-semitism-selected-incidents-around-the-world-in-2016
Armstrong, Karen, *Fields of Blood: Religion and the History of Violence*, New York: Alfred Knopf, 2015.
Baer, Daniel, "U.S.–Vietnam Bilateral Relations," Deputy Assistant Secretary, Bureau of Democracy, Human Rights, and Labor, Prepared Statement to the House Committee on Foreign Affairs Subcommittee on Asia and the Pacific, June 5, 2013, Washington, D.C.
Bangs, Dupertuis, "Dutch Contributions to Religious Toleration," *Church History,* Vol. 79, No. 3 (September 2010), pp. 585–613.

Barkey, Karen, *Empire of Difference,* Cambridge, UK: Cambridge University Press, 2008.

Barsa, John, "Remarks on USAID Advancing Religious Freedom," August 17, 2020. https://www.usaid.gov/news-information/speeches/aug-17-2020-usaid-advancing-religious-liberty-usaid-acting-administrator-john-barsa

Bayram, Mushfig, "Supreme Court Challenge to Student Hijab Ban," *Forum 18*, April 29, 2019. http://www.forum18.org/archive.php?article_id=2472

Beitz, Charles, "Human Dignity in the Theory of Human Rights: Nothing but a Phrase?" *Philosophy and Public Affairs,* Vol. 41, No. 3 (Summer 2013), pp. 259–90.

Bennoune, Karima, "Report on Cultural Rights," July 17, 2017, A/72/155. https://undocs.org/en/A/72/155

Berlin, Isiah, "The Originality of Machiavelli," in Against the Current*: Essays in the History of Ideas*, New York: Viking Press, 1980, pp. 25–79.

Bielefeldt, Heiner, "Misperceptions about Freedom of Religion or Belief," *Human Rights Quarterly*, Vol. 35 (2013), pp. 33–68.

Bielefeldt, Heiner, *Report on Mission to Viet Nam*, January 30, 2015, A/HRC/28/66/Add.2.

Bielefeldt, Heiner, *Freedom of Religion or Belief: Thematic Reports of the UN Special Rapporteur, 2010–2016*, Bonn: Culture and Science Publications, 2017.

Bielefeldt, Heiner, and Michael Wierner, *Religious Freedom Under Scrutiny*, Philadelphia: University of Pennsylvania Press, 2020.

Bierschank, Thomas, "Religion and Political Structure: Remarks on Ibadism in Oman and the Mizah (Algeria)," *Studia Islamica,* Vol. 68 (1988), pp. 107–27.

Birdsall, Judd, "Obama and the Drama Over International Religious Freedom Policy: An Insider's Perspective," *The Review of Faith and International Affairs,* Vol. 10, No. 3 (Fall 2012), pp. 33–41.

Blinken, Antony, Press Release, "Religious Freedom Designations," November 14, 2021.

Blinken, Antony, Press Release, "The United States Promotes Accountability for Human Rights Violations and Abuses," December 10, 2021.

British Broadcasting Corporation, "German Jews Warned Not to Wear Kippas After Rise in Anti-Semitism," May 26, 2019. https://www.bbc.com/news/world-europe-48411735?ocid=socialflow_twitter

Brown, Nathan, and Michele Dunne, "Who Will Speak for Islam in Egypt–and Who Will Listen?" Carnegie Endowment for International Peace, June 7, 2021. https://carnegieendowment.org/2021/06/07/who-will-speak-for-islam-in-egypt-and-who-will-listen-pub-84654

Brownback, Samuel, "Faith Angle Podcast with Wajahat Ali," December 31, 2019.

Brownback, Samuel, Ambassador at Large for International Religious Freedom, Briefing, May 14, 2020.

Bush, Kenneth, and Diana Saltarelli, *The Two Faces of Education in Ethnic Conflict: Towards a Peacebuilding Education for Children*, Florence: UNICEF, 2000.

Butterfield, Herbert, *Toleration in Religion and Politics*, New York: Council on Religion and International Affairs, 1980.

Cairo Institute for Human Rights Studies, "Islamist Groups Must Stop Inciting to Sectarian Violence; Protection of Christians Responsibility of the State," August 7, 2013.

Carroll, James, *Constantine's Sword: The Church and the Jews*, New York: Houghton Mifflin Company, 2001.

Chayes, Sarah, *Thieves of the State: Why Corruption Threatens Global Security*, New York: W.W. Norton and Company, 2015.
Clark, Ann Marie, "Nongovernmental Organizations," in *Encyclopedia of Human Rights* (Vol. 4), David P. Forsythe, editor-in-chief, Oxford: Oxford University Press, 2009, pp. 87–96.
Cole, Wade, "Mind the Gap: State Capacity and the Implementation of Human Rights Treaties," *International Organization,* Vol. 69 (Spring 2015), pp. 405–41.
Cornell, Svante, and Jacob Zenn, "Religion and the Secular State in Uzbekistan," in *Uzbekistan's New Face*, edited by S. Frederick Starr and Svante Cornell, Lanham, MD: Rowman and Littlefield, 2018, pp. 193–219.
Cornell, Vincent, "Theologies of Difference and Ideologies of Intolerance in Islam," in *Religious Tolerance in World Religions*, edited by Jacob Neuser and Bruce Chilton, West Conshohocken, PA: Templeton Foundation Press, 2008, pp. 274–96.
Cox, Harvey, *The Future of Faith*, New York: Harper One, 2009.
Crone, Patricia, *God's Rule – Government and Islam*, New York: Columbia University Press, 2004.
Crowley, Michael, "Trump Says He Avoided Punishing China Over Uighur Camps to Protect Trade Talks," *New York Times*, June 21, 2020. https://www.nytimes.com/2020/06/21/us/politics/trump-uighurs-china-trade.html
Dallas, Kelsey, "What Does the International Religious Freedom Ambassador Do?" *Desert News,* July 30, 2017.
Diamond, Larry, *Ill Winds*, New York: Penguin Press, 2019.
Doumato, Abdella, "Saudi Arabia: From 'Wahhabi' Roots to Contemporary Revisionism," in *Teaching Islam: Textbooks and Religion in the Middle East*, edited by Elanor Abdella Doumato and Gregory Starret, Boulder, CO: Lynne Rienner, 2006, pp. 153–176.
Dunn, Geoffrey, *Tertullian*, New York: Psychology Press, 2004.
Dunne, Michele, and Katie Bentivoglio, "Is Sisi Islam's Martin Luther?" January 16, 2015. https://carnegie-mec.org/diwan/57738
Durham, W., and Brett Scharffs, *Law and Religion: National, International and Comparative Perspectives*, New York: Wolters Kluwer, 2019.
Edqvist, Gunnar, "Freedom of Religion and New Relations Between Church and State in Sweden," *Studia Theologica*, Vol. 54 (2000), pp. 35–41.
Egyptian Initiative for Personal Rights, Press Release, "A Report on the 'Shiite Massacre' in the Abu Muslim Corner in Giza," June 26, 2013. http://eipr.org/pressrelease/2013/06/26/1750
Embassy of Uzbekistan, "The Ministry of Justice, the Republic of Uzbekistan Announced the Number of Religious Organizations Registered in the Country," February 21, 2020. https://www.uzbekistan.org/news/view?id=312
Epstein, Susan, and K. Alan Kronstradt, "Pakistan: US Foreign Assistance," Congressional Research Service, October 4, 2012.
Evans, Malcom, "Historical Analysis of Freedom of Religion or Belief as a Technique for Resolving Religious Conflict," in *Facilitating Freedom of Religion or Belief: A Deskbook,* edited by Tore Lindholm, W. Cole Durham, and Bahia G. Tahzib-Lie, Leiden: Martinus Nijhoff Publishers, 2004, pp. 1–17.
European Parliament Intergroup on FoRB and RT, "2014 Annual Report: The State of Freedom of Religion or Belief in the World," Brussels, Belgium. https://www.oursplatform.org/wp-content/uploads/European-Parliament-Intergroup-on-Freedom-of-Religion-2014-Report-State-of-Freedom-of-Religion-or-Belief-in-the-World.pdf

Fahmi, Georges, "The Egyptian State and the Religious Sphere," Carnegie Middle East Center, September 18, 2014. https://carnegie-mec.org/2014/09/18/egyptian-state-and-religious-sphere-pub-56619

Farouk, Mahmoud, Amy Hawthorne, and Ahmed Rizk, *Prayers Unanswered: Assessing the Impact of Egypt's 2016 Church Construction Law*, Project on Middle East Democracy, December 2018. https://pomed.org/wp-content/uploads/2018/12/CCL_Report_181212_FINAL.pdf

Farr, Thomas, "Examining the Government's Record on Implementing the International Religious Freedom Act," Testimony before the Subcommittee on National Security of the House Committee on Oversight and Government Reform, June 13, 2013, Washington, D.C.

Ferguson, Barbara, "The Cyrus Cylinder—Often Referred to as the First Bill of Human Rights," *Washington Report on Middle East Affairs*, May 2013.

Fordham University, *Jewish History Sourcebook: The Black Death and the Jews 1348–1349 CE*. https://sourcebooks.fordham.edu/jewish/1348-jewsblackdeath.asp

Forsythe, David, *Human Rights in International Relations*, 4th edition, New York: Cambridge University Press, 2017.

Forsythe, David, and Barbara Ann Rieffer-Flanagan, *The International Committee of the Red Cross: A Neutral Humanitarian Actor*, New York: Routledge, 2016.

Forum 18, "Uzbekistan: Raids, Eviction Threat for Urgench Baptists," October 22, 2019. http://www.forum18.org/archive.php?article_id=2515

Fox, Jonathan, "Religious Freedom in Theory and in Practice," *Human Rights Review*, Vol. 16, No. 1 (2015), pp. 1–22.

Freedom House, "Saudi Arabia's Curriculum of Intolerance," 2006, https://freedomhouse.org/sites/default/files/CurriculumOfIntolerance.pdf

Freedom House, "Has Mirziyoyev Really Brought Religious Liberty to Uzbekistan?" January 16, 2019. https://freedomhouse.org/blog/has-mirziyoyev-really-brought-religious-liberty-uzbekistan

Freedom House, "Freedom in the World Report 2020: Vietnam," https://freedomhouse.org/country/vietnam/freedom-world/2020

Fukuyama, Francis, *Political Order and Political Decay*, New York: Farrar, Straus, and Giroux, 2014.

Galeotti, Anna Elisabetta, *Toleration as Recognition*, Cambridge, UK: Cambridge University Press, 2002.

Galli, Marc, "Good Morning, Vietnam!" *Christianity Today*, May 2007, pp. 25–32.

Garnsey, Peter, "Religious Toleration in Classical Antiquity," in *Persecution and Toleration*, edited by W. J. Sheils, London: Basil Blackwell, 1984, pp. 1–27.

Gaustad, Edwin, *Roger Williams*, Oxford: Oxford University Press, 2005.

George, Robert, Testimony before the Africa, Global Health, Global Human Rights and International Organizations Subcommittee of the House Foreign Affairs Committee, July 16, 2016, Washington, D.C.

Gidda, Mirren, "How Much Longer Can Oman Be an Oasis of Peace in the Middle East?" *Newsweek*, February 10, 2017.

Gill, Anthony, "Religious Liberty and Economic Development: Exploring the Causal Connections," *The Review of Faith and International Affairs*, Vol. 2, No. 4 (2013), pp. 5–23.

Gillespie, John, "Human Rights as a Larger Loyalty: The Evolution of Religious Freedom in Vietnam," *Harvard Human Rights Journal*, Vol. 27, pp. 107–49.

Goldstein, Joseph, and Ahmad Shakib, "A Day After a Killing Afghans React in Horror, but Some Show Approval," *New York Times*, March 20, 2015.

Gottschalk, Peter, *American Heretics*, New York: Palgrave Macmillan, 2013.
Government Affairs Office (GAO), "International Religious Freedom Act: State Department and Commission Are Implementing Responsibilities but Need to Improve Interaction," GAO Report 13-196, March 26, 2013. https://www.gao.gov/products/gao-13-196
Green, William Scott, "The 'What' and 'Why' of Religious Toleration: Some Questions to Consider," in *Religious Tolerance in World Traditions*, edited by Jacob Neuser and Bruce Chilton, West Conshohocken, PA: Templeton Foundation Press, 2008, pp. 3–11.
Grim, Brian, Greg Clark, and Robert Edward Snyder, "Is Religious Freedom Good for Business? A Conceptual and Empirical Analysis," *Interdisciplinary Journal of Research on Religion,* Vol. 10, No. 4 (2014), pp. 2–19. https://www.religjournal.com/pdf/ijrr10004.pdf
Grim, Brian, and Roger Finke, *The Price of Freedom Denied*, New York: Cambridge University Press, 2011.
Groiss, Arnon, "Jews, Christians, War and Peace in Egyptian School Textbooks," 2004. http://www.impact-se.org/docs/reports/Egypt/EgyptMarch2004.pdf
Gunatilleke, Gehan "Criteria and Constraints: The Human Rights Committee's Test on Limiting the Freedom of Religion or Belief," *Religion and Human Rights*, Vol. 15 (2020), pp. 20–38.
Haefeli, Evan, *New Netherlands and the Dutch Origins of Religious Liberty*, Philadelphia: University of Pennsylvania Press, 2012.
Hasimova, Umida, "Religion, Beards, and Uzbekistan's Secular Government," *The Diplomat*, September 9, 2019. https://thediplomat.com/2019/09/religion-beards-and-uzbekistans-secular-government/
Hassan, Sanaa, *Christians versus Muslims in Egypt: The Century-Long Struggle for Coptic Equality*, Oxford: Oxford University Press, 2003.
Hawthorne, Amy, "Hearing on Egypt: Trends in Politics, Economics, and Human Rights," Testimony before the Subcommittee on Middle East, North Africa, and International Terrorism, House of Representatives, September 9, 2020, Washington, D.C. https://docs.house.gov/Committee/Calendar/ByEvent.aspx?EventID=110989
Hayward, Susan, "Understanding and Extending the Marrakesh Declaration in Policy and Practice," US Institute of Peace, September 2016. https://www.usip.org/sites/default/files/SR392-Understanding-and-Extending-the-Marrakesh-Declaration-in-Policy-and-Practice.pdf
Hess, Robert, and Judith Torney, *The Development of Political Attitudes in Childhood*, Chicago: Aldine, 1967.
Higgins, Nicholas, "Hobbes's Paradoxical Toleration: Inter Regentes Tolerantia, Tolerans Intolerantia Inter Plebein," *Politics and Religion*, Vol. 9 (2016), pp. 139–61.
Hirst, Paul, *From Statism to Pluralism*, London: UCL Press, 1997.
Hirst, Paul, "Statism, Pluralism, and Social Control," *British Journal of Criminology*, Vol. 40, No. 2 (2000), pp. 279–95.
Hoffman, Valerie, "Ibadism: History, Doctrines, and Recent Scholarship," *Religion Compass,* Vol. 9, No. 9 (2015), pp. 297–307.
Holt, Mack, *The French Wars of Religion, 1562–1629*, New York: Cambridge University Press, 1995.
Houben, Hubert, *Roger II of Sicily: A Ruler between East and West,* translated by Graham Loud and Diane Milburn, Cambridge, UK: Cambridge University Press, 2002.

Howard-Hassmann, Rhoda, *In Defense of Universal Human Rights*, Cambridge, UK: Polity Press, 2018.
Hudson, David, "President Obama Praises Freedom of Religion at the National Prayer Breakfast," February 6, 2014. https://obamawhitehouse.archives.gov/blog/2014/02/06/president-obama-praises-freedom-religion-national-prayer-breakfast
Hudson Institute, "Ten Years On: Saudi Arabia's Textbooks Still Promote Religious Violence," September 16, 2011, https://www.hudson.org/research/8309-ten-years-on-saudi-arabia-s-textbooks-still-promote-religious-violence
Human Rights Society of Uzbekistan, "Report on Civil and Political Rights: Uzbekistan," 2014. https://www.ecoi.net/en/file/local/1321622/1930_1408022470_int-ccpr-ico-uzb-17837-e.pdf
Human Rights Watch, "Republic of Uzbekistan: Crackdown in the Farghona Valley: Arbitrary Arrests and Religious Discrimination," 1998. https://www.hrw.org/legacy/reports98/uzbekistan/
Human Rights Watch, "Human Rights Watch Submission to the European Union for the EU–Vietnam Human Rights Dialogue," February 18, 2002. https://www.hrw.org/news/2020/02/18/human-rights-watch-submission-european-union-eu-vietnam-human-rights-dialogue
Human Rights Watch, "Saudi Arabia: Christians Arrested at Private Prayer," January 30, 2012.
Human Rights Watch, "Egypt: Lynching of Shia Follows Months of Hate Speech," June 27, 2013.
Human Rights Watch, "Uzbekistan: A Year into New Presidency, Cautious Hope for Change," October 25, 2017. https://www.hrw.org/news/2017/10/25/uzbekistan-year-new-presidency-cautious-hope-change
Ibrahim, Ishak, "Egypt's Officials Don't See Unrecognized Religious Minorities," The Tahrir Institute for Middle East Policy, June 2, 2021. https://timep.org/commentary/analysis/egypts-officials-dont-see-unrecognized-religious-minorities/
Ibrahim, Mina, "Ashura: A Day in History of Discrimination against Egyptian Shi'as" *Daily News Egypt*, October 24, 2015. http://www.dailynewsegypt.com/2015/10/24/ashura-a-day-in-history-of-discrimination-against-egyptian-shias/
Imamova, Navbahov, "Where Freedoms are Expanding—Slowly," *The Atlantic*, October 5, 2019. https://www.theatlantic.com/international/archive/2019/10/uzbekistan-freedom-slowly-expanding/599446/
Imamova, Navbahov, "Pompeo in Central Asia: State Department Spokesperson says America Brings a New Focus to the Region," February 7, 2020. https://www.amerikaovozi.com/a/5277696.html
Inboden, William, "Promoting Religious Freedom from the Oval Office," February 19, 2015. Berkeley Center. https://berkleycenter.georgetown.edu/essays/promoting-religious-freedom-from-the-oval-office
Institute on Religion and Public Policy, "Religious Freedom in Uzbekistan," October 7, 2008.
International Center for Not-for-Profit Law, "The Presidential Decree on Measures to Further Reform Judicial and Legal System, and Enhance Guarantees for Sound Protection of Rights and Freedoms of Citizens," October 23, 2016. https://www.icnl.org/research/library/uzbekistan_merax/
International Center for Religion and Diplomacy, "The State of Curricular Reform in the Kingdom of Saudi Arabia," June 2012.
International Commission of Jurists, "ICJ welcomes the first visit of the UN Special Rapporteur on the Independence of Judges and Lawyers to Uzbekistan," September

20, 2019. https://www.icj.org/icj-welcomes-the-first-visit-of-the-un-special-rapporteur-on-the-independence-of-judges-and-lawyers-to-uzbekistan/

International Crisis Group, "Education Reforms in Pakistan," June 23, 2014. https://protectingeducation.org/wp-content/uploads/documents/documents_international_crisis_group_-education-reform-in-pakistan.pdf

International Labour Organization, *Third Party Monitoring on Child and Forced Labour in Uzbekistan.* https://www.ilo.org/moscow/projects/WCMS_704979/lang--en/index.htm

Ishay, Michele, *The History of Human Rights*, Berkeley: University of California Press, 2008.

Jantera-Jareborg, Marrit, "Religion and the Secular State in Sweden," in *Religion and the Secular State: National Reports*, edited by Javier Martinez Torron and W. Cole Durham, Madrid: Servicio de Publicaciones de la Facultad de Derecho de la Universidad Complutense, 2015, pp. 669–86.

Jasser, M., Testimony before the Committee on Foreign Affairs, Subcommittee on Africa, Global Health, Global Human Rights and International Organizations, House of Representatives, December 10, 2013, Washington, D.C.

Jefferson, Thomas, *Notes on the State of Virginia*, edited by William Peden, Chapel Hill: University of North Carolina Press, 1955.

Johnson, Noel, and Mark Koyama, *Persecution and Toleration: The Long Road to Religious Freedom,* Cambridge, UK: Cambridge University Press, 2019.

Jones, Jeremy, and Nicholas Ridout, *Oman, Culture and Diplomacy*, Edinburgh: Edinburgh University Press, 2012.

Jones, Jeremy, and Nicholas Ridout, *A History of Modern Oman,* New York: Cambridge University Press, 2015.

Kalim, Ibrahim, "Sources of Tolerance and Intolerance in Islam," in *Religious Tolerance in World Religions*, edited by Jacob Neuser and Bruce Chilton, West Conshohocken, PA: Templeton Foundation Press, 2008, pp. 239–73.

Karabell, Zachary, *Peace Be Upon You*, New York: Knopf, 2007.

Keck, Margaret, and Katherine Sikkink, *Activists Beyond Borders*, New York: Cornell University Press, 1998.

Keith, Charles, *Catholic Vietnam: A Church from Empire to Nation*, Berkeley: University of California Press, 2012.

Kerry, John, "Remarks on the Release of the International Religious Freedom Report," May 20, 2013. Washington, D.C.

Khalid, Adeeb, *Islam After Communism: Religion and Politics in Central Asia*, Berkeley: University of California Press, 2007.

Kirkpatrick, David, and Merna Thomas, "Egyptian Leader Visits Coptic Christmas Eve Service," *New York Times*, January 6, 2015. https://www.nytimes.com/2015/01/07/world/middleeast/egyptian-leader-visits-coptic-christmas-eve-service.html

Kittelmann Flensner, Karin, *Discourses of Religion and Secularism in Religious Education Classes*, Cham: Springer, 2017.

Klauber, Martin I. (Ed.), "The Edict of Nantes," in *The Theology of the French Reformed Churches: From Henri IV to the Revocation of the Edict of Nantes*, Grand Rapids, MI: Reformation Heritage Books, 2014.

Kleining, John, and Nicholas Evans, "Human Flourishing, Human Dignity, and Human Rights," *Law and Philosophy,* Vol. 32, No. 5 (September 2013), pp. 539–64.

Kozak, Mike, Special Briefing, Bureau of Democracy, Human Rights, and Labor, August 15, 2017, Washington, D.C.

Kozak, Michael, Testimony before the House Oversight and Government Reform Subcommittee on National Security, October 11, 2017, Washington, D.C.
Krajeski, Jenna, "The Daring Plan to Save a Religious Minority from ISIS," *The New Yorker,* February 19, 2018. https://www.newyorker.com/magazine/2018/02/26/the-daring-plan-to-save-a-religious-minority-from-isis
Kuok, Lynn, "While the World Sleeps, Myanmar Burns," *Foreign Affairs*, September 28, 2017.
Lacorne, Denis, *The Limits of Tolerance: Enlightenment Values and Religious Fanaticism*, New York: Columbia University Press, 2019.
Laine, James, *Meta-Religion: Religion and Power in World History*, Berkeley: University of California Press, 2015.
Landler, Mark, and Adam Goldman, "U.S. Will Withhold Security Aid from Pakistan," *New York Times,* January 4, 2018. https://www.nytimes.com/2018/01/04/us/politics/trump-pakistan-aid.html?action=Click&contentCollection=BreakingNews&contentID=66316241&pgtype=Homepage&_r=0
Lantos Swett, Katrina, Testimony before the House Committee on Foreign Affairs: Subcommittee on Africa, Global Health, Global Human Rights and International Organizations, February 27, 2013, Washington, D.C.
Lantos Swett, Katrina, Testimony before the National Security Subcommittee of the House Committee on Oversight and Government Reform, June 13, 2013, Washington, D.C.
Lederer, Edith, "UN Investigator: Rights of Minorities to Worship Undermined," *Associated Press*, November 4, 2020. https://apnews.com/article/religion-maldives-freedom-of-religion-discrimination-north-korea-16c8581a5a00b5d4f0887e803e8c40dc
Lees, Sean, "Final Evaluation of Joint Project of UNDP, USAID and Supreme Court of Uzbekistan Rule of Law Partnership in Uzbekistan," August 2017.
Leiter, Brian, *Why Tolerate Religion?* Princeton, NJ: Princeton University Press, 2013.
Levey, Stuart, "Loss of Moneyman a Big Blow for al-Qaeda," *Washington Post,* June 6, 2010. http://www.washingtonpost.com/wp-dyn/content/article/2010/06/04/AR2010060404271_pf.html
Liljestrand, Johan, "Education for Citizenship in Swedish RE: Approaches and Dilemmas in Teacher's Talk," *Religion and Education*, Vol. 44, No. 3 (2017), pp. 317–30.
Limbert, Mandana, "Oman: Cultivating Good Citizens and Religious Virtue," in *Teaching Islam: Textbooks and Religion in the Middle East,* edited by Eleanor Abdella-Doumato and Gregory Starett (Boulder, CO: Lynne Rienner, 2007), pp. 103–24.
Lindkvist, Linde, *Religious Freedom and the Universal Declaration of Human Rights*, New York: Cambridge University Press, 2017.
Lipton, Sara, *Dark Mirror: The Medieval Origins of Anti-Jewish Iconography*, New York: Metropolitan Books/Henry Holt and Company, 2014.
Locke, John, *A Letter Concerning Toleration*, edited by James Tully, Indianapolis, IN: Hackett Publishing Company, 1983.
Lone, Wa, Kyaw Soe OO, Simon Lewis, and Antoni Slodkowski, "How Myanmar Forces, Burned, Looted and Killed in a Remote Village," *Reuters*, February 8, 2018. https://www.reuters.com/article/us-myanmar-rakhine-events-specialreport/special-report-how-myanmar-forces-burned-looted-and-killed-in-a-remote-village-idUSKBN1FS3BH

Mahmood, Saba, "Religious Freedom, Minority Rights, and Geopolitics," in *Politics of Religious Freedom,* edited by Winnifred Fallers Sullivan, Elizabeth Shakman Hurd, Saba Mahmood, and Peter Danchin, Chicago: University of Chicago Press, 2015, pp. 142–8.

Mahmood, Saba, and Peter Danchin, "Immunity or Regulation? Antinomies of Religious Freedom," *The South Atlantic Quarterly*, Vol. 113, No. 1 (2014), pp. 129–59.

Makari, Peter, *Conflict and Cooperation: Christian–Muslim Relations in Contemporary Egypt*, Syracuse, NY: Syracuse University Press, 2007.

Manor, Yohanan, "Inculcating Islamist Ideals in Egypt," *Middle East Quarterly*, (Fall 2015). https://www.meforum.org/5480/inculcating-islamist-ideals-in-egypt

Mantilla, Giovanni, *Lawmaking Under Pressure: International Humanitarian Law and Internal Armed Conflict*, New York: Cornell University Press, 2020.

Markham, David, "Was Napoleon an Anti-Semite? Napoleon, the Jews and Religious Freedom," Speech, Tel Aviv, Israel, May 31, 2007.

Markkola, Pirjo, "The Long History of Lutheranism in Scandinavia. From State Religion to the People's Church," *Perichoresis*, Vol. 13, No. 2 (2015), pp. 3–15.

Marrakesh Declaration, "Executive Summary," Marrakesh Declaration on the Rights of Religious Minorities in Predominantly Muslim Majority Communities, January 27, 2016. https://www.marrakeshdeclaration.org/declaration/index.html

Marshall, John, *John Locke, Toleration and Early Enlightenment Culture*, Cambridge, UK: Cambridge University Press, 2006.

Marshall, Katherine, "Towards Enriching Understandings and Assessments of Freedom of Religion or Belief: Politics, Debates, Methodologies, and Practices," CREID Working Paper, Vol. 2021, No. 6, January 2021.

Marx, Karl, *Critique of Hegel's Philosophy of Right*, translated by Joseph O'Malley, Cambridge, UK: Cambridge University Press, 1970.

Mathews, Jessica, "America's Indefensible Defense Budget," *The New York Review of Books,* July 18, 2019.

McDonough, Denis, "International Religious Freedom: A Human Right, a National Security Issue, a Foreign Policy Priority," July 31, 2012. https://obamawhitehouse.archives.gov/blog/2012/07/31/international-religious-freedom-human-right-national-security-issue-foreign-policy-p

McDougall, Walter, *Promised Land, Crusader State: The American Encounter with the World Since 1776*, New York: Mariner Books, 1998.

Meacham, Jon, *American Gospel*, New York: Random House, 2007.

Menocal, Maria Rosa, *The Ornament of the World*, New York: Brown, 2003.

Michalak, Michael, "Vietnam Religious Freedom Update – The Case Against CPC," E.O. 12958. https://www.theguardian.com/world/us-embassy-cables-documents/244345

Mill, John Stuart, *On Liberty*, edited by Stefan Collini, Cambridge, UK: Cambridge University Press, 1989.

Moosvi, Shireen, "Akbar's Enterprise of Religious Conciliation in the Early Phase, 1561–1578: Spontaneous or Motivated," *Studies in People's History*, Vol. 4, No. 1 (2017), pp. 46–52.

Moratinos, Miguel, "The UN's First Anti-Semitism Envoy: A Conversation with High Representative for the UN Alliance," August 13, 2020. https://www.ajc.org/news/the-uns-increased-focus-on-antisemitism-a-conversation-with-high-representative-miguel

Moratinos, Miguel, "Remarks at the WJC International Meeting of the Special Envoys and Coordinators Combating Anti-Semitism," November 19, 2020. https://www.unaoc.org/2020/11/remarks-international-meeting-of-the-special-envoys-and-coordinators-combating-anti-semitism/

Moyn, Samuel, "Religious Freedom and the Fate of Secularism," in *Religion, Secularism, and Constitutional Democracy*, edited by Jean Cohen and Cecile Laborde, New York: Columbia University Press, 2016, pp. 27–46.

Mozur, Paul, "A Genocide Incited on Facebook, with Posts from Myanmar's Military," *New York Times*, October 15, 2018. https://www.nytimes.com/2018/10/15/technology/myanmar-facebook-genocide.html

Muasher, Marwan, *The Second Arab Awakening and the Battle for Pluralism*, New Haven, CT: Yale University Press, 2014.

Murphy, Andrew, *Liberty, Conscious, and Toleration: The Political Thought of William Penn*, New York: Oxford University Press, 2016.

Myint-U, Thank, "Myanmar's Coming Revolution," *Foreign Affairs*, Vol. 100, No. 4 (July/August 2021), pp. 132–45.

Nagakoshi, Yuzuki, "The Scope and Implications of the International Criminal Court's Jurisdictional Decision over the Rohingya Crisis," *Human Rights Quarterly,* Vol. 43, No. 2 (2021), pp. 259–89.

Najibullah, Farangis, "Uzbek Imam Fired After Deviating from the Script," *Radio Free Europe*, September 10, 2018.

Nardi, Dominic, Policy Analyst USCRIF, "Country Update: An Assessment of Vietnam's Law on Belief and Religion," November 2019.

Nauert, Heather, Press Release, "Designations Under the International Religious Freedom Act of 1998," January 4, 2018, Washington, D.C.

Neuser, Jacob, and Bruce Chilton (Eds.), *Religious Tolerance in World Religions*, West Conshohocken, PA: Templeton Foundation Press, 2008.

Norwich, John, *The Kingdom in the Sun 1130–1194*, New York: Faber and Faber, 2010.

Nussbaum, Martha, *The New Religious Intolerance*, Cambridge, MA: Belknap Press, 2012.

Obama, Barack, Statement, August 7, 2014, Washington D.C. https://obamawhitehouse.archives.gov/the-press-office/2014/08/07/statement-president

Office of the Press Secretary, "Remarks by the President on the Situation in Egypt," August 15, 2013. https://obamawhitehouse.archives.gov/the-press-office/2013/08/15/remarks-president-situation-egypt

Office of the Press Secretary, "Background Briefing by Senior Administration Officials on Iraq," August 8, 2014. https://obamawhitehouse.archives.gov/the-press-office/2014/08/08/background-briefing-senior-administration-officials-iraq

Office of the Press Secretary, "Promoting and Protecting Religious Freedom Around the Globe," August, 10, 2016. https://obamawhitehouse.archives.gov/the-press-office/2016/08/10/fact-sheet-promoting-and-protecting-religious-freedom-around-globe

Paddock, Richard, "U.N. Court Orders Myanmar to Protect Rohingya Muslims," *New York Times,* January 23, 2020. https://www.nytimes.com/2020/01/23/world/asia/myanmar-rohingya-genocide.html

Pardo, Eldad J., "A Further Step Forward: Review of Changes and Remaining Problematic Content in Saudi Textbooks 2021–22," IMPACT-se, September 2021. https://www.impact-se.org/wp-content/uploads/A-Further-Step-Forward-Review-of-Changes-and-Remaining-Problematic-Content-in-Saudi-Textbooks-2021%E2%80%9322.pdf

Patterson, Eric, "What They Say and Do: Religious Freedom as a National Security Lens," *The Review of Faith and International Affairs,* Vol. 2, No. 1, (Spring 2013), pp. 22–30.

Pettersoon, Per, "State and Religion in Sweden: Ambiguity between Disestablishment and Religious Control," *Nordic Journal of Religion and Society*, Vol. 24, No. 2 (2011), pp. 119–35.

Petty, Marty, "U.N. Religion Expert Concerned over 'Interrupted' Vietnam Visit," *Reuters*, July 31, 2014.

Pew Forum on Religion and Public Life, "Latest Trends in Religious Restrictions and Hostilities," February 26, 2015. https://www.pewresearch.org/religion/2015/02/26/religious-hostilities/

Pew Research Center, "Trends in Global Restrictions on Religion," June 23, 2016. http://assets.pewresearch.org/wp-content/uploads/sites/11/2016/06/Restrictions2016-Full-Report-FINAL.pdf Pew Research Center

Pew Research Center, "Global Uptick in Government Restrictions," June, 21, 2018. https://www.pewforum.org/2018/06/21/global-uptick-in-government-restrictions-on-religion-in-2016/

Pew Research Center, "A Closer Look at How Religious Restrictions Have Risen Around the World," July 15, 2019. https://www.pewforum.org/2019/07/15/a-closer-look-at-how-religious-restrictions-have-risen-around-the-world/

Pew Research Center, "In 2018, Government Restrictions on Religion Reach Highest Level Globally in More Than a Decade," November 10, 2020. https://www.pewforum.org/2020/11/10/in-2018-government-restrictions-on-religion-reach-highest-level-globally-in-more-than-a-decade/

Pew Research Center, "Globally, Social Hostilities Related to Religion Decline in 2019, While Government Restrictions Remain at Highest Levels," September 30, 2021. https://www.pewforum.org/2021/09/30/globally-social-hostilities-related-to-religion-decline-in-2019-while-government-restrictions-remain-at-highest-levels/

Philpott, Daniel, "Religious Freedom and Peacebuilding: May I Introduce You Two?" *The Review of Faith and International Affairs*, Vol. 11, No. 1 (2013), pp. 31–7.

Pinto, Thiago Alves, "An Empirical Investigation of the Use of Limitations to Freedom of Religion or Belief at the European Court of Human Rights," *Religion and Human Rights*, Vol. 15, No. 1–2 (2020), pp. 96–133.

Poe, Ted, Opening Statement, "Saudi Arabia's Troubling Educational Curriculum," House of Representatives, Subcommittee on Terrorism, Nonproliferation and Trade, July 19, 2017, Washington, D.C.

Polishook, Irwin, *Roger Williams, John Cotton and Religious Freedom*, Hoboken, NJ: Prentice Hall, 1967.

Pompeo, Michael, "Keynote Address at the Ministerial to Advance Religious Freedom," July 18, 2019, Washington, D.C. https://2017-2021.state.gov/secretary-of-state-michael-r-pompeo-keynote-address-at-the-ministerial-to-advance-religious-freedom/index.html

Pompeo, Michael, Press Statement, "United States Takes Action Against Violations of Religious Freedom," December 20, 2019, Washington, D.C.

Postman, N. *The End of Education: Redefining the Value of School*, New York: Vintage Books, 1996.

Power, Samantha, Remarks at the 2021 International Religious Freedom Summit, July 14, 2021.

Preston, Andrew, *Sword of the Spirit, Shield of Faith,* New York: Anchor Books, 2012.

Project on Middle East Democracy (POMED), “Fact Sheet – Egypt’s ‘New’ NGO Law: As Draconian as the Old One,” September 23, 2019.
Rawls, John, *The Laws of Peoples,* Cambridge, MA: Harvard University Press, 1999.
Reimer, Reg, and Hien Vu, “Towards the Rule of Law for Freedom of Religion and Belief in Vietnam,” *The Review of Faith and International Affairs,* Vol. 14, No. 4 (October 2016), pp. 78–88.
Rich, Bruce, *To Uphold the World: A Call for a New Global Ethic from Ancient India*, Boston: Beacon Press, 2010.
Richard, Anne, “U.S. Humanitarian Assistance in Response to the Iraq Crisis,” Testimony before the House Foreign Affairs Subcommittees on Africa, Global Health, Global Human Rights and International Organizations and the Middle East and North Africa, September 10, 2014, Washington, D.C. https://docs.house.gov/meetings/FA/FA16/20140910/102642/HHRG-113-FA16-Wstate-RichardA-20140910.pdf
Rieffer-Flanagan, Barbara Ann, *Evolving Iran*, Washington, D.C.: Georgetown University Press, 2013.
Rieffer-Flanagan, Barbara Ann, “Rhetoric versus Reality: American Foreign Policy and Religious Freedom in the Middle East” in *Routledge Handbook on Human Rights and the Middle East and North Africa*, edited by Anthony Tirado Chase, New York: Routledge, 2017, pp. 317–29.
Rigterink, Jurgen, First Vice President of the European Bank for Reconstruction and Development, Speech, Berlin, Germany, January 14, 2019. https://www.ebrd.com/news/speeches/reforming-uzbekistan-challenges-and-opportunities.html
Roberts, Andrew, *Napoleon: A Life*, New York: Viking, 2014.
Rosenthal, Gert, “A Brief and Independent Inquiry into the Involvement of the United Nations in Myanmar from 2010 To 2018,” May 29, 2019. https://www.un.org/sg/sites/www.un.org.sg/files/atoms/files/Myanmar%20Report%20-%20May%202019.pdf
Rowen, Herbert H. (Ed.), *The Low Countries in Early Modern Times: A Documentary History*, New York: Harper and Row, 1972.
Roy, Oliver, “The Transformation of the Arab World,” *Journal of Democracy*, Vol. 23, No. 3 (July 2012), pp. 5–18.
Rubin, Alissa, “French ‘Burkini’ Bans Provoke Backlash as Armed Police Confront Beachgoers,” *New York Times,* August 24, 2016. https://www.nytimes.com/2016/08/25/world/europe/france-burkini.html
Ruffini, Francesco, *Religious Liberty*, New York: G. P. Putnam’s Sons, 1912.
Rutherford, Bruce, *Egypt After Mubarak*, Princeton, NJ: Princeton University Press, 2008.
Sahgal, Neha, and Brian Grim, “Egypt’s Restrictions on Religion Coincide with Lack of Religious Tolerance,” Pew Research Center, July 2, 2013. http://www.pewresearch.org/fact-tank/2013/07/02/egypts-restrictions-on-religion-coincide-with-lack-of-religious-tolerance/
Saiya, Nilay, *Weapons of Peace,* Cambridge, UK: Cambridge University Press, 2018.
Saperstein, David, Ambassador-at-Large for International Religious Freedom, Statement for the House Foreign Affairs Committee Subcommittee on Africa, Global Health, Global Human Rights, and International Organizations, June 16, 2016, Washington, D.C.
Saperstein, David, Panel Discussion, “Tolerance: A Key to Religious Freedom,” February 9, 2017, Washington, D.C.

Scheible, Kristin, "Towards a Buddhist Policy of Tolerance: The Case of King Ashoka," in *Religious Tolerance in World Religions*, edited by Jacob Neuser and Bruce Chilton, West Conshohocken, PA: Templeton Foundation Press, 2008, pp. 317–30.

Schwarzfuchs, Simon, *Napoleon, the Jews and the Sanhedrin*, London: Routledge, 1979.

Scolnicov, Anat, *The Right of Religious Freedom in International Law*, New York: Routledge, 2010.

Scott, Rachel, "Managing Religion and Renegotiating the Secular: The Muslim Brotherhood and Defining the Religious Sphere," *Politics and Religion,* Vol. 7 (2014), pp. 51–78.

Seiple, Chris, "Understanding Uzbekistan," Foreign Policy Research Institute, May 6, 2005.

Seiple, Chris, Testimony before the Senate Finance Committee, July 12, 2006, on "S.3495—A bill to authorize the extension of nondiscriminatory treatment (normal trade relations treatment) to the products of Vietnam." https://www.finance.senate.gov/hearings/to-hear-testimony-on-s3495a-bill-to-authorize-the-extension-of-nondiscriminatory-treatment-normal-trade-relations-treatment-to-the-products-of-vietnam

Seiple, Chris, "Revisiting the Geo-Political Thinking of Sir Halford John Mackinder: United States–Uzbekistan Relations 1991–2005," November 2006. https://globalengage.org/_assets/docs/771_seiple_dissertation.pdf

Seiple, Chris, "The Essence of Exceptionalism: Roger Williams and the Birth of Religious Freedom in America." *The Review of Faith and International Affairs* Vol. 10, No. 2 (Summer 2012), pp. 13–19.

Sever, Mjusa, "Judicial and Governance Reform," in *Uzbekistan's New Face*, edited by S. Frederick Starr and Svante Cornell, Lanham, MD: Rowman and Littlefield, 2018, pp. 115–45.

Shaheed, Ahmed, *Report of the Special Rapporteur on Freedom of Religion or Belief on His Mission to Uzbekistan*, February 22, 2017, A/HRC/37/49/Add.2.

Shaheed, Ahmed, "The United Nations Addresses Antisemitism as a Human Rights Issue: A Historic Achievement," September 19, 2019. https://www.ajc.org/the-united-nations-addresses-antisemitism-as-a-human-rights-issue-a-historic-achievement

Shaheed, Ahmed, "Gender-Based Violence and Discrimination in the Name of Religion or Belief," August 24, 2020. A/HRC/43/48. https://undocs.org/A/HRC/43/48

Shaheed, Ahmed, "Conversation with the Council on Foreign Relations Religion and Foreign Policy Webinar Series," September 22, 2020.

Shaheed, Ahmed, "UN Special Rapporteur for Freedom of Religion or Belief, Ahmed Shaheed's Message to UCC SoR Students," *Study of Religions, UCC, Ireland,* February 11, 2021. https://www.youtube.com/watch?v=uRFUv2rR5dE

Shaheed, Ahmed, "Conversation with USCIRF Spotlight Podcast," June 11, 2021. https://www.uscirf.gov/news-room/uscirf-spotlight/top-priorities-un-special-rapporteur-freedom-religion-or-belief

Shakman Hurd, Elizabeth, *Beyond Religious Freedom: The New Global Politics of Religion*, Princeton, NJ: Princeton University Press, 2015.

Shakman Hurd, Elizabeth, Testimony before the House Foreign Affairs Committee, Tom Lantos Human Rights Commission, July 13, 2021, Washington, D.C.

Sheff, Marcus, and David A. Weinberg, "Saudi Textbooks Revised, but Still Incite Hate," March 30, 2020. https://www.longwarjournal.org/archives/2020/03/saudi-textbooks-revised-but-still-incite-hate.php

Skolverket, "Curriculum for the Upper Secondary School," 2013. https://www.skolverket.se/publikationsserier/styrdokument/2013/curriculum-for-the-upper-secondary-school
Smith, George, *Religion and Trade in New Netherlands: Dutch Origins and American Development*, Ithaca, NY: Cornell University Press, 1973.
Smith-Cannoy, Heather, *Insincere Commitments: Human Rights Treaties, Abusive States, and Citizen Activism*, Washington, D.C.: Georgetown University Press, 2012.
Starr, S. Frederick, "Change and Continuity in Uzbekistan, 1991–2016," in *Uzbekistan's New Face*, edited by S. Frederick Starr and Svante E. Cornell, Lanham, MD: Rowman and Littlefield, 2018, pp. 18–40.
State Department, *International Religious Freedom Report for 2005*. Washington, D.C.: US State Department. https://www.state.gov/j/drl/rls/irf/2005/51535.htm.
State Department, *International Religious Freedom Report for 2009*. Washington, D.C.: US State Department. https://2009-2017.state.gov/j/drl/rls/irf/2009/127374.htm
State Department, *International Religious Freedom Report for 2010*. Washington, D.C.: US State Department.
State Department, *International Religious Freedom Report for 2011*. Washington, D.C.: US State Department.
State Department, "Uzbekistan 2012." http://www.state.gov/documents/organization/193949.pdf
State Department, *International Religious Freedom Report for 2013*. Washington, D.C.: US State Department.
State Department, *International Religious Freedom Report for 2014*. Washington, D.C.: US State Department.
State Department, "Executive Summary," *International Religious Freedom Report for 2015*. Washington, D.C.: US State Department.
State Department, *International Religious Freedom Report for 2016*. Washington, D.C.: US State Department.
State Department, *International Religious Freedom Report for 2017*. Washington, D.C.: US State Department.
State Department, *International Religious Freedom Report for 2018*. Washington, D.C.: US State Department.
State Department, "Ministerial on Religious Freedom," July 2019. https://www.state.gov/ministerial-to-advance-religious-freedom-schedule-of-events/
State Department, *International Religious Freedom Report for 2019*, June 10, 2020. Washington, D.C.: US State Department. https://www.state.gov/wp-content/uploads/2020/06/CHINA-INCLUDES-TIBET-XINJIANG-HONG-KONG-AND-MACAU-2019-INTERNATIONAL-RELIGIOUS-FREEDOM-REPORT.pdf
State Department, "Joint Statement: A Shared Vision for Advancing Freedom of Religion or Belief for All," November 17, 2020. https://www.state.gov/a-shared-vision-for-advancing-freedom-of-religion-or-belief-for-all/
State Department, *International Religious Freedom Report for 2020*, May 12, 2021, Washington, D.C.: US State Department. https://www.state.gov/reports/2020-report-on-international-religious-freedom/
State Department, Bureau of Democracy, Human Rights, and Labor, "Religious Freedom and National Security," August 17, 2011, Washington, D.C.: US State Department.

Stevenson, Alexandra, "Facebook Admits it Was Used to Incite Violence in Myanmar," *New York Times,* November 6, 2018. https://www.nytimes.com/2018/11/06/technology/myanmar-facebook.html

Subedi, Surya, "Protection of Human Rights through the Mechanism of UN Special Rapporteurs," *Human Rights Quarterly,* Vol. 33, No. 1 (February 2011), pp. 201–28.

Swerdlow, Steve, "Charting Progress in Mirziyoyev's Uzbekistan," Human Rights Watch, October 7, 2019. https://www.hrw.org/news/2019/10/07/charting-progress-mirziyoyevs-uzbekistan#

Tadros, Mariz, "Vicissitudes in the Entente between the Coptic Orthodox Church and the State of Egypt," *International Journal of Middle East Studies*, Vol. 41, No. 2 (2009), pp. 269–87.

Tadros, Samuel, *Motherland Lost: The Egyptian and Coptic Quest for Modernity*, Stanford, CA: Hoover Institution Press, 2013.

Tadros, Samuel, Congressional Testimony, "Egypt: Trends in Politics, Economics, and Human Rights," September 9, 2020, Washington, D.C. https://foreignaffairs.house.gov/hearings?ID=56A33A4A-8ACB-4D21-B321-A4AFC0118F98

Tadros, Samuel, IDC webinar, "Briefing on Egypt: Egypt Must Confront Christian Persecution," January 15, 2021. https://religionunplugged.com/news/2021/1/15/are-egypts-christians-persecuted-why-copts-say-no

Tahrir Institute for Middle East Policy, "A Fragile Egypt in a Changing World: Six Years After the Revolution," 2017. https://timep.org/wp-content/uploads/2017/05/Fragile-Egypt-in-a-Changing-World.pdf

Tashkent Times, "Uzbekistan's Development Strategy for 2017–2021 has been Adopted Following Public Consultation," August 2, 2017. http://tashkenttimes.uz/national/541-uzbekistan-s-development-strategy-for-2017-2021-has-been-adopted-following-

Taylor, Alan, *American Colonies,* New York: Penguin, 2001.

Taylor, Philip, "Modernity and Re-enchantment in Post-revolutionary Vietnam," in *Modernity and Re-enchantment,* edited by Philip Taylor, New York: Lexington Books, 2007, pp. 1–56.

Tayyeb, Ahmed, "Al Azhar Document," 2012. http://danutm.files.wordpress.com/2012/04/al-azhar-document-for-basic-freedoms.pdf

Thames, Knox, "A Real Opportunity for Religion Law Reform in Uzbekistan," *The Diplomat,* October 16, 2020. https://thediplomat.com/2020/10/a-real-opportunity-for-religion-law-reform-in-uzbekistan/

Thames, Knox, "Teaching Tolerance and Promoting Pluralism: Challenges and Opportunities," Remarks to the Institute of Gulf Affairs, October 22, 2020. https://www.knoxthames.com/post/remarks-to-institute-of-gulf-affairs

Thorkildsen, Dag, "West Nordic and East Nordic Religiousness and Secularity: Historical Unity and Diversity," in *Secular and Sacred? The Scandinavian Case of Religion in Human Rights, Law and Public Square*, edited by Rosemarie van den Breemer, Jose Casanova, and Trygve Wyller, Gottingen, Germany: Vandenhoeck and Ruprecht, 2014, pp. 85–101.

Toft, Monica Duffy, Daniel Philpott, and Timothy Samuel Shah, *God's Century: Resurgent Religion and Global Politics*, New York: W. W. Norton and Company, 2011.

Toosi, Nahal, "The Genocide the U.S. Didn't See Coming," *Politico*, March/April 2018. https://www.politico.com/magazine/story/2018/03/04/obama-rohingya-genocide-myanmar-burma-muslim-syu-kii-217214/

Trump White House, *National Security Strategy of the United States of America*, December 18, 2017. https://trumpwhitehouse.archives.gov/wp-content/uploads/2017/12/NSS-Final-12-18-2017-0905.pdf

Tunheim, John, "Nurturing Rule of Law in Young Uzbekistan," January 31, 2013. https://blog.usaid.gov/2013/01/nurturing-rule-of-law-in-uzbekistan/

United Nations (UN), "Charter." https://www.un.org/en/about-us/un-charter/full-text

UN High Commissioner for Refugees (UNHCR), "General Overview." https://reporting.unhcr.org/sites/default/files/Myanmar%20factsheet%20August%202021.pdf

UNHCR, "Bangladesh Operational Update," July 2021. https://reporting.unhcr.org/sites/default/files/Bangladesh_Operational%20Update_July%202021.pdf

UN Human Rights Committee, "Concluding Observations on the Fifth Periodic Report of Uzbekistan," May 1, 2020, CCPR/C/UZB/CO/5.

UN Human Rights Council, "Resolution 16/18, Combating Intolerance, Negative Stereotyping and Stigmatization of, and Discrimination, Incitement to Violence, and Violence Against Persons Based on Religion or Belief," March 24, 2011, A/HRC/RES/16/18. https://www2.ohchr.org.A.HRC.RES.16.18_en.pdf

UN Human Rights Council, "Annual Report of the High Commissioner for Human Rights," January 11, 2013, A/HRC/22/17/add.4.

UN Human Rights Council, "Report of the Special Rapporteur on the Situation of Human Rights in Myanmar," March 14, 2017, A/HRC/34/67.

UN Human Rights Council, "Resolution 34/22, Situation on Human Rights in Myanmar," March 24, 2017, A/HRC/RES/34/22.

UN Human Rights Council, Press Release, "Myanmar: Worsening Cycle of Violence in Rakhine Must Be Broken Urgently, UN Expert Warns," August 31, 2017. https://www.ohchr.org/EN/NewsEvents/Pages/DisplayNews.aspx?NewsID=22018

UN Human Rights Council, "Human Rights Situations that Require the Council's Attention, Report of the Independent International Fact-Finding Mission on Myanmar," September 12, 2018, A/HRC/39/64.

UN Human Rights Council, "Report of the Independent International Fact-Finding Mission on Myanmar," September 28, 2018, A/HRC/39/64.

UN Human Rights Council, "Countering Islamophobia/Anti-Muslim Hatred to Eliminate Discrimination and Intolerance Based on Religion or Belief," February 25, 2021, A/HRC/46/30.

UN News, "Rohingyas Could Face Further Violence if They Return to Myanmar, UN Adviser Warns," March 13, 2018. https://news.un.org/en/story/2018/03/1004842

UN News, "Six Years after Genocide, International Community Must Prioritize Justice for Yazidi Community," August 3, 2020. https://news.un.org/en/story/2020/08/1069432

UN Office of the High Commissioner of Human Rights, "Human Rights Council Starts Interactive Dialogue with the Special Rapporteur on Freedom of Religion or Belief," March 10, 2015. https://www.ohchr.org/EN/NewsEvents/Pages/DisplayNews.aspx?NewsID=15678

UN Security Council, "Security Council Presidential Statement Calls on Myanmar to End Excessive Military Force, Intercommunal Violence in Rakhine State," November 6, 2017. S/PRST/2017/22. https://www.un.org/press/en/2017/sc13055.doc.htm

United States Agency for International Development (USAID), "Uzbekistan Passes Law on Gender Equality," December 19, 2019. https://www.usaid.gov/uzbekistan/program-updates/dec-2019-uzbekistan-passes-law-gender-equality

USAID, "Basic Education Fact Sheet," July 2020. https://www.usaid.gov/sites/default/files/documents/USAIDEgypt_Education-Basic_Fact_Sheet_2020_EN.pdf
United States Commission on International Religious Freedom (USCIRF), "Connecting the Dots: Education and Religious Discrimination in Pakistan," November 2011. https://www.uscirf.gov/sites/default/files/resources/Pakistan-ConnectingTheDots-Email(3).pdf
USCIRF, Annual Report of the U.S. Commission on International Religious Freedom, April 2013.
USCIRF, Office of the Spokesperson, Media Note, "Meeting on Religious Freedom in Vietnam," July 25, 2013, Washington, D.C.
USCIRF, Press Release, "USCIRF Urges President Obama to Raise Religious Freedom with Vietnamese President," July 22, 2013.
USCIRF, Press Release, "USCIRF Urges President Obama to Raise Religious Freedom with Vietnamese President," July 22, 2013.
USCIRF, "2017 Annual Report." http://www.uscirf.gov/sites/default/files/2017.USCIRFAnnualReport.pdf
USCIRF, "Religious Freedom in Vietnam: Assessing the Country of Particular Concern Designation 10 Years after its Removal," February 2017. https://www.uscirf.gov/sites/default/files/Vietnam.%20Assessing%20the%20Country%20of%20Particular%20Concern%20Designation%2010%20Years%20after%20its%20Removal.pdf
USCIRF, "Vietnam: Religious Prisoner of Conscience Pastor Nguyen Cong Chinh Released," July 31, 2017.
USCIRF, "Special Report: Study Revealed Numerous Passages in Saudi Textbooks Advocating Intolerance and Violence," May 2018. https://www.uscirf.gov/reports-briefs/special-reports/study-revealed-numerous-passages-in-saudi-textbooks-advocating
USCIRF, "2019 Annual Report," April 2019. https://www.uscirf.gov/sites/default/files/2019USCIRFAnnualReport.pdf
USCIRF, "Country Update: Uzbekistan," January 2020. https://www.uscirf.gov/reports-briefs/policy-briefs-and-focuses/uzbekistan-country-update
USCIRF, "Religious Freedom in Cuba in 2019," March 2020. https://www.uscirf.gov/sites/default/files/2020%20Cuba%20Policy%20Update.pdf
USCIRF, "2020 Annual Report." https://www.uscirf.gov/publications/2020-annual-report
USCIRF, "Vietnam." https://www.uscirf.gov/sites/default/files/Vietnam.pdf
USCRIF, "2021 Annual Report." https://www.uscirf.gov/sites/default/files/2021-05/Saudi%20Arabia%20Chapter%20AR2021.pdf
USCIRF, Press Release, "USCIRF Concerned by new Uzbekistan Religion Law," July 16, 2021.
USCRIF, "Spotlight Podcast with Nadine Maenza," August 25, 2021. https://www.uscirf.gov/news-room/uscirf-spotlight/fourth-anniversary-rohingya-genocide
Valeri, Marc, *Oman: Politics and Society in the Qaboos State*, New York: Columbia University Press, 2009.
Van Hoang, Chung, *New Religions and State's Response to Religious Diversification in Contemporary Vietnam*, Cham, Switzerland: Springer, 2017.
Vatican, "Declaration on the Relation of the Church to Non-Christian Religions Nostra Aetate, Proclaimed by His Holiness Pope Paul VI," October 28, 1965. https://www.vatican.va/archive/hist_councils/ii_vatican_council/documents/vat-ii_decl_19651028_nostra-aetate_en.html

Vu, Hien, Stephen Bailey, and James Chen, "Engaging Vietnam and Laos on Religious Freedom," *The Review of Faith and International Affairs*, Vol. 14, No. 2 (2016), pp. 86–92.

Wade, Francis, *Myanmar's Enemy Within*, London: Zed Books, 2017.

Wahid Hanna, Michael, "Public Order and Egypt's Statist Tradition," *The Review of Faith and International Affairs*, Vol. 13, No. 1 (2015), pp. 23–30.

Wallace, E. Gregory, "Justifying Religious Freedom: The Western Tradition," *Penn State Law Review*, Vol. 114, No. 2 (2009), pp. 485–570.

Walsh, Declan, and Nour Youseff, "Gunmen Attack Coptic Christian Convoy in Egypt killing at least 26," *New York Times*, May 26, 2017.

Walzer, Michael, "Liberalism and the Art of Separation," *Political Theory*, Vol. 12, No. 3 (August 1984), pp. 315–30.

Wang, Yuting, "Prospects for Covenantal Pluralism in the People's Republic of China: A Reflection on State Policy and Muslim Minorities," *The Review of Faith and International Affairs*, Vol. 19, No. 2 (2021), pp. 14–28.

Weinberg, David Andrew, "Prepared Statement for the Subcommittee on Terrorism, Nonproliferation, and Trade, House of Representatives," July 19, 2017, Washington, D.C.

Weinberg, David Andrew, "Egyptian Textbooks Send Mixed Messages about Jews," ADL, June 22, 2021. https://www.adl.org/blog/egyptian-textbooks-send-mixed-messages-about-jews

Weiner, Scott, "Religious Freedom Conditions in Saudi Arabia," USCRIF, September 2021. https://www.uscirf.gov/sites/default/files/2021-09/2021%20Saudi%20Arabia%20Country%20Update.pdf

Weitz, Richard, "Uzbekistan's New Foreign Policy: Change and Continuity Under New Leadership," in *Uzbekistan's New Face*, edited by S. Frederick Starr and Svante Cornell, Lanham, MD: Rowman and Littlefield, 2018, pp. 41–81.

Werthmuller, Kurt, Webinar, "Are Egypt's Christians Persecuted? Why Some Copts Say No," January 15, 2021. https://religionunplugged.com/news/2021/1/15/are-egypts-christians-persecuted-why-copts-say-no

White House, Office of the Press Secretary, "Joint Statement: Between the United States and the Socialist Republic of Vietnam," May 23, 2016.

Wilken, Robert Louis, *Liberty in the Things of God: The Christian Origins of Religious Freedom*, New Haven, CT: Yale University Press, 2019.

Winter, Ofir, "Egypt Enhances its Peace Education, One Step at a Time," An Impact Brief, March 2016. https://www.impact-se.org/wp-content/uploads/Egypt-Report-Ofir-Winter.pdf

Worsnip, Patrick, "Bush Promotes Religious Freedom at UN Gathering," *Reuters*, November 13, 2008. http://www.reuters.com/article/us-un-interfaith-idUSTRE4AC75Y20081113

Zagorin, Perez, *How the Idea of Religious Toleration Came to the West*, Princeton, NJ: Princeton University Press, 2003.

Zogby Research Service, "After Tahrir: Egyptians Assess their Government, their Institutions, and their Future," June 2013. http://static.squarespace.com/static/52750dd3e4b08c252c723404/t/52928b8de4b070ad8eec181e/1385335693242/Egypt%20June%202013%20FINAL.pdf

Index